PRAISE FOR

Hedge Hunters
Hedge Fund Masters on the Rewards, the Risk, and the Reckoning

BY KATHERINE BURTON
BLOOMBERG NEWS

One of Amazon.com's Best Books of 2007
Top 10 Editors' Picks: Finance & Investing

"A readable, relevant book, with lessons a new generation of hedge-fund managers, in a decidedly less hospitable investment climate, would do well to take to heart."

—*BARRON'S*

"A fine introduction to hedge funds for both the interested reader and those contemplating a career in this area of investment."

—*LIBRARY JOURNAL*

"Great descriptions of the backgrounds, philosophies, and practices of the best managers, told in a rapid, entertaining narrative—I learned quite a lot."

—DAVID EINHORN

Manager, Greenlight Capital Hedge Fund

"This is a page-turner, with insights from some of the legends of the hedge fund industry. And it's written in a wonderfully engaging style by a veteran journalist with unprecedented access to these titans of Wall Street."

—ANDREW W. LO

Harris & Harris Group Professor
Director, MIT Laboratory for Financial Engineering
MIT Sloan School of Management

"Burton . . . break[s] new ground by profiling thirteen up-and-coming managers selected by ten acknowledged 'leaders and legends.' Well written."

—PUBLISHERS WEEKLY

HEDGE
HUNTERS

Also available from
Bloomberg Press

Complicit:
How Greed and Collusion Made the Credit Crisis Unstoppable
By Mark Gilbert

Confidence Game:
How a Hedge Fund Manager Called Wall Street's Bluff
By Christine Richard
(April 2010)

———

A complete list of our titles is available at
www.bloomberg.com/books

HEDGE
HUNTERS

How Hedge Fund Masters Survived

KATHERINE BURTON
Bloomberg News

BLOOMBERG PRESS
NEW YORK

Portions of this book were published as *Hedge Hunters: Hedge Fund Masters on the Rewards, the Risk, and the Reckoning*, by Katherine Burton, ISBN 978-1-57660-245-4, © 2007 by Bloomberg L.P.

First edition published 2010
1 3 5 7 9 10 8 6 4 2

Library of Congress Cataloging-in-Publication Data

Burton, Katherine.
　Hedge hunters : how hedge fund masters survived / Katherine Burton. -- 1st ed.
　　p. cm.
　Includes index.
　Summary: "A rare look at the hedge fund industry's top performers that introduces the most talented new managers, handpicked by the masters themselves. With unprecedented candor and detail, the most successful hedge fund managers reveal their personal journeys, their individual strategies for producing outstanding returns, attributes most important to the job, and how they survived the subprime crisis"--Provided by publisher.
　ISBN 978-1-57660-363-5 (pbk. : alk. paper)
　1. Hedge funds. 2. Investment advisors. I. Title.

HG4530.B87 2010
332.64'5240922--dc22   2009048376

To Colin

Contents

Preface to the 2009 Edition

At 11:42 P.M. on December 31, 2008, as the most tumultuous year in financial markets since the Great Depression was coming to a close, I got a text message from a friend in the hedge fund industry: "RIP" was all it said.

The reaction was understandable. Hedge funds, on average, lost 19 percent during the year, their worst annual showing ever. The industry shrunk to roughly $1.2 trillion, down from its peak of $1.8 trillion just six months earlier, as a result of losses and client withdrawals. Funds were shutting down and people were losing their jobs at a record pace. In 2009 and perhaps beyond, compensation would be a fraction of the fat paychecks industry players had received as recently as 2007. Hedge funds had lost their swagger.

The losses in 2008 had been the calamitous denouement to years of easy credit that fueled consumer spending and created the biggest real estate bubble the United States had ever experienced. The first signs of trouble appeared in 2007—just as I was writing the first edition of this book—when the value of mortgages made to people with bad credit started to tumble. Bank CEOs and government officials initially assured the world that the crisis would be contained to these so-called subprime mortgages. They were wrong.

By the fall of 2008, the scope of the damage was plain: Federal officials had engineered JPMorgan Chase's purchase of Bear Stearns, and the government bailed out insurer AIG (American International Group) and seized Fannie Mae and Freddie Mac. Bank of America bought Merrill Lynch, and Lehman Brothers declared bankruptcy. The government banned short-selling in more than 940 financial stocks. Banks stopped lending. Hedge funds and other money managers rushed to sell their holdings to reduce their level of borrowing, cut losses, and raise cash to meet redemptions of clients unhappy with their performance.

The fallout was a massive liquidation that wreaked havoc in almost everyone's portfolio. The stocks and bonds that everyone thought were the healthiest fell the most in price because they were the easiest to sell. Securities that managers were shorting because they viewed them as most likely to plummet in value jumped in price as traders bought them to cover their positions.

Although most of the "smart money" knew that credit had been too easy, that the markets were due for some sort of correction, and that the global economy would certainly slow, few investors foresaw the swiftness and magnitude of the move. Call it a matter of myopia or a lack of imagination, but many traders remained too focused on their area of expertise—be it stocks, bonds, or commodities. They failed to give enough weight to the big picture, to contemplate the havoc that would ensue from a triple threat: the possibility that banks would stopped lending, investors would all want their money back, and everyone would try to sell everything all at once.

Experience didn't help much. Managers who had been in the markets for decades were often even more handicapped because they reacted as if this downturn would be much like those they'd seen in the previous ten or twenty years. Even many of the managers profiled in this book, the majority of whom had never before posted a losing year, faltered. Most of them lost at least 20 percent of their assets in a matter of weeks. About 500 firms shut down in 2008, or about 15 percent of the total at the end of 2007.

Hedge fund managers, for the most part, have been humbled. They recognize that they amassed too much money, which caused them to stray into investments beyond their core areas of competency. As they grew, many hedge funds shifted capital into private companies— investments they couldn't unload quickly. Because so much of their portfolios had become illiquid, more than 20 percent of hedge fund assets were subject to some sort of limit on withdrawals.

Only three of the seventeen managers profiled in this book—Jim Chanos, Julian Robertson, and Bruce Ritter—made money in 2008. Two, Bernay Box and Dwight Anderson, returned all their investor capital in their main funds. Only one hedge fund group, Canyon Partners, limited client withdrawals at the end of the year.

Despite their troubles, the profiled managers have entered 2009 re-energized. As Daniel Loeb told investors, "After suffering through a year like 2008, the best thing to do is to stand up, take your lumps, and clear the portfolio of dead wood."

The theme for 2009 is back to the future. Assets of many firms have dropped to levels not seen for three or four years. Managers are returning to the strategies they know best and have made them money year after year. In the wake of the Bernard Madoff's $65 billion Ponzi scheme, investors are demanding more transparency as to what their managers are doing and how they're marking their investments. And they're getting more answers. Overall, hedge funds are more investor friendly. They're giving clients more opportunities to exit the funds, or offering them lower fees if they agree to stay in the fund for a longer period of time. It's a buyer's market.

For hedge fund investors, 2008 was proof that integrity matters as much, if not more, than money-making prowess. The best managers acknowledged their mistakes and learned from them, rather than blaming losses on unprecedented market moves or on government actions. They did everything they could to give clients their money back as quickly as possible when they wanted out. They never forgot whose money it really was.

Former hedge fund manager Michael Steinhardt pulled much of his money from hedge funds in the wake of a disastrous 2008. "I remember myself and others being much more idealistic and caring overwhelmingly about the investor," he says. "In some respects, the hedge fund industry is not the glorious and ennobled field I thought it was."

Despite the extreme disappointment of investors like Steinhardt, no one expects hedge funds to go away. After all, hedge fund clients still did better in 2008 than they would have with traditional money managers who bet only on rising prices.

As it turns out, *Hedge Hunters* came out at the top of the market when what some might say was a hedge fund bubble was ready to burst. Indeed, the lessons that can be gleaned from the managers profiled here may be even more valuable in the context of a difficult economic environment than they were during a bull market. It is the managers who find ways to prosper during these tumultuous times who will surely be considered the masters of their craft.

— K. B.
September 2009

Preface to the 2007 Edition

IN THE MID-90S, when I began covering hedge funds for Bloomberg News, and during much of the decade that followed, the people who ran these funds occupied a quirky, little-known corner of the financial services industry. Once in a while, a name like George Soros, renowned as "the man who broke the Bank of England" for forcing the British pound out of the European monetary system, or John Meriwether, who nearly started a financial crisis with $4 billion in losses at Long-Term Capital Management, would make its way into the mainstream press. But most of the time, no one paid any heed to these eccentric sorts who managed money in a way that few others dared.

Unlike the managers of mutual funds and other traditional portfolios—which invest only in securities expected to rise in price—the people running hedge funds would also try to profit by wagering on securities whose value they expected would fall. The goal was to make money under any market conditions. They sometimes borrowed cash to make these bets, and they charged outsized fees—initially, 1 percent of assets under management (now, more often 2 percent) and 20 percent of any gains they made.

Hedge fund managers were considered cowboys, colorful personalities who didn't fit within the confines of a large organization. They wanted to run their own show by their own rules. The conventional wisdom back then was that size was anathema to performance. Funds routinely returned capital to their investors. By the late 1990s, only two managers, Tiger Management's Julian Robertson and Soros Fund Management's George Soros, had ventured across the $20 billion threshold. Neither manager lasted long at that lofty height.

A lot has changed since then. What was once a handful of renegade investment professionals—one early practitioner told me that if he hadn't become a hedge fund manager, he would have ended up as a bookie—has morphed into a buttoned-down industry of substantial size. Today, in 2007, there are roughly twenty-four hundred single-manager hedge fund firms worldwide, overseeing $1.7 trillion. The two largest fund groups are affiliated with major financial institutions—JPMorgan Chase & Company and the Goldman Sachs Group—and at the beginning of 2007, the seven largest firms accounted for almost $200 billion of industry assets.

As new entrants have crowded the field, performance has suffered. The average annual return for a hedge fund between the start of 2000 and July 2007 was less than 9 percent, a dramatic decline from 18 percent in the previous decade. Finding ways to make money in the markets is harder now, especially because the bigger the firm, the less impact each individual trade has on overall performance.

The hot topic as this book goes to press is the debt crisis and the resulting flight to quality that has caused some significant—and in a few cases, mortal—losses at several hedge fund firms. After years of tight credit spreads and rising stock markets, some funds have suffered what Edward Vasser, chief investment officer at Wolf Asset Management International, calls a "crisis of complacency." So far, most of the damage has been contained to funds that trade debt using a lot of borrowed money and to quantitative funds that use computer models to make their buy and sell decisions. The managers profiled in this book are not "quants," and no more than one or two of them use much leverage. Overall, most funds are making it through these tumultuous times, perhaps a little bruised, but still standing.

This backdrop of a maturing industry seems the right time to ask some very basic questions: What makes a great hedge fund manager? What accounts for the ability to thrive under conditions that make mere survival an achievement? Finding that out would go a long way toward uncovering which of the hundreds of new entrants are destined to be management stars—and maybe provide some essential tips for the young men and women who'd settle for a lesser place among this select group of investors.

To find the answers, I sought out the industry's leaders and legends—hedge fund masters who have all successfully weathered the vagaries of the financial markets for a decade or more and produced returns that far outstrip those of their peers. I chose them because of the parts they've played in the evolution of hedge funds. They excel at different strategies and some either honed their investment skills under notable mentors or became mentors themselves, influencing practices throughout the industry. Michael Steinhardt is among the industry's founders as is Julian Robertson, who is renowned for developing investment talent at Tiger Management. Tiger Cubs Lee Ainslie and Dwight Anderson were with Robertson in the early days before heading out on their own. Kynikos Associates' Jim Chanos, who makes money solely on stocks he expects to tumble, is the longest-surviving short seller with the most assets and was an obvious choice for the book, as was Boone Pickens, the grandfather of commodities trading. Richard Perry helped build the famed merger arbitrage desk at Goldman Sachs under Robert Rubin, which launched some of today's most successful hedge fund managers. Canyon Partners' Mitch Julis and Josh Friedman have created a $16.5 billion multistrategy firm, trading in everything from high-yield bonds to stocks and bank debt. Daniel Loeb still posts some of the best returns around even as his Third Point has grown large enough to float a publicly traded fund on the London Stock Exchange. And Avenue Capital Group's Marc Lasry, the most institutionally focused of the group, produces resolutely steady returns and has created one of the fastest-growing firms in the business, pulling in billions in assets from pension funds and other relatively conservative clients.

I talked to these managers about their training, their work, the lessons they've learned in the business, and the qualities they think are necessary to success. Although they're among the biggest names in the industry, some of them had never before agreed to an in-depth interview. A few common traits were immediately apparent. They all work incredibly hard, and they all think more about the bets that might sink them than about the trades that can make them a lot of money. "Live to trade another day" is one manager's motto. How each ensures his survival, however, can be astonishingly different. One went into mind-numbing market minutiae to describe why he put on a particular position. Another told of making an investment call based on a visceral instinct honed from years of decision making. He couldn't account for the thought process that got him there, but he knew he was right. Their personal styles are equally disparate. Several of these hedge fund mavens care deeply about training and mentoring their employees; others—even some who were tutored by investment greats in their youth—say they simply don't have the patience for it.

With the goal of turning the spotlight on little-known virtuosos, I also asked the masters to talk about the up-and-coming or undiscovered hedge fund professionals whose skills they admire. I interviewed these lesser-known traders to get a handle on how they had won the respect of the established players. Initially, I expected these new hedge fund stars to be in their twenties or early thirties, with funds only a few years old. Instead, the candidates were all over the map in terms of age and experience: Some of the picks have been in business for well over a decade but have remained under the radar because they've curtailed asset growth. Others just opened up shop recently. Their ages range from mid-thirties to late fifties. The variety is intriguing, but, for the most part, the veterans' explanations for their choices were single-minded and unembroidered: They make money.

In exploring the talents of all these men—whether veterans or young turks—I had hoped to uncover the winning recipe for outstanding performance, to find out what separates investment and business-building geniuses from the average joes. But there is no such recipe. That's because the approaches to investment management they've cooked up are as varied as their backgrounds and personalities. Some of them traded stocks and constructed portfolios while still in their teens. Several earned MBAs. Others took a more circuitous route to stardom: One had spent time in Israel studying the Talmud. Another had practiced law. Their threshold for money-losing pain also varies. One manager uses options liberally as insurance against a market tumble. Another never hedges.

The basic skills of money management—portfolio construction, risk management, company analysis, and research—can be taught. Yet the secret sauce, the emphasis each manager places on these investment tools, is invariably infused with the elements that drive their varied personalities—whether geeky or hip, outgoing or retiring, down-home or academic. Each style is represented in the stories of these mavericks.

Whatever their training, education, or risk tolerance, they share many qualities: they're skeptical, intellectually curious, and independent thinkers. Passionate about their profession and their goals, they take the long view. With integrity as much of a priority as performance, they built a track record first, a business second. Perhaps the most challenging hurdle they've cleared is to balance confidence and conviction with the recognition that they're fallible. Egerton Capital's John Armitage puts it most succinctly: "You have to be obsessive, you have to have guts, you have to know when to stick to your convictions and when to walk away." To make those crucial distinctions, they assemble the facts and question their investment premises. The process can result in sleepless nights and grouchy clients, but these managers don't waver once they're convinced they're right.

And when it comes to what really matters, they usually are.

Acknowledgments

First and foremost, I'd like to thank all the managers who so graciously agreed to be interviewed. Without their generosity of time and their willingness to educate me about how they do what they do, there would be no book.

At Bloomberg, special thanks to Matt Winkler for giving me the opportunity to drop my daily gig for six months to work on this project—and for taking a chance on me fourteen years ago when he hired me for my first full-time journalism job. To Jared Kieling and Ron Henkoff for supporting this project from the get-go, and to Charles Glasser for his keen legal reading of the manuscript. To Tim Quinson and Larry Edelman for so diligently respecting my book leave, and to Jenny Strasburg for pulling all the weight during my absence. To Evan Burton for ensuring that all the interview transcriptions got done in a timely manner and to Dru-Ann Chuchran for her stellar copyediting skills. To my editors Mary Ann McGuigan, who provided excellent guidance and editing, and Sophia Efthimiatou, who took what started as a casual conversation and shepherded the idea into this final product. Without her enthusiasm, encouragement, and counsel it wouldn't have happened.

To my industry sources—who always prefer to remain anonymous—who helped steer me toward the managers I should interview and provided background and insight into their businesses. Thank you all for so kindly sharing your stories and knowledge with me over the past decade. And thanks to Scott Esser at Hedge Fund Research for providing data on the industry, which are used throughout the book.

Finally, thanks to my family and friends for making sure I remained sane and balanced during the months I was sprinting toward my deadline.

HEDGE
HUNTERS

Chapter 1

Mark Yusko
What It Takes to Be the Best

In 2004, a twenty-one-year-old New York University student named Hakan Yalincak told the world he was going to run a hedge fund. With his mother, Ayferafet, he rented office space in Greenwich, Connecticut, and filled it with computers, fancy furniture, and Bloomberg terminals. They hired temps to man the screens. Wealthy investors paraded through the offices to check out the boy wonder and were told the story of a young stock-picking genius born into a wealthy Turkish family worth $800 million. The mother-son duo raised more than $7 million.

Yalincak never bought any stocks. Instead, prosecutors said he used the money to purchase a Porsche and expensive jewelry and gave $1.25 million—the first installment of what he said would be a $21 million gift—to New York University, where he was then a senior studying history. The young Turkish national was later arrested and pleaded guilty to bank and wire fraud. Yalincak was sentenced to forty-two months in prison; his mother's sentence was two years in prison, after she pleaded guilty to conspiracy to commit wire fraud.

This sad tale speaks volumes about the world of hedge funds. A con can happen in any industry. But it's the golden aura of hedge funds, with its promise of unparalleled riches, that made this unlikely scam possible and allowed a kid barely old enough to order a beer to raise millions of dollars from adults with real jobs and big bank accounts.

1

Everyone, it seems, wants a piece of the hedge fund business. MBA students across the country are eschewing jobs at major investment banks to join the funds, many of which won't be around in ten years. Managers trying to find an edge have opened funds trading such unlikely assets as art and wine.

The hedge fund world didn't always garner such attention. One friend in the industry tells of a visit home to his parents during which the mother of a childhood pal asked how his successful landscaping business was going: "Your mother said something about hedges?" The history of hedge funds—private partnerships in which the manager bets on falling as well as rising prices of stocks, bonds, and other financial instruments and then takes a piece of the profits—dates back at least as far as 1923, when Benjamin Graham, the godfather of value investing, opened just such a fund. Yet it's taken almost eighty years for the trend to become widely known.

Nowadays, the bartender, the massage therapist, and just about everybody's neighbors all know that hedge fund managers are the new masters of the universe. They make the cover of *New York* magazine; in fact, just about every kind of publication—from the *New York Post* to *Vanity Fair*—runs stories about them. They're even hip enough for HBO to develop a series about them. The amount of money they manage isn't huge compared with other large capital pools. Even accounting for leverage, the hedge fund industry's assets probably come to less than half the $10 trillion that mutual funds control. Yet the biggest hedge fund managers wield power far beyond the world of stocks and bonds. They are the Carnegies and Rockefellers of the twenty-first century: some of the biggest philanthropists, the largest political donors, and the most influential art collectors.

In 1990, there were only a few hundred hedge fund managers, with $39 billion in assets. At the end of 2006, the two biggest hedge fund operators together managed more than $65 billion. In total that year, there were roughly twenty-four hundred managers, with $1.5 trillion in assets. New entrants continue to rush in, and average returns have fallen as competition increases. As the number of hedge funds grows, so do the odds of their having mediocre leadership. Finding the best managers is even harder than it used to be.

But Mark Yusko seems to have the knack. He has been investing in hedge funds for more than a dozen years, first as senior investment director at the University of Notre Dame and later as chief investment officer at the University of North Carolina at Chapel Hill (UNC). In his six-and-a-half-year tenure at UNC, he increased the endowment's investment in hedge funds to about 55 percent of its $1.2 billion in assets. In 2004, he left UNC to form Morgan Creek Capital Management in Chapel Hill. The firm advises institutions and wealthy individuals on how and where to invest their money and farms out money to hedge funds and other investment firms.

In the years that Yusko has been picking managers, he has invested with most of the established hedge fund managers interviewed in this book and many others in the top tier. He has worked closely with Julian Robertson, who managed money for UNC for almost a decade and who owns a small minority stake in Morgan Creek. Robertson also provided seed capital for Tiger Select Fund Management, a group of funds Yusko runs that invests in other hedge funds.

"I joke that it may take me five years to figure out if I want to invest with someone," says Yusko, "but I know in five minutes if I'll never invest with somebody. When they don't have it, it's immediately obvious." The *it*—that special something that characterizes managers who seem to be divining rods for investment returns—is hard to define. Yusko has not found any one identifiable characteristic they all share that's central to success, but in some cases, that edge—whatever it may be—is apparent from the first meeting. "The moment I met David Bonderman [founder of buyout firm Texas Pacific Group], I threw my wallet at him and said, 'Here. Take all my money.' The guy has it," says Yusko. "I had a similar experience with Julian and with John Griffin." Griffin was once president of Robertson's Tiger Management and now runs hedge fund Blue Ridge Capital in New York.

The essentials for success may be elusive, but in his years of picking hedge fund managers, Yusko has developed some ideas about what constitutes great talent and how it can be nurtured. At its core, it's all about the people, he says, and mentoring is a vital part of the process. "Money is managed by people, not institutions," says Yusko.

"A lot of people get hung up on the idea that a great manager has to come out of a certain educational institution, or requires a certain credential, or has to have worked at one of the big uglies like Goldman Sachs. It's exactly the opposite." The investment business is about craftsmanship, he says, and a craftsman is an apprentice first.

Yusko likens the process of learning how to manage a fund to the way artists learned to paint hundreds of years ago. The master would set up his easel, and the apprentices would set up their easels in a circle around him. They would proceed by copying his palette, his brushstrokes, his use of light. Eventually, great painters—with styles all their own—were born from the great masters. "When Julian ran Tiger, they sat around a big round table," says Yusko. "Julian was the master and these young guys were there to copy his brushstrokes." They paid attention to how he made decisions and processed information and wisely followed suit.

Paying attention has always paid off. Before, say, the 1990s, many of the biggest winners were those who knew things before other investors did. But these days, information is much easier to get, and there are many more managers trying to parse it. With such intense competition, having a good mentor to show you the ropes has gone from necessary to critical. "Once the industry shifted into information overload, running a fund became more about process and practices and the ability to synthesize," says Yusko. "Those are learned skills."

But whether it's gleaned from a mentor or a Ouija board, what managers must learn is how to gain the advantage and identify the opportunity. In markets, when one person wins, another one loses. "Ultimately, we buy managers for their edge. You pay those high fees to great managers because they know how to extract alpha, or wealth, from the pool, where it's a zero-sum game."

When Robertson launched Tiger Management in 1980, Yusko explains, he believed he had a great advantage over most institutional investors, which were primarily mutual funds or traditional investors who bought and held stocks. "Julian had a great line when he got into the business: 'It's me and the patsies,'" says Yusko. Robertson didn't mean that his competition lacked smarts, but he saw that they were rule bound. The fund's prospectus forced them to stay inside the box. The rules might allow them to own one type of security and not another. They might prohibit short selling or forbid ownership of more than a certain percentage of a company.

"These managers were like poker players who can't hold aces," says Yusko. "If you can't hold aces, you're going to have a tough time winning a poker hand."

As time went on, a swarm of new players looked to join the fun. "People who didn't have these rules came into the business," says Yusko. All the young analysts and portfolio managers wanted to leave the Fidelity Investments of the world and open the next Soros Fund Management. There were more traders with fewer restrictions, yet many of them didn't know the finer points of the game so the renegade no longer had the advantage.

"Now, with the explosion of hedge funds," says Yusko, "there is a whole new set of patsies in the game again." This new generation of pigeons wasn't trained by the masters; they don't understand portfolio construction. Many of them presume that because they were talented analysts, they will be superb portfolio managers, says Yusko. In fact, he argues, the personality traits of a good analyst and a good portfolio manager are completely different. "What you need to be an analyst is an attention to detail, a fundamental research mindset, the ability to do active due diligence, and the skill to do financial modeling. It's very quantitative. Being a portfolio manager is almost the direct opposite. It's all about nuance and extrapolation and interpolation. It's about reading between the lines, understanding the elements that *aren't* printed in the factual statements, what the management *doesn't* say when they make a public statement, what they omitted when they were writing up their notes for the financial statements."

And ultimately it's about having the courage to pull the trigger, to put the money on the line.

The right combination of skills is not the set that most people would expect in a fund manager, says Yusko. The best in the business today are not necessarily the finest analysts, and many of them are not even the most quantitatively oriented. "Great portfolio managers are great thinkers," says Yusko. "They're smart guys who were drawn to the work and were trained about the markets by great thinkers."

Robertson is probably the best at spotting that kind of talent. "He has a process for it," says Yusko. "He is wired that way. He's a mentor. He guides them. He passes them the tools." The tools are critical: Managers need a process and a philosophy—a vision. If they don't have the tools, they won't succeed.

Some great managers are not so great at cultivating top talent, a deficiency that Yusko says may simply be a function of age—or rather the lack of it. "You cannot have wisdom without age. To be a great mentor, you have to be older, more mature, and wiser." Yusko believes that the younger the manager, the harder it is for him to command the respect of an apprentice: "'He's not that much older than I am,' the apprentice is thinking, 'Can he really be so much better?'"

Having interviewed and worked with hundreds of hedge fund managers over the years, Yusko has come up with some attributes that he believes are essential to being the best.

Independence. The word *contrarian* is often linked to investment smarts, but Yusko prefers the term *independent thinker.* After all, merely doing the opposite of what other investors are doing doesn't necessarily put you ahead of the crowd. "Sometimes the consensus is right and momentum can work for a period of time," he says.

Likewise, the modus operandi for some contrarians is to work on the assumption that things like interest rates and stock market returns are mean reverting, a conviction that markets get out of whack but eventually revert back to long-term average values. "The problem, of course, is that markets can remain irrational longer than the rational investor can remain solvent," says Yusko, quoting economist John Maynard Keynes. Being early, he points out, is often a euphemism for being wrong.

To capture the essence of the true nonconformist, Yusko prefers the definition used by Dean LeBaron, founder and former chairman of Batterymarch Financial Management in Boston: "Contrary thinking is most like intellectual independence, with a healthy dash of agnosticism about consensus views."

Managers who are independent thinkers are constantly challenging consensus and doing their own research. "You can't just accept what other people say," says Yusko, "or accept what other people put in reports."

Guts. What distinguishes a great investor is the willingness to take intelligent risk, says Yusko. Even for the willing, the odds are intimidating. "A legendary investor like Michael Steinhardt, Julian Robertson, or George Soros is right 58 or 59 percent of the time," says Yusko. "That's frightening when you think about it. Most investors are right only about 30 to 40 percent of the time. If you can be right even 51 percent, the odds work in your favor."

Clearly, without risk, there can be no substantial return. Around 2000, more institutions, like pension funds, began investing in hedge funds, and these institutions demand steadier returns, even if that means lower profits. To meet the needs of their new clients, some managers have tended to reduce the magnitude of the swings in their performance, a tendency that makes for lower gains and smaller losses.

Some managers are inclined to be less aggressive because they focus more on the 2 percent management fee they earn on the assets they oversee than on the 20 percent performance fee they pocket on the money they make. If a hedge fund manager oversees, say, $20 billion, he earns $400 million just for coming to work every day, and only a portion of that goes to keeping the lights on and paying employees. Why take unnecessary chances and risk losing lots of money and clients?

"The people you really want," Yusko insists, "are the ones who understand intelligent risk and have the guts to bet big." They have that rare chutzpah depicted in *Ocean's Eleven*, the movie about a casino heist, starring George Clooney and Brad Pitt. Clooney's character, Danny Ocean, is talking about why it's so hard to win at gambling in Vegas: "'Cause the house always wins. You play long enough, never change the stakes, the house takes you. Unless, when that perfect hand comes along, you bet big, and then you take the house."

To illustrate, Yusko points to Soros and Stanley Druckenmiller, Soros's chief investment strategist, who bet on a fall in the British pound, loaded up the boat, and earned $1 billion, and to Sir John Templeton, a legendary value investor, who in 1939 bought $100 worth of every stock listed on the New York Stock Exchange that was trading below a dollar, wagering that World War II was about to start and these stocks would soar. Within three years, 100 of the 104 made him money.

Humility and Intellectual Honesty. Top managers constantly reevaluate their positions, says Yusko. They look for data that contradict their thesis, rather than focusing on information that bolsters their view. When a position moves against them, their first question is: Am I early or am I wrong? Is this conviction or pigheadedness?

The best managers aren't afraid to say they made a mistake, says Yusko. "When they're wrong, they change their minds. Arrogance doesn't work in this business because the market will smack you down. You can be confident, but you can't be arrogant."

Roy Neuberger, founder of money management firm Neuberger Berman, whom Yusko lists among the greatest investors of all time, is widely believed to have said there are three rules to managing money: Rule 1: Do not lose money. Rule 2: Do not lose money. Rule 3: Never forget rules 1 and 2. And if adhering to those rules means you may have to eat crow, the only decision remaining is which fork to use. "The difference between a mistake and an error," says Yusko, "is that an error is a mistake you don't correct. Managers who press a bad position, insisting the market is wrong, usually don't survive it. The good managers don't cling to the mast as the ship goes down. They jump in a lifeboat and go look for another ship."

And they jump quickly. On the Friday before the October 1987 stock market crash, Druckenmiller famously decided to switch his portfolio. He shifted from wagering that U.S. stocks would fall to betting that shares would rise. He even borrowed money to goose returns. After the close that day, he had a conversation with Soros (who was not yet his boss), and over the weekend a talk with Jack Dreyfus, founder of the Dreyfus Fund, that convinced him he was dead wrong. On Black Monday, the market opened 200 points lower, and Druckenmiller acted with lightning speed, selling his entire position early in the day and going net short. He ended the month with a profit.

Connections. The best managers know the value of networking. Yusko sometimes finds great managers by talking to other investment professionals he respects. About once a year he has dinner with Hugh Sloane, cofounder of Sloane Robinson, a hedge fund company in London, and makes a point of asking him if he's given anyone money to manage. Yusko knows that any manager Sloane mentions is worthy of serious consideration. He takes it as a given that the person is smart. "That's because I know how smart Hugh is," says Yusko, "and how savvy and how discriminating, so it helps narrow my search."

Clearly, the value of a network depends on who's in it. Yusko is convinced that we become like the people we spend our time with: "Find out who the three or four most important people are in someone's life, and you'll know what kind of person he is." The goal, ideally, is to network with people whom you and others respect. Most people don't. In fact, Yusko believes that most people would be sadly disappointed if they examined their close associates, because they'd see that these people are not a help to them. "The great managers have great mentors and great friends and great sources," says Yusko.

The greater the manager, the greater the associates are likely to be. "Knowing who these guys spend time with, who they respect and admire, and who their mentors are is key to getting a sense of who *they* are," says Yusko. He tells the story of being in Robertson's office one day when he received a phone call. Robertson listened for a bit, then said, "You go next door and tell Putin that if he lets Yukos go down the tubes, there's going to be hell to pay." The fellow on the other end of the line was sitting next door to Russian President Vladimir Putin at the Kremlin, discussing the Russian oil company Yukos, then run by billionaire Mikhail Khodorkovsky. In the end, Putin didn't heed the warning—Khodorkovsky was convicted in 2005 of fraud and tax evasion, and the company was declared bankrupt in 2006—but the fact that Robertson was in a position to issue one speaks volumes.

Ambition. Hedge fund managers may be among the most intense players in financial markets. "Every manager I think highly of is very, very competitive," says Yusko, and they all have some hobby or interest that suits their competitive nature. Marc Lasry, who runs Avenue Capital Group in New York, is renowned for hosting high-stakes poker games in which the take can be as high as $20,000. Many of them look for the same kind of relentless drive in the people they bring into the firm. Robertson, for one, likes to hire college athletes because of their competitive nature as well as their sense of discipline and teamwork. The theory goes: if they take no prisoners on the golf course, on the soccer field, or at the poker table, they will be the same way in the markets.

Smarts. Even an abundance of guts and the most exclusive network can't help the cerebral lightweight. "Raw intellectual horsepower has to be there," says Yusko. That horsepower can have a range of fuels. Some are mathematically gifted; others have photographic memories. "Some of them just have a knack for being able to extrapolate and interpolate trends," he says. "They have a feel for the changes in the markets. They are sensors or seers." He cites David Bonderman's ability to see trends before they happen, a skill related to pattern recognition. But Yusko insists that masters like Bonderman simply have "different wiring." Some of the best managers are woefully inarticulate about why they see things that other investors miss. As the *New Yorker*'s Malcolm Gladwell points out in his best-selling book *Blink*, they can't explain it because the decisions, based on years of experience, are being made at the unconscious level. They just know.

Respect for Employees. The top managers treat their employees well. They pay them handsomely, and they listen to their ideas. "If you're approachable and admired by the people who work for you, you get their best ideas and their best thinking," says Yusko. If employees feel cheated or mistreated, they will walk. There is always another hedge fund that will hire them. Treating them fairly doesn't mean that a manager won't lose his temper now and then, especially when an employee messes up. "They are brutally harsh when mistakes are made," says Yusko, "but an employee learns from that not to make mistakes."

Integrity. "Integrity might be the defining characteristic of most great managers," says Yusko. "They don't cut corners. They do it the right way." In his view, if a manager cheats on little things—an advantageous call on the tennis court, a small lie on his résumé—he might well cheat on bigger things. He might be tempted to value the contents of his portfolio incorrectly or lie to investors about his returns. Some of the biggest hedge fund frauds in the industry to date—from Michael Berger's Manhattan Capital Management to Sam Israel's and Daniel Marino's Bayou Group—started with little lies that turned into hundreds of millions of dollars of undisclosed losses.

In addition to identifying top managers, Yusko's job involves monitoring them once they have his clients' money in hand. This review requires a different set of questions: Are they disciplined in their investment style, or are they creeping into areas where they don't have expertise? Are they less hungry than they were in their younger days? Has something changed in their life that has taken their focus away from the job? The following are some of the red flags he looks for.

The Red Ferrari Syndrome. The hedge fund business is lucrative, and people can change when they start making serious coin. As the cash starts to roll in, some managers get lazy or focus more attention on acquiring new toys than on investing in the markets. There are some telltale signs: Does he have a fleet of new sports cars? Is she building a fourth vacation home? Is his golf handicap dramatically lower? Yusko tells the story of a tongue-in-cheek wager that Steven Feinberg, head of New York hedge fund Cerberus Capital Management, made with him as proof he'd never succumb to the Red Ferrari Syndrome. Feinberg declared that if he ever moved out of his house in Greenwich or bought a new car, he'd double the return Yusko made on his investment in Cerberus. Yusko says technically he could have called in that bet a couple of years ago because Feinberg bought a new Chevy pickup when his old one clocked 260,000 miles. Yusko chose to overlook it.

Calling in Rich. In 2000, after George Soros's Quantum Fund lost 20 percent in the first two weeks of April when technology stocks tumbled, Soros told investors he was going to change the way the $8.5 billion fund was managed. Much of the money in Quantum was his, and he said he was more interested in preserving capital than in making more of it. "When people have too much of their personal money in the fund, they tend to become too careful," says Yusko. "I don't hire these guys to be conservative."

Personal Tragedy. "People experience tragedy and loss, and that usually impairs them—many times beyond repair," says Yusko. An ugly divorce, for example, can take a manager's eye off the ball, and some investors may even pull their money out of a fund until the legal battle is over. Nevertheless, Yusko says there are many examples of managers who come back stronger after a grave illness or a huge loss. In 1998, John Meriwether's Long-Term Capital Management lost 92 percent of its money and prompted a bail-out orchestrated by the Federal Reserve. A year later, he founded JWM Partners in Greenwich, Connecticut, and has produced steady returns ever since.

WHAT MAKES A MANAGER GREAT? What separates the run-of-the-mill stock pickers from the market superstars? Brains, courage, and humility, for starters. You're not likely to find one who lacks these strengths. Yet, what makes the managers profiled in this book most interesting is not so much what they have in common but how each is so different from the rest. Money management is far from a science, and none of these managers, even those trained by the same mentors, do what they do in exactly the same way. Some are skilled at betting on securities whose prices are tumbling, others are excellent traders, some have inexhaustible patience, others thrive on risk. The approaches they take and the choices they make are influenced and informed by their backgrounds and early successes and by their failures. Taken together, these professionals can offer considerable insight into the art of the trade.

AFTER THE CRISIS

Getting Real

"When the tide goes out, you see who's swimming naked," says Yusko, quoting an aphorism made famous by investor Warren Buffett. In 2008, the tide receded farther and faster than it had at any time in fifty years.

The previous five years had produced some relatively easy times for making money. After the Internet bubble burst in the early years of the decade, stock markets across the globe took off, jumping by about 2.5 times off their lows. Economies around the world, both developed nations and the likes of China, Russia, India, and Brazil, were on a tear. Borrowing was easy. Inflation was low.

With investment dollars plentiful, hedge funds mushroomed. Their assets reached $1.8 trillion by the end of 2007, double what they were five years earlier.

The lush times caused a bit of market amnesia among hedge fund managers. They forgot that market booms beget market busts. They forgot that there can be periods when prices jump around irrationally, and in those times, it's often better to get out of the way. They lost sight of the dangers of crowded trades and of buying hard-to-sell assets. They forgot that clients might want their money back. They didn't consider the perils of using borrowed money in volatile times. They forgot that markets go down. "A lot of people were ill-prepared to deal with what happened because they weren't good at the short side," or betting on the decline of stocks, bonds, currencies, and commodities, says Yusko.

Clients, including Yusko himself, were guilty of going too easy on the people who were handling their money, he says. "We didn't judge managers as stringently as we should have." Investors should have focused more on how well their managers could shift their portfolio between cash and wagers on falling and rising securities, as markets changed, and on how adept they were at limiting losses when a trade didn't go their way. In 2008, it became abundantly clear that these attributes mattered at least as much as being a strong analyst.

Many of the managers Yusko invested with in 2008, including some of the largest, lost money and limited withdrawals. Still, he sees the aftermath of the disastrous year as positive for the industry as managers return to sound practices of doing business. The message for 2009: Back to basics.

That doesn't mean managers aren't concerned about growing their businesses. Almost every manager wants to raise money after losing as much as 50 percent of assets from losses and redemptions. Even the top-performing traders whose funds had been closed to new investors for years decided to open the doors at the end of 2008. Some of the biggest names in the industry have been making more of an effort to meet with clients and speak at investor gatherings.

Even so, Yusko says 2009 has been about making money. That's particularly important after a losing year, because the managers who are down won't get to charge their 20 percent performance fee until the previous year's losses are recouped. "The industry will move from gathering assets to managing assets," he says. Managers will depend less on borrowed funds to make money and focus their efforts on generating returns no matter the market direction.

Yusko also sees a return to the "sole practitioner" model of investing, in which one person calls the shots. "Hedge funds gave into the temptation to hire lots of people. What they forgot is that groups don't make good decisions," he says. "An investment committee should have an odd number of members and three is too many."

He also sees a change on the horizon in fee structures and other terms for clients. Some funds have told their investors that they will trade only liquid securities and will allow clients to leave the fund every quarter, or even monthly, rather than making them wait a year or more to exit. Other managers who want to lock up their investors for longer periods of time are paying for that privilege by lowering their fees.

Overall, Yusko says, if 2008 taught us anything, it's that everything is cyclical.

The question that remains is why so many managers, even the smart ones, forgot that.

Chapter 2

Michael Steinhardt
A Passion for Performance

WHEN MICHAEL STEINHARDT was thirteen, his bar mitzvah gift from his father was two hundred shares of stock worth more than $5,000: one hundred of Penn Dixie Cement and one hundred of Columbia Gas System. The shares got Steinhardt's attention right away. He was fascinated with the notion that the companies' stock prices would fluctuate continuously and that he could be wealthier one day and poorer the next. He became so intrigued with the stock market that nearly every day after school he would leave his friends and ride the subway to downtown Brooklyn to the offices of Bache & Company, a brokerage firm. There he watched the ticker tape and observed the brokers placing their trades. He soon began reading company annual reports and other financial data; and by the time he was sixteen, he had opened a trading account in Manhattan at Merrill, Lynch, Pierce, Fenner and Smith, where he would go and read research on various companies and invest his money.

He was hooked. "I came to love the risk taking associated with trading and the rush that comes when the risk pays off," he says. "I have no doubt that I inherited this love of the rush from my father, who lived his life taking risks and pushing boundaries. Psychologically, emotionally, and perhaps even intellectually, gambling and the manner in which I then invested may not have been importantly different."

15

Maybe not, but Steinhardt had a gift for keeping the odds on his side. The hedge fund he opened in New York in 1967, when he was twenty-six, posted a gain of 99 percent in its first full year. During the next twenty-eight years, the fund produced average annual returns of 24 percent, after fees, one of the longest and best track records of any hedge fund in the industry.

Although Steinhardt started his career as a stock picker, he later became known as one of the preeminent macro managers, chasing macroeconomic trends by wagering on the direction of stocks, bonds, and, to a lesser extent, currencies. One key to Steinhardt's success was his intensity, his view that every day was a new opportunity to make money. "It means thinking about one's portfolio all the time," says Steinhardt. "What made me feel fulfilled and rewarded was having superb performance. I didn't have the ability to separate my sense of self from my performance. When things weren't good, I couldn't be happy. I was immersed in my misery."

When Steinhardt's fund lost 31 percent in 1994—its only major annual decline in his career—he was devastated. The following October, with the $2.6 billion fund up about 20 percent on the year, he announced his retirement at fifty-four years old.

At Steinhardt's office in midtown Manhattan, a glass case displays some of the Judaica he collects, silver pieces including a menorah and several Torah breastplates. At sixty-six, he's portly and mostly balding, with a white mustache and glasses. Although he's known as a difficult boss, he's soft-spoken and quick to laugh. His conversation is peppered with Yiddish words like *dreck* and *schlepper*, byproducts of his youth in Bensonhurst, Brooklyn, which in the 1940s was a predominately lower-middle-class neighborhood with a large Jewish population.

Steinhardt's childhood was different from that of most of his school friends. His mother, Claire, had divorced his father, Sol, a chronic gambler, after less than two years of marriage. She raised Michael alone, with some assistance from her mother, who lived with them. Although his father's presence in Steinhardt's early years was sporadic, the elder Steinhardt did not want his son to miss out on the advantages enjoyed by children of wealth. After graduating from high school at sixteen, Steinhardt decided to attend college at the City University of New York, primarily because the education would be essentially free. His father had other ideas. He took the young Steinhardt to dinner one night and told him to apply to the Wharton School at the University of Pennsylvania. He promised to pay if Steinhardt was accepted. He was, and Steinhardt's father made good on his promise.

Still, Steinhardt didn't like the odds. Fearful that his father would somehow fail to come up with all the tuition money needed for a four-year education, Steinhardt pushed to finish Wharton in three years. While Steinhardt was in college, his father was arrested—Frank Hogan, the district attorney at the time, called him the biggest jewel fence in America—and eventually spent almost two years in prison. Still, he managed to pay all Steinhardt's tuition.

A three-year push made it impossible to complete the requirements for a major in finance at Wharton, so Steinhardt majored in sociology. It was hardly the usual route for a student bent on a Wall Street career, but Steinhardt says that studying sociology and statistics proved to be an advantage. Sociology taught him a systematic approach to considering human behavior in making decisions about the market. Statistics allowed him to figure out how to apply probability theories in calculating the likelihood of various events. He became comfortable making wagers with incomplete information, a necessary skill for investing.

After a brief stint in the army and a few years working as an analyst at brokerage firm Loeb Rhoades & Company, Steinhardt and two friends, Howard Berkowitz and Jerrold Fine, decided to start their own hedge fund: Steinhardt, Fine, Berkowitz & Company, the predecessor to Steinhardt Management Company (Fine left the firm in 1976; Berkowitz left in 1979). He was five months shy of his twenty-seventh birthday. The firm opened its doors in July 1967 with eight employees and $7.7 million in capital, gathered primarily from family and friends. Steinhardt had the trading talent; his two partners focused more on stock analysis.

From June 30, 1970, to the last day of 1972, Standard & Poor's 500 Index (S&P 500) climbed almost 76 percent, with dividends reinvested. Steinhardt and his partners did not ride that wave. For the fiscal year ending September 30, 1970, the fund gained only 8.7 percent. And although it was up 42.2 percent for the year that followed, in 1972 the fund underperformed the market. That's because they were betting on the tumble of the very stocks—Eastman Kodak, General Electric, Johnson & Johnson, among others—that had driven stock indexes higher. Steinhardt didn't believe these so-called Nifty Fifty stocks were worth the price. They appealed to the buy-and-hold investors, but Steinhardt, knowing that no investment goes up forever, saw them as a fad. Validation came the next two years when Steinhardt made huge profits as the benchmark index plummeted 43 percent by September 1974, a decline led by the Nifty Fifty. In true contrarian spirit, Steinhardt and his partners started buying close to the bottom in late 1974, when most managers were despairing that stocks would continue to tumble.

Steinhardt's ability to profit from these extreme ups and downs exhibited his talent for what he calls "variant perception." The way to make a lot of money was to have a view that was based on a better understanding and greater knowledge than anyone else had, a view that was very different from what the rest of the market was thinking. Informed by that understanding, he would make a concentrated bet.

Steinhardt's first big bond bet, made in 1981, may be one of his most dramatic examples of variant perception. As the 1980s began, the U.S. economy faced massive inflation and a huge deficit. Interest rates for short-term paper and 30-year bonds were on the rise, reaching yields in the midteens in 1981. Wall Street analysts were predicting that inflation would continue to rise, forcing interest rates higher and bond prices lower. Steinhardt held an opposing view. He believed that U.S. Federal Reserve Chairman Paul Volcker was serious about curbing inflation and that he would be relentless about raising rates to do so, sending the economy into a recession. Steinhardt was on the lookout for any signs of a slowdown; he even created an index of New York taxis to track how many of them were going without passengers.

In the spring of 1981, he started to bet that the U.S. economy would slow more quickly than expected and that interest rates would drop and bond prices would jump. So Steinhardt made a big wager. He was then managing about $75 million in assets, and he borrowed money to place a $250 million wager that the price of U.S. 10-year Treasuries would rocket. He added to the position, even as bond prices fell. At one point, he was down $10 million on paper. Some investors pulled their money from the fund because

Steinhardt had cut his teeth as a stock jock, not a bond trader. The value of his portfolio fluctuated wildly, but by September 30, 1981, the end of Steinhardt's fiscal year, it had returned 10 percent. The next year, he posted a staggering 97 percent gain, thanks primarily to the bond call.

A few years later, Steinhardt had another variant perception of note. In April 1987, in a letter to investors, he outlined his reasons for concern about the U.S. stock market. The ratio of companies' earnings relative to their stock price was high; dividends were low. There were few cheap stocks, and he didn't believe that the environment of low growth, low inflation, and low interest rates would continue for much longer. He was convinced that either the economy would weaken or, if it picked up, interest rates would likely rise. He also expected wilder moves in the stock market. "With the advent of so-called program trading, and the proliferation of new derivatives instruments, potential volatility has greatly increased," Steinhardt wrote to his investors, adding that 50-point or 100-point moves in the Dow Jones Industrial Average would no longer be considered shocking. "I am inclined to be much more cautious in these circumstances despite the obvious risk, given the current momentum of the market, of missing a further substantial rise in stock prices," he wrote.

Steinhardt's portfolio had been more heavily weighted to stocks he expected to fall, but within a few months, as shares kept going up, the "obvious risk" of being short got the better of him, and he began to buy stocks. As they kept going up, he bought more. As September ended, Steinhardt was up about 45 percent. Even though the S&P 500 plunged about 5 percent on October 16, Steinhardt wasn't worried. The following Monday, the market went into a free fall, and Steinhardt, thinking the panic was overdone, bought more shares on the way down. By the end of that week, he'd erased nearly all the gains he'd made so far that year.

Even with a disappointing 1987, Steinhardt was a moneymaker, and he claims one of the keys to his success was to be simultaneously a buy-and-hold investor and a day-to-day or even hour-to-hour trader. "I don't think you can achieve absolutely superior performance without being sensitive to the short term," he says. "I've held a lot of things long term, but I viewed my arena as all opportunities in the market, whether they were long term or short term."

Nor was he inclined to cut his losses quickly. "I was very stubborn." Still, he continuously reexamined the ideas behind his positions to ensure that he wasn't wrong, or that the situation hadn't changed.

Steinhardt counts his early exposure to stocks as a critical factor in becoming a top-ranking money manager. "I was involved in the stock market when I was thirteen," he says. "By the time I graduated from Wharton at nineteen, I was experienced. I had already made a lot of mistakes. The earlier you do it and the earlier you learn from it, the better."

For Steinhardt, the best lessons always came from the biggest mess-ups, whether it was foreseeing the 1987 stock market crash, and then losing money when it came, or his wrong-way bet on bonds in 1994 that caused the fund to lose almost one-third of its value. "I couldn't remember the good trades," he says. "All I could remember were the horror stories, because those are the ones I learned from. You learn much more from your losers than your winners."

"When he made mistakes, he was very quick to realize them, and he demanded the same of his staff," says John Lattanzio, Steinhardt's longtime head trader, who now runs his own shop, Lattanzio Management, out of Steinhardt's offices. If an analyst went to Steinhardt and freely admitted that he had made a mistake, Steinhardt wouldn't yell, says Lattanzio. "He'd say, 'Fine. You made a mistake. Get the monkey off your back and move on.' Michael has made more mistakes than most and that's why he's great." The screaming would start only if the analyst resisted the idea that he had made an error.

It took Steinhardt most of his career to realize that there was a distinct, and unvarying, pattern to the way he managed money, whether he was betting that a stock, a bond, or a currency would increase or decrease in value. "I would almost invariably get in too soon," he says. "I was always interested in things that were out of favor, and I was perfectly comfortable buying things near or at their lows, things that looked terrible in the charts. I liked to buy things that were selling well below prior prices. It's that Lower East Side Jewish mentality: If it once sold for $9 and I could buy it for $3, I was buying it cheap."

A bargain is what Steinhardt had in mind in mid-1993 as he considered IBM. Right after Louis Gerstner Jr. became chief executive, Steinhardt started buying shares of the computer maker. The company had repeatedly taken large write-offs and because it was a strong competitor in the industry, Steinhardt figured it would recover. The shares were trading in the high forties when he started buying, and he watched them drop into the thirties. "I bought several million shares," he says. "The stock started to turn, and I started to sell it in the fifties because I had made my point. I was smart enough to anticipate the bottom, that the stock was cheap. It had gone from the thirties—its low for oodles of years—and climbed into the fifties, at which point I started to scale out. The question of how high it would go had very little interest to me. The intellectual drama was gone. I would buy things too soon, stubbornly stick around, often start out with losses, and take my profits much too soon. That was my continuous pattern."

Betting on shares he expected to tumble was agonizing for Steinhardt. "The short side was filled with angst," he says. "I would go against the world's favorite companies, the most glamorous stocks. Sometimes I didn't have the courage to stick around, but often I did. Even when I made money, I wouldn't think about how much money I could make. I would invariably cover too soon. I had that pattern throughout my career. I would buy on weakness—buy like a contrarian. I was insensitive to maximizing the potential gain because the intellectual reward wasn't so great, or so I contended. It was all about where my motivations lay."

Steinhardt admits this approach was flawed. "You have to think about maximizing your gains, not just about satisfying your ego," he says. "I didn't think about the gains as much as I did about the intellectual challenge." Still he managed to produce top returns. At the time Steinhardt announced his retirement, he said that a dollar invested with him from the beginning was then worth $462.24. The same investment in the S&P 500 would have been worth $17.06. "In terms of being a money manager with the best possible return on capital, I was better than anybody."

No formula exists for how a manager gets that good, but for Steinhardt, a trader's life is one that demands great instincts and the conviction to listen to them. "You don't learn consciously as much as you learn subconsciously," says Steinhardt. "In the heat of battle, we'd talk about a trade. Someone would come in and tell me a story and I'd say, 'No, that doesn't feel right.'" Steinhardt couldn't always articulate the reasons for his doubts, but his intuition was solid, and he trusted it. He claims he wasn't born with good instincts; he acquired them. His subconscious would sift through the facts, incomplete as they were, and lead him to certain conclusions. "They weren't always right, but they were worth listening to." And when he didn't listen, he'd often come to regret it. "I didn't want to impose myself on people I was working with. They'd done serious work. So sometimes I'd go along with them, and they'd be wrong."

Getting it right, however, was not solely a matter of intuition. He learned by doing. "My instinct was very good because of my intensity and the extent of experience," says Steinhardt. "The best of the highly experienced traders understand this in ways others in the investment-management world won't." The more you do it, the better you get. "In the course of a career, a money manager can make x decisions or 50 times x decisions. He who makes 50 times x decisions learns more."

The cumulative effect of making those choices is to strengthen the skills, including intuition, that come into play in investing. "Implicit in any decision," he explains, "are all sorts of facts, judgments, charts, and price histories that don't necessarily come into your conscious mind but somehow register in your subconscious."

But even the most experienced traders (no matter how clearly their intuition speaks to them) must contend with the temptations of the market: the alluring opportunity that can make them put aside basic principles and go for it. Such a mistake, Steinhardt's biggest, came in 1994. In the previous few years, he had started to expand into global stock and bond markets as a way to find new places to invest his growing assets, which in 1993 had reached almost $5 billion. He bought more than $30 billion worth of foreign bonds, thanks to the ease of borrowing money from Wall Street brokerage firms, and that year, he was up more than 60 percent.

Steinhardt and many other hedge funds were betting on rising bond prices in the United States and overseas. The Federal Reserve had been cutting interest rates for five years. Inflation was at a relatively low 2.7 percent, suggesting that prices weren't moving high enough to justify a rate increase. Then, on February 4, 1994, the Federal Reserve unexpectedly raised interest rates a quarter of a percentage point, following the publication of data that showed economic growth was on the rise. The move sent U.S., and especially foreign, bonds tumbling. Steinhardt says his mistakes over the years were many, but in this case he had broken one of his cardinal rules because he didn't know more than anyone else about the market. He had gotten cocky and his positions were too large relative to the amount of trading done in those markets. He had failed to ask himself the question he was always asking his analysts: "What do you know about this investment that the rest of the world doesn't?"

Steinhardt pays close attention to who knows what in hedge fund management. Wall Street loves to slice and dice the ways investors manage a portfolio. From candle charts to intermarket analysis, from sector rotation to the Elliott Wave, there's a tool for every trader. Steinhardt's measure of a great manager is simple: who has the best returns? In this camp, he places John Armitage, cofounder of Egerton Capital in London. His flagship European stock fund, launched in November 1994, has returned about 20 percent a year, on average, since inception. "You can't be a great money manager unless you have good numbers," says Steinhardt. "When I look at the list of forty or so hedge funds in which I invest at the end of every month, I look at their numbers. I don't care what they say about why they did well or didn't do well."

Steinhardt contends that talking to a manager can actually be misleading. "I used to say that I lost more money dealing with articulate people than I did any other way because articulate people have the ability to persuade you, but they aren't necessarily right," he says. "We can all be persuaded by other people, but in the end, it's the numbers that matter." And he makes decisions fairly quickly about whether someone has what it takes to achieve them.

That doesn't mean that Steinhardt will drop a manager if he goes through a bad spell. "If I have faith in a person with long experience, I'm prepared to endure periods of not getting good numbers, but that's based on a long period of good performance."

Steinhardt admits that his idea of success is a lot narrower than those of most other investors or traders. "There are very successful money managers whose overall performance is half or less than what mine was," he says. "They set out to do something very different from what I did. They didn't intend to have the best performance in the United States; they didn't intend to make money in up markets and down markets. Yet they became successful in very important ways. My focus was very narrow. All I cared about was the performance. I didn't particularly care about building an organization or about building assets under management. What made me feel fulfilled and rewarded was having superb performance. I felt terrible when my performance did not meet my unrealistic standards. Other people have a more balanced perspective, and they are prepared to do things a lot differently. They build a business, they cultivate clients, they build an organization. They are serving a very different vision of what their role is."

Steinhardt freely admits he wasn't all that good at managing people. He sometimes failed to trust his analysts, and he tells the story of selling one analyst's position while he was out at lunch. "I couldn't build an organization," he says. "That didn't interest me." As he sees it, organization building conflicted with his monomaniacal focus on performance. "If I had it to do over again, I would be less intense. I'd give people I worked with more space."

Still, one suspects he would still be obsessed with making out-sized profits. Steinhardt is dismayed by the falling returns of today's hedge funds, given the standard 2 percent management fees and 20 percent of profits they charge. "The contrast between hedge fund managers of the 1960s, the 1970s, and the 1980s and those working today is just extraordinary," says Steinhardt. "There was an élan, a sense of elitism, and that related to performance. It's not that way anymore. People can have a career managing hedge funds without having distinguished performance."

Even so, Steinhardt has found managers whose returns continue to impress him. He invests in roughly forty funds and looks for a fairly conservative result: He never wants to lose money in a year, but he doesn't expect that most funds will return more than 20 percent. Armitage fits the mold. "John is a man who has grace and humility while at the same time, the sort of competitive intensity one wishes to have in a money manager," says Steinhardt. "He is as good as they get."

Although Armitage is younger than Steinhardt by about two decades, he's hardly a newcomer. He's built Egerton into a $6 billion hedge fund firm. Lattanzio, who calls Armitage a "very good stock picker and a big moneymaker," first met the British manager when he joined up with William Bollinger, a former Tiger Management analyst, to form Egerton. Steinhardt was the firm's first client, giving them a line of capital to invest in European stocks on behalf of Steinhardt's funds.

Lattanzio says what makes Armitage great is that he's intellectually honest. Like Steinhardt, if he makes a mistake he is quick to admit it. "He doesn't fall in love with his positions. It's only a piece of paper," says Lattanzio. Armitage goes over his holdings again and again, asking himself if he would be willing to buy them at the current price. If the answer is no, he sells them, says Lattanzio.

Since his retirement, Steinhardt has had no difficulty broadening his focus. He is now a major philanthropist, primarily supporting Jewish causes. Although he is an avowed atheist, his goal is to revitalize Jewish identity through educational, religious, and cultural initiatives. He has funded such programs as Birthright Israel, which has provided about 130,000 free trips to Israel for Jews between the ages of eighteen and twenty-six who have never been to the Holy Land. In 2004, he bought a stake in New York–based WisdomTree Investments, which creates a variety of specialized index funds that trade on stock exchanges. He also collects art, including works on paper of Paul Klee, Jackson Pollock, and Pablo Picasso, among others, as well as Judaica and antiquities. As we talked in his office, he tried to convince his wife, Judy, to consider selling a Pollock piece that he bought six or seven years earlier for $2.7 million and which his art dealer had just called to say might fetch $20 million.

He was not successful.

AFTER THE CRISIS

No Excuses

The first time Steinhardt walked away from hedge fund investing was in 1995, when he shut down his fund after two years of sub-par performance. He turned his back a second time in 2008, firing

60 percent of the hedge fund managers with whom he invests because they lost too much money. "When I was a manager, I thought it was a near disaster to have a down year," he says. "I don't think that managers today think in such terms."

For Steinhardt, the worst credit crisis in fifty years was no excuse for losing money. Hedge funds are supposed to make a profit in good times and bad, and most funds failed last year in part because few of them were good at betting on securities they expected to tumble. Nor were they adept at managing risk, he says. Stocks tumbled 37 percent in 2008, convertible bonds fell 29 percent, and oil dropped from a high of $145 in July to $44.60 by the end of December. Hedge funds could have made money on any of these downward trends.

"Hedge funds have a place. But I think the place should be constrained to those who really have shown or have the potential for truly superior investment results," says Steinhardt. That's why he has only fifteen hedge funds left in his portfolio, down from forty at the beginning of 2008. Industry-wide, hedge funds lost 19 percent, on average, and many multibillion-dollar funds dropped even more than that.

For Steinhardt, deciding which managers to keep didn't depend solely on the size of their losses. "To some degree, it was a function of their performance and of personal relationships. Broadly speaking, it was how I do a lot of things—it was intuitive," he says. "The hedge fund managers that I still have are terrific. They are people I have known for an extensive period of time, people who are reliable and decent. They're hard working. With no exception, they take their business seriously, and take losses with pain."

He also paid close attention to how the managers treated their clients as the markets turned down. Steinhardt was upset by managers who limited withdrawals from their funds rather than giving money back to clients who wanted to exit. "People who restricted withdrawals are ignoring the rights of their investors and I think that is a major negative in considering future investments with them."

Curtailing risk is important for Steinhardt, who is sixty-eight years old. "I don't care that much about making a lot of money at this point. It's a little bit more about preservation of capital."

With that in mind, Steinhardt took the money he'd taken out of hedge funds and put it into short-term debt. He doesn't expect he'll be reallocating that cash to hedge funds anytime soon, not even to the managers he kept in his investment stable. "If you're older or don't have all that much money, or are less secure, you'll probably have to swallow deep and go into some intermediate bonds of considerable quality and settle for 4 or 5 or 6 percent," he says of the current market environment.

For Steinhardt, the world of hedge funds has always been about performance. "If I had a down year, I was ready to commit hari-kari. I used to say to my investors that we should make no less than 15 percent per year, and never lose money. Well, we did lose money—once very badly, and once or twice marginally in twenty-nine years. But the idea was that because we were—pardon the expression—hedged, we should not lose money."

Steinhardt says that many of today's managers don't share his attitude about the responsibility that goes along with managing other peoples' money. "I don't think they have the high standards and they don't achieve superior performance. But they charge superior compensation fees. And the investors, who once were defined as sophisticated, aren't sophisticated anymore."

"I remember myself and others being much more idealistic and caring overwhelmingly about the investor," he says. "In some respects, the hedge fund industry is not the glorious and ennobled field I thought it was."

Chapter 3

John Armitage
Reasoned and Unrattled

JOHN ARMITAGE WAS looking a bit stressed when I met him on March 1, 2007. He was attentive to my questions about Egerton Capital, the $6 billion hedge fund firm he runs in London, but he was uneasy as he spoke, glancing repeatedly at his BlackBerry for messages. One eye was bloodshot.

His jitters were understandable. It had been a rough time in the markets. The Dow Jones STOXX 50 Index, the benchmark index of the fifty largest European companies, had plummeted 5 percent since the close on February 26—its biggest slump since 2003—on concerns that the global economy was slowing. After being up about 4 percent for the year, the three main Egerton hedge funds had erased all their gains in less than seventy-two hours. The funds had also lagged the benchmark index in January. "We had a good year last year," said Armitage. "I had about a month to enjoy the success."

As it turned out, he needn't have worried. By the end of March, the funds were back up 4 percent, and by late August they had returned about 5 percent, even with the turbulent markets of July and early August.

• • •

Armitage founded Egerton in 1994 with William Bollinger, a former Goldman Sachs analyst and Tiger Management alumnus, and the hedge fund firm is one of the largest and oldest in London. Racking up average annual returns of about 21 percent, after fees, between inception and mid-2007, the funds never posted a losing year.

Armitage likes to find undervalued European companies in industries that he and his team understand. He looks for stocks that can do substantially better than the market. *Better*, as Armitage defines it, is a significant hurdle: He buys only stocks he expects will go up 30 percent over twelve months. Although his strategy is biased toward shares he expects to rise, he also shorts stocks. Those picks make up about 5 percent to 15 percent of the portfolio.

Despite his gray hair, Armitage, forty-seven, has the endearingly disheveled appearance of a British public school boy. In fact, he attended Eton and studied history at Cambridge. The day I met him, he was wearing a blue broadcloth shirt that had managed to work its way out of the back of his navy cotton trousers, and his socks had slipped to his ankles. The gold ring on his finger was so old that I could no longer make out the insignia.

Disarmingly modest—the very opposite of the alpha-male-finance stereotype so popular in the New World—Armitage ascribes Egerton's success to hard work and to focus and discipline rather than any preternatural ability to spot winners. He's been known for such humility since his days at Morgan Grenfell, now owned by Deutsche Bank, where he managed a top-rated European stock mutual fund. Armitage likens his place in the hedge fund universe to that of the anonymous artisans in the Middle Ages who sculpted cathedral facades. They weren't creative geniuses like da Vinci or Michelangelo, but they were well trained and what they did was worthwhile. "What we do here is a cookie-cutter skill. It can be taught," he says.

Armitage's humility is matched only by his drive. "I've wanted to be successful," he says, and adds after a pause, one that speaks volumes about taking nothing for granted, "I've had tremendous periods of self-doubt."

The brief equity meltdown in late February and early March 2007 may have been stressful, yet as the market plunged, Armitage didn't waver, neither buying nor selling shares aggressively. That discipline is the hallmark of how he manages money. "We don't like selling stocks in a different way than we buy them," he says. "We don't buy stocks just because they're going up, so we don't sell them just because they're going down." He and his team hadn't used borrowed money to make their bets, and they owned some puts on the stock index (an agreement that gives the buyer the right to sell the index at a specific price by a specific date) to protect against a tumble in share prices. Armitage didn't make any purchases as stocks came crashing down, however. "That's probably cowardly," he says.

Eight portfolio managers help Armitage run Egerton. "I have to be on board if the position is big," he says. "If I don't like it, I prefer not to have it in the portfolio." He tends to drop into people's offices, rather than running formal meetings.

Egerton generally holds sixty to eighty positions, twenty of which account for about 60 percent of assets. He analyzes companies, picks the best in terms of potential returns, and ranks them according to which will make him the most money. His biggest position in early 2007 accounted for 7 percent of the portfolio. He focuses primarily on mid-cap and large-cap stocks and spends a lot of time talking to management. "You can only make a judgment if you meet or talk to companies," he says.

Although Armitage looks for stocks that are selling at an inexpensive price relative to the company's moneymaking potential, he's not especially interested in companies in need of fixing. "I like to own good businesses," he says. "I don't want to see headlines in the *Financial Times* in the morning that make me sick. The ones I want are not necessarily the best in their group, but they're good." He likes companies that have good management, generate a lot of cash, have strong balance sheets, and demonstrate considerable potential for growth. Filling that bill in early 2007 was Spanish bank Banco Bilbao Vizcaya Argentaria (BBVA), which Egerton had owned since late 2005 and in 2007 counted as its biggest holding. The bank has a strong presence in Latin America, including Mexico. "It's a very good retail bank," he says, with conservative accounting. By 2007, BBVA accounted for 30 percent of the Mexican market, helped by the purchase of Grupo Financiero Bancomer, then Mexico's biggest bank, in 2000. Armitage sees strong growth for at least a decade, given that 45 percent of Mexicans don't yet have bank accounts and the total mortgages outstanding are equivalent to those made in any one year by a single savings and loan in the United Kingdom. The

Mexican operations helped to increase BBVA's first-quarter profit by about 31 percent in 2007.

The fund's second-largest position was in the American depositary receipts of OAO VimpelCom, Russia's No. 2 cell-phone company. Most of the company's growth was organic, rather than through acquisitions, allowing for expansion that came at a relatively low cost and without carrying a lot of debt—all of which endears it to Armitage. Although cell-phone subscriptions in Russia total about 152 million, almost 10 million more than the country's population, the saturation isn't as high as it seems because many Russians own more than one phone, Armitage says. The country's standard of living is on the rise, and cell-phone use is growing along with it. In the first quarter of 2007, VimpelCom reported cash flow at record levels, and through July its shares had climbed 36 percent, following a nearly 80 percent jump the previous year.

Another large holding was Randstad Holding, a temporary-employment company in Diemen, Netherlands. It does most of its business in the Netherlands and Germany, although it also operates in France, Spain, and Portugal. Providing temps is a small but growing enterprise in Europe. "Management runs the business in a very disciplined fashion. If I had a private business, I'd want them running it," says Armitage. Like the fund's other two major holdings, Randstad generates cash and posted earnings in the first quarter of 2007 that rose almost 50 percent from a year earlier.

Armitage analyzes and reexamines his positions continually. "I don't have as quick a mind as I would like," claims Armitage. "I need to go over things again and again and again and again. I think of more questions to ask each time. I develop a better understanding over time, and I begin to feel good or bad about the stock." An avid researcher who drags around pounds of financial documents when he's away from the office, he once told an interviewer that his hobby was reading annual reports.

His penchant for deliberation in decision making developed over time. "I invest less naïvely than I used to," says Armitage. "I was probably a faster decision maker and quicker to jump on a position when I was younger." Now, he reminds himself that if you don't own it, it can't kill you.

Homework, however extensive, can't offer insights into every business, which may be why Armitage gravitates toward companies and industries he understands, although he may buy more esoteric stocks, like those of biotechnology companies, if the circumstances are right—for example, if the U.S. Food and Drug Administration has already approved a drug. "If the FDA approves an oncology drug, then that's good enough for me," he says. He tends to shy away from technology companies, however, because it's hard to judge which hot, new thing today will be obsolete tomorrow. "Who knows whether Google will be the best thing since sliced bread in five years?"

Constant studying also helps him to decide when to sell. He's continually reassessing the company's growth potential as he learns more about its business, which is why he doesn't use precise price targets to tell him when to exit a trade. Nor is he comfortable using stop-losses, preset limits that would force him out of a stock if it reached a certain price. There was a time in the markets when stop-losses worked, he says, but that was when they were dominated by buy-and-hold investors and short-term moves were more rational. If a stock suddenly plunged, it was probably because someone knew something the rest of the world didn't. Today, markets tend to be more volatile, with more hot money trading in and out of shares. In a bear market, he finds stops can shake an investor out of good companies that have temporarily tumbled along with the indexes.

To detect which stocks are in trouble, he and his team perform the same in-depth research they would in looking for shares to buy. During the market plunge of 2001 and 2002, they did well shorting companies with flawed accounting, as well as companies with negative cash flow. If an enterprise is hemorrhaging cash, it's just a matter of time before it goes out of business, he says.

When interest rates are low, and it's easy to borrow money, turning a profit by shorting—borrowing shares and then selling them in the hopes that you can buy them back later at a cheaper price—becomes more difficult and he tends to hold fewer of them in his portfolio. Just before the minicorrection in early 2007, Armitage told me the shorts had been hurting performance. "Some investment approaches are innate; shorting stocks is not," says Armitage. "Most of the time, the stock market goes up or is flat. With shorting, the dice are stacked against you," which is why he makes relatively few short bets. "We are the most conventional of any of the funds you're talking to, and that reserve comes from a sense of our limitations."

• • •

Unlike many top managers, who were drawn to the markets early and started honing their investment skills while they were in their teens, Armitage entered money management by accident. He had never considered a career in finance, never ran home from school to pore over stock charts. The impetus was far less complicated: In 1981, after he graduated from university, he needed a job and merchant banks were hiring. "I figured they were meritocracies, and the work would be fast moving and exciting," says Armitage. "I was light years from the way people plan their careers now." He landed at Morgan Grenfell. "I was very lucky."

Starting out as an analyst, Armitage wasn't captivated by the work right away. "It took me a period of time to enjoy what I was doing, and it took me five or six years to become passionate about it." In 1988, Michael Dobson—who became chief executive of Morgan Grenfell a year later—gave Armitage a mutual fund to manage: the Morgan Grenfell European Growth Trust. Armitage was thrilled, and he set out to make it a success. "It was very childish, but I wanted something that would be advertised in the *Financial Times*."

It was. During the six years Armitage ran it, the fund was the top-ranked European mutual fund ahead of eighty-four rivals, beating the average annual return of the index by 10 percentage points. Then Bollinger came to him with a proposition. Former hedge fund manager Michael Steinhardt (see Chapter 2) was willing to give Bollinger some money to invest in European stocks on behalf of Steinhardt's hedge fund, and Bollinger asked Armitage to join him in starting a firm. The idea took Armitage by surprise. "I thought I was going to stay at Morgan Grenfell for the rest of my life," he says. "I was well paid. It felt like a small company."

Bollinger's proposal to manage the Steinhardt account and to start a hedge fund firm began to grow on him. He liked Bollinger and trusted him. What's more, Bollinger had about five years' experience running a hedge fund after leaving Tiger Management in 1987, so he came equipped with a set of skills that would complement Armitage's strengths. Armitage had never had to worry about the business side of things, but he had a proven track record in investing.

Bollinger brought an investment track record to the table, too. At Goldman, he had been an oil-services analyst beginning in 1980 when oil was trading at $40 a barrel, and during his tenure there he watched it tumble toward $10, a price it finally hit in 1986. Under those conditions, Bollinger had learned a thing or two about shorting shares, skills that led Tiger Management's Julian Robertson (see Chapter 15) to hire him.

Aside from his greater experience wagering on falling stocks, Bollinger was also more fundamentally risk averse than Armitage. He tended to take a broader, macroeconomic view of the world, whereas Armitage drilled down into company details. Bollinger, Armitage says, served as ballast in turbulent markets, pondering how much cash they should hold or the number of index puts to buy. "He was always worrying about what was around the corner."

After the Internet bubble burst and global stock markets were collapsing at the beginning of the decade, their differing styles served the fund's investors well. They ended 2001 up 1 percent as the European stock market tumbled 17 percent that year, and in 2002, the flagship funds jumped nearly 12 percent, probably their best performance ever relative to the benchmark, which fell 32 percent. They had not held many Internet stocks, and although their long positions didn't gain much, they owned index puts, which made money when stocks tumbled, as well as puts on the dollar, which fell about 15 percent against the euro that year.

In 2005, after more than a decade, Bollinger left Egerton to pursue philanthropic endeavors, although he remains a partner in the firm, an investor in its funds, and a close friend of Armitage. With Bollinger's departure, Armitage realized he would have to change the way he ran the portfolios. He knew he couldn't do alone what Bollinger's contribution had allowed them to do together. "I couldn't split my personality down the middle," says Armitage. "I couldn't worry about losing money and making money." The new strategy for managing the funds had to be one that matched his strengths, one with which he could be comfortable. That meant he would primarily buy stocks he expected would climb, allowing his net exposure on long investments to be between 70 percent and 100 percent of assets. He would own index puts as "disaster insurance," in case markets fell 20 percent or more. All he had to do was pick the right stocks and stay away from leverage, the latter being unusual for stock funds, which generally borrow some money to make their wagers. "You shouldn't need leverage to perform well," he says. "The best way to die poor if you've been born rich is to borrow money and invest badly."

He knew the approach was doable. He had run the Morgan Grenfell mutual fund and produced average annual returns of 27 percent a year. Since March 1995, he'd also managed a long-only fund at Egerton, which had racked up profits of more than 24 percent annually. Armitage also knew that this style might mean more volatile returns, so he told investors he'd lower his performance fee in exchange for their paying him more than they normally would after a losing year.

Most funds have what's called a high watermark, which means that if the manager loses money in a year, he doesn't collect a fee on any subsequent gains until the investors are made whole. The high watermark has proven disastrous for some funds. If a fund loses 20 percent in a year, a manager has to return 25 percent before he can start charging fees again. Often, investment staff will jump ship after such a loss, knowing they probably won't see a bonus until the fund is again in the black. Some managers have closed their doors rather than try to claw their way back into positive territory.

With those dangers in mind, Armitage made a deal with his investors. For those who were amenable, he reduced their fees from a 1 percent management fee and 20 percent performance fee to 1 and 15 (with founding investors paying 1 and 10). In the event of a losing year, the investors would pay only half the fees as performance rebounded until Armitage made up twice the loss. For example, if the fund's net asset value fell from 100 to 90, investors would pay half their fee—7.5 percent—until the fund's net asset value hit 110. Under this fee structure, Armitage could still pay his people while he was digging himself out of a hole. The new arrangement gave him confidence. "I'd be less prone to sell stocks when they collapsed," he says. "I'd be better at staying in the market, and better at ignoring the market wiggles."

And he was. In May and June of 2006, when the benchmark European index tumbled almost 10 percent, he was ready. Before the stock market's big move down, Armitage had been selling some of his holdings because the prices of shares he owned had produced big gains. His funds were about 75 percent net long, but he owned a fair number of index puts and held some cash. Armitage sensed there might be trouble ahead. "It had been quite easy to make money and that worried me," says Armitage.

As the markets plunged, he and his team bought some shares. Although the stocks he already owned dropped about 1.3 times the rate of the market, they bounced back with a lot more force than the overall index did. "We were not very aggressively positioned, so we weren't forced sellers," Armitage explains. He ended the year up 26 percent after fees, compared with 14 percent for the index.

The market challenges in 2006 demanded skills that Armitage says are key to investing well. "You have to be obsessive, you have to have guts, you have to know when to stick to your convictions and when to walk away," says Armitage. Just as important is being able to face that you won't always know when that moment has arrived. Be prepared to make mistakes, he says, because you'll make a lot of them. Armitage reckons that a good investor is right about 60 percent of the time. "If you didn't make a lot of mistakes, you wouldn't be working. You'd be on a beach."

Selling too soon is one of the most common errors investors make—and one Armitage admits he's made his share of as well. "I've bought stocks that have gone down, and they sear on your soul, but selling winners, that's the big mistake," he says. "I've been a very bad seller of shares. I've sold lots of winners." He points to Hennes & Mauritz (H&M) in Stockholm, Europe's second-largest clothes retailer, which he sold in 1995. Since then, H&M's stock has climbed 35 percent a year on average.

What makes the temptation to bail out early so difficult to resist? "Investors confuse rates of return with the potential for absolute gain," Armitage explains. "You make the mistake of not understanding the true potential." If a stock has already gone up 20 percent or 30 percent, and it looks to be fairly valued for the next six months, it becomes impossible to imagine it will repeat that performance. And you're probably already eyeing another stock that's cheaper, he says.

These essentials of managing a fund successfully—having confidence in your picks, being decisive, and surviving in difficult market conditions—came to Armitage from respected associates and mentors, he says, including his former boss Dobson, colleague Werner Wanke, and his current partners William Bollinger, Marcello Sallusti, and Ralph Kanza.

Armitage acknowledges that greatness in a handful of other investors whom he admires and knows: Michael Steinhardt; Nick Roditi, a manager who used to work for George Soros and now runs money in London; Christopher Hohn, who runs the activist hedge fund TCI Fund Management in London; Anthony Bolton, who helped turn Fidelity International into the United Kingdom's largest mutual fund company; and Donald Cecil, who founded Cumberland Associates in New York. "They have supernormal intellectual gifts that set them apart from ordinary people," he says. "They've got the guts to take big positions and to stand out from the crowd."

Armitage says that there's a danger in talking too much to investors he respects. "When you know how good someone is and you know they're normally right, you're going to be seduced," he says, and you may end up seeing only what they see. "At the end of the day, we all have to do things for ourselves."

But Armitage never seems to have much trouble doing that.

AFTER THE CRISIS

Assessing the Unknown

Armitage's Egerton European fund dropped 26 percent in 2008, his worst annual loss in more than twenty years of investing. Even so, the fund has returned almost 17 percent a year on average since its inception in November 1994.

As was the case with many managers in 2008, Armitage experienced the lion's share of the damage between the end of May and the end of November. His biggest mistake, he says, was paying too much attention to individual companies rather than focusing on the macroeconomic situation and its effects on global stock markets as investors ran for the exits en masse to raise cash and reduce debt. "Our focus on companies and managements' views and their businesses, with hindsight, proved very unhelpful because it did not allow for the fact that financial markets themselves caused the slowdown and the drop into a recession," Armitage told clients in January 2009.

As stock prices slid, he cut his exposure in the stocks he was expecting to rise in value. But he didn't move fast enough, he says. His average net exposure (his longs minus his shorts) fell from 62 percent in June to 33 percent by the end of the year, roughly the same exposure he had during the last bear market of 2001 and 2002.

His holdings in the early part of 2009 included a stake in DIRECTV Group Inc., a U.S. satellite pay TV business that also operates in Brazil, Mexico, and other Latin American countries. Armitage liked the company's prospects because it was adding more subscribers and services, had little debt, and would most likely be buying back shares.

He also owned Anheuser-Busch InBev NV, the world's largest beer maker, created in late 2008 through the $52 billion merger of Belgian brewer InBev NV with the maker of Budweiser. The company "blends the most efficient cost-driven and cash-focused management we know with the strongest brewing franchise in the United States," Armitage told investors in April 2009.

In the first quarter of 2009, the Egerton fund fell about 40 basis points, compared to a drop of nearly 12 percent for the FTSE World Series Europe Index. By mid-July the fund had returned 2.8 percent, while the FTSE Index had rebounded, climbing about 6 percent for the year and 35 percent from its lows in early March. The fund lagged the market because Armitage chose to reduce net exposure to 31 percent in early April, even as European stocks were beginning to climb. "It is always hard to understand whether a rally after a major decline is just a bear-market rally, or whether it constitutes a turning point," he told investors. "This is an environment where one should tread carefully."

His fear was that the Europe and emerging markets had more losses ahead. The U.S. economy had been faltering for many months, but the downturn in Europe and emerging markets had only begun after September 2008, when Lehman Brothers declared bankruptcy. That meant that companies operating in these countries could be facing a big hit to their bottom line, and subsequently to their stock prices. Rather than jump into the markets, Armitage chose to hold 40 percent of his portfolio in cash while he waited to see the extent of the earnings decline. "If what is happening is 'unprecedented,' then "I do not know," is the appropriate response until we have strong convictions," he said.

By the end of September, Armitage's flagship fund had climbed about 9 percent as he cut his cash position to 17 percent of assets and increased his net exposure to 75 percent.

Chapter 4

Marc Lasry

An Intolerance for Losing

BEFORE MARC LASRY BUYS the debt of a troubled company, he considers everything that can go wrong. "Most investors focus on how much they're going to make rather than on how much they could lose," says Lasry. "Our focus is on the downside." So when his analysts do their homework, he wants to know the worst that could happen. "I don't want to hear how great the investment is. I want to hear how we could get hurt. Once we know that our downside is protected, then we look at what we can make on it."

That's not the typical hedge fund manager's approach, but Lasry, forty-eight, took an atypical route to creating New York–based Avenue Capital Group, one of the world's largest hedge funds trading bank debt, loans, and other securities of companies in or near bankruptcy. As a young adult, Lasry never imagined a career in finance. Instead he went to law school and started his professional life as a bankruptcy attorney. In 1995, eleven years after he got his degree, he formed Avenue Capital with his sister, Sonia Gardner, establishing perhaps the only brother and sister team in the hedge fund universe.

In 2001, assets in Lasry's fund totaled only $1 billion. By 2007, Lasry's deliberate, conservative approach helped him build Avenue's hedge fund assets to $14.5 billion. The firm also manages $3.1 billion in collateralized loan obligations, loans that are packaged together to form new securities. Lasry attracts billions of dollars from large stodgy institutions like the state pension funds of California and Pennsylvania, which generally pay him 2 percent of assets and 20 percent of any profit he makes—not for having the highest returns but for having steady performance.

And they get what they pay for. From its inception through mid-2007, Avenue's flagship fund returned about 10 percent a year after fees on average, beating the benchmark stock index by 3.3 percentage points. Lasry's biggest loss of any year was for 1998, when his Avenue fund dropped 8.7 percent—an almost painless slip compared with the 31 percent the Standard & Poor's 500 Index lost in 2001 and 2002 as the Internet bubble burst.

Stacked against the earnings of the more aggressive types, Lasry's numbers tell a modest story. For example, Avenue's returns are less than half those of David Tepper, a well-respected distressed-securities manager who started his firm, Appaloosa Management, in 1993 after leaving Goldman Sachs, where he was the head of junk-bond trading. Tepper's Palomino Fund averaged returns of close to 30 percent a year between its start on December 31, 1994, and July 2007. But the more important difference between the two is that Tepper's performance is much more volatile. His biggest drawdown, or loss from peak to trough, was between February and September of 1998, when the fund tumbled by nearly half. "David likes to take risks," says Lasry. "He likes playing at the bottom of the capital structure, and if he's right, he does extremely well. If he's wrong, he gets hurt."

But getting hurt—at least seriously—is something Avenue's institutional investors must avoid. The firm's prominence among hedge funds—it ranked No. 32 in terms of assets at the end of 2006, up from No. 82 the year before—reflects the changing nature of the industry. More institutions, especially corporate and public pension funds, are investing in these private partnerships. These investors tend to be more cautious. If California loses money investing for its pension fund, the state might be forced to cut programs or increase taxes to pay its retirees. With such consequences at stake, these institutions flock to managers who take less risk, even if it means they don't produce supersized profits. Avenue's better-than-equity returns with milder swings in performance fit their needs quite nicely.

Lasry's style suits his institutional clients. His looks echo Main Street more than Wall Street. His wavy hair has more salt than pepper, and he favors casual slacks and sweaters—the sleeves pushed up above the elbows as if he was preparing to do manual labor or play a friendly game of basketball that he fully intends to win. His office in midtown Manhattan is quite large and accommodates a substantial desk, a small round table and four chairs, a leather couch, and white lamps deserving of a place in a living room. One wall bears a photo of Lasry with Nelson Mandela and Bill Clinton, whose daughter Chelsea works for the firm. Lasry is a big supporter of Hillary Clinton.

Like many attorneys, Lasry is a careful guy. He doesn't use borrowed money to make bets, and he buys only loans and bonds that are at the top of the capital structure, which means he gets paid first if things go horribly wrong. He mostly declines to discuss individual positions—even those no longer in the port-folio—for fear of getting into trouble with the fund's lawyers, including his sister Sonia, who is Avenue's general counsel. His youngest sister, Ruth, also has a law degree and works at Avenue as a bank debt trader.

Lasry's modus operandi is to buy senior bank loans or bonds cheaply, generally at $0.40 to $0.60 on the dollar. Senior debt is first in line to be paid if disaster strikes. "We've done it in Europe, in Asia, and in the U.S.," says Lasry. If he's wrong about the fundamentals of a company, the fund may not make money, but it won't lose any either. "Our downside is we'll get back our cost three years from now." If he buys debt at, say, $0.50, and the company liquidates its assets, or eventually gets taken over, he'll generally get out what he put in. If he's right, he'll end up selling out at $0.90 or $1.00 in three years. His upside is limited because the debt will be paid off at par, or $1.00. Buyers of subordinated debt, which gets paid off after the senior debtors have been made whole, sometimes get shares in the new corporate entity that emerges from bankruptcy, so their potential profit can be much higher.

Lasry is comfortable giving up the possibility of a greater payday. If he buys debt at $0.50 and ends up with $1.00 three years later, he has made at least a 25 percent annualized return. That's as good as or better than what stocks can offer. "I've generated an equity-like return and taken substantially less risk," says Lasry. "That's a lot of what we do. We're getting overpaid for that risk. We would rather protect our downside."

Investing in distressed debt is a cyclical business. In recessionary times, investment ideas mushroom. When economic times are good, there are fewer opportunities to make money. In 2003, it became a lot harder to produce top returns because default rates began to drop. By 2007, the default rate was about 1 percent, compared with 13 percent in 2002. The market of distressed debt—bonds trading at 10 percentage points or more above comparable U.S. Treasuries— peaked in 2002 at $950 billion and remained between $600 billion and $700 billion through 2006.

That squeeze in supply forced Avenue to research more and smaller companies. "You invest only in the opportunities you see. I have no problem sitting on cash," he says. He has about thirty to forty positions across his various funds. "We have a large team. We like to do private equity–type research, go out and meet with the company. Our analysts look at maybe ten companies each." He reckons most hedge fund analysts cover thirty companies.

Avenue often finds good investments in industries that are facing rapid changes, economic difficulty, or regulatory pressures. When Lasry is deciding whether to buy, he looks for answers to some key questions. The most important is whether there is a reason for the troubled company to stay in business. "If it ceased to exist, would it matter?" he wants to know. "Are there real assets there? Is there a consistency to the cash flow? Current problems aside, is this a company that is going to be able to survive? Does it have something that's unique that its competitors want?"

An investor looking at discount retailer Caldor's when it filed for Chapter 11 bankruptcy in 1995 needed only to consider the store's business plan to gauge its potential for future success. "A company like that buys goods cheap and sells them," says Lasry. "There's no barrier to entry and lots of other retailers are doing the same thing. If Caldor's goes out of business, it's not going to be a big deal." Indeed, the retailer ceased operations in 1999, unable to fight the increased competition from other discount stores including Wal-Mart Stores.

The situation is different with companies like Northwest Airlines, which exited bankruptcy protection in May 2007. "It's much harder for airlines to go out of business," says Lasry, at least when they have routes that are valuable to other players. Eastern Airlines no longer exists because it traveled only the East Coast—a corridor well served by other airlines. Northwest has valuable Asian routes. "Most airlines would love to have those slots."

Lasry also looks to buy from sellers who are unloading their holdings for what he calls noneconomic reasons. Maybe a bank needs to get nonperforming loans off its books. Maybe a company's bonds have just been downgraded to a rating that precludes a mutual fund from owning them. Most people don't like to own things that are in trouble, he says. Avenue might first start looking at a company's debt because it's trading cheaply, then decide through a series of quantitative and qualitative screens whether it's worthy of pursuit.

About 5 percent of Lasry's U.S. investments are in trade claims, which are accounts receivable of a troubled company: Perhaps a supplier ships $1 million of goods to a cash-strapped retailer, and the retailer subsequently files for Chapter 11. The supplier then becomes an unsecured creditor. If the unsecured bonds are trading at $0.50, Avenue can buy the trade claim for anywhere from $0.20 to $0.40 because there is no public market for them, meaning each supplier needs to be contacted individually. Once a company is in bankruptcy, suppliers who continue to do business with it are first in line to get paid. Even so, some suppliers will sell their accounts receivable for $0.95 as insurance in case the troubled company suddenly goes into liquidation. When Avenue was smaller and bankruptcies were higher, the firm had 20 percent to 30 percent of assets in trade claims.

The possibility of liquidation poses a risk, of course, but Lasry's biggest mistakes have come not from the bottom falling out but from getting involved with companies that were lying to their investors. "We've gotten hurt relying on the numbers and on meetings with the company and getting to a certain comfort level and then finding out there is fraud. How do you come up with a system to catch fraud? It's hard. The guys committing fraud are good at lying and hiding. In the past, we thought such behavior was an aberration. It's not." The firm's analysts now make a point of talking to a lot of people, including the chief financial officer, the comptroller, and competitors, to ensure that what company management is telling them is true.

• • •

Lasry's journey toward success in the world of hedge funds didn't result from any grand plan on his part. Indeed, life threw him its share of misunderstandings and false starts. Born in Marrakech, Morocco, he immigrated to Hartford, Connecticut, when he was seven. When he arrived in the United States, he spoke only French and understood Arabic. His parents enrolled him in public school and when his mother went to a parent-teacher conference a few months later, she got a disturbing report. "We think your son is a little bit retarded," the teacher said. "We speak to him, but he never speaks back." Mrs. Lasry explained that her son was still learning English. "But that can't be the reason," the teacher responded. "We speak Spanish to him."

Lasry's postgraduate studies likewise got off to a seemingly unpropitious start. He was interested in learning, but he had no burning desire to be a lawyer. The summer before he started New York Law School, he had worked as a UPS truck driver and considered ditching his academic plans. "These drivers make a lot of money. I thought I could get into management," he told a group of students in a speech at his alma mater in 2007. "But my wife didn't want me to be a truck driver. She wanted me to go to law school." So he went.

He remained uncertain about what kind of law he wanted to pursue until he took a course in corporate law and bankruptcy reorganization and his professor recommended him for a clerkship with the Honorable Edward Ryan, then the chief bankruptcy judge in the Southern District of New York. After graduating in 1984, he went to work in the bankruptcy practice of Angel & Frankel in New York.

Like any first-year associate, he worked like a dog, clocking twelve-to-fifteen-hour days and seeing precious little of his wife and young daughter. Lasry had married his college sweetheart, Cathy, whom he met through his sister Sonia, when the three of them were at Clark University in Worcester, Massachusetts. Lasry and his wife have five children.

Fed up with the schedule at Angel & Frankel, he jumped at the chance a year later to be a lawyer at Smith Vasiliou Management

Company, in New York, an investment-management firm that was buying trade claims. He befriended an analyst there and began learning the investment side of the business.

A quick learner, he was soon suggesting possible investments. At first, his boss gave Lasry's ideas little notice, citing the young man's lack of experience. Lasry countered that he was confident enough to be willing to invest his entire net worth in the idea. "That's only $25,000," his boss scoffed.

Even then, Lasry employed his downside theory of risk. He had nothing to lose in trying to get into the investment game. If his boss didn't listen, nothing would change. He'd still have his job as attorney. "Even if the boss didn't buy into the investment, he'd know I was right if the price went up. I'd have a chit. You have to get a lot of chits," he says. "If you're wrong at any time, you're screwed. I'm just telling you. That's how it is."

But Lasry is a big believer in sticking his neck out. His recommendations made the firm $25 million his first year. His salary was $50,000, and he decided to ask for half of 1 percent of the money he'd made them as a bonus, or $125,000. His boss applauded him for having done a fabulous job and offered him $10,000. "I realized this firm wasn't the place for me," says Lasry.

He moved to Cowen & Company as codirector of its bankruptcy and reorganization department. There he was given a partner's capital to invest, and he hired Sonia, who had just earned a law degree from New York's Benjamin N. Cardozo School of Law at Yeshiva University. One of the groups that coinvested with them was the Bass family of Dallas, Texas, who had earned their wealth as wildcatters in their home state.

Lasry and his sister left Cowen in 1989 to work for a company affiliated with the Robert M. Bass Group, and ended up under the investment tutelage of David Bonderman, who was then chief operating officer for Bass. Bonderman later cofounded Texas Pacific Group in 1993, one of the largest private equity shops in the world. At Bass, the firm made an average 73 percent a year return for six years.

Lasry's years at Bass taught him a great deal. And he credits Bonderman for much of it. "Bonderman is a pretty unique individual," says Lasry. "There were very few people managing a couple of billion dollars then. Bonderman was investing in equities, distressed debt, everything. He's at the high end of street smarts and book smarts." Lasry strongly recommends that young people seek opportunities to work for someone who's smarter than the rest and willing to teach. "In business, you quickly learn that there aren't that many people who impress you right away," he says. "Everyone thinks he's smart, but when you meet someone you think is head and shoulders above you, that's what creates a phenomenal place to work."

At Bass, Lasry was surrounded by graduates of the top law schools in the country, including Yale, Harvard, and Stanford. Their pedigrees did not intimidate him, and he still puts a lot of faith in people with street smarts—the ones who can think on their feet and come up with novel ideas. "There are always going to be very smart people," he says. "The thing that will set you apart is if you have a real love: if you really want to kill for that job and you show you can figure things out a little bit differently. You can't be shy about voicing your opinions."

He looks back on Bass as a great experience. Even after some people left the firm, they ended up working together, coinvesting in deals, he says. Other investors associated with Bass include Richard Rainwater, the Texas billionaire who helped create the Bass family fortune; Dan Stern, cofounder and chief executive of Reservoir Capital Group; and real estate investor Thomas Barrack, who runs Colony Capital. "It was a pretty large group," he says. Bonderman still holds sway with Lasry. "I run my own firm, but if David suggests something, I do it."

In 1990, Lasry and his sister opened their own brokerage business, Amroc Investments, which dealt in bank debt and trade claims. Five years later, they started Avenue with $10 million, building it into a $1 billion hedge fund firm within the first five years. Lasry closed down the brokerage business in 2001, although an entity called Amroc still exists to find trade claims for Avenue to buy.

Starting Avenue was a grueling experience. "For those first five years, all I did was invest money and travel to meet investor after investor after investor after investor," says Lasry. "I was putting in twelve-to-eighteen-hour days. When the government of Singapore says, 'We'd love to invest. But please come by at the end of the week, otherwise we won't have time to see you for another three months,' you make a day trip to Singapore. It was a huge amount of work."

The effort paid off. Avenue now has nine offices across Asia, including China, Thailand, and the Philippines. As part of his efforts to build a bigger business, Lasry decided in 2006 to sell a roughly 15 percent stake in Avenue to Morgan Stanley, the second-biggest U.S. securities firm, for $280 million. "It brought in a world-class partner who could increase our information flow," says Lasry. "It was the next logical step in continuing to build our firm."

Success in fund management takes more than legwork and strategic partnerships. For Lasry, investing is all about knowing more than anyone else, understanding the risk, and having the conviction to stick to your guns. "Every investment has a risk," he says. "Ultimately, it's the assessment of those risks and having the confidence that what you think will happen ultimately does happen."

The better you know the investment you're making, the greater your conviction will be. "The person who is better prepared, the person who has done the most work, has a huge edge because most people are lazy," he says. If you have done a lot of research, you're prepared for what happens. Imagine you buy a bank loan at $0.50 on the dollar, and you've estimated that it could drop to $0.40 because the company could report quarterly earnings below analysts' estimates. Ultimately, you believe the loans are worth $0.80 on the dollar. If the company does miss earnings and the price of the loan starts dropping, you aren't upset. You anticipated the decline. And you believe that you know more than other investors. You're convinced that eventually the price will move higher.

Avenue's bet on Delta Air Lines, which filed for bankruptcy in September 2005, is an example of in-depth research, strong conviction, and a little luck. After Delta filed for Chapter 11, Avenue started buying up loans that were secured by airplanes. Then the company's senior unsecured bonds started falling from $0.50 to $0.25. As the bonds tumbled, Avenue bought them, ending up with close to $250 million of the senior unsecured bonds. Lasry's contention was that they were buying at a price at or close to liquidation value, but he also believed Delta management would be able to turn the company around. Lasry figured it would take two or three years for the bonds to climb to $0.40. Instead, they more than doubled in about six months.

Lasry's credit analysis on Delta may have been right, but he also got lucky. In August 2006, the U.K. authorities uncovered a terrorist plot to blow up airplanes flying from the United Kingdom to the United States. If that plan hadn't been foiled, the entire industry would have been crippled. Instead, air travel picked up. Three months later came another happy coincidence: Rival carrier U.S. Airways Group made a hostile bid of $10.2 billion to buy Delta, and the bonds Lasry owned jumped to about $0.70, so Lasry sold a large portion of his position. Creditors later rejected the bid, but Lasry had already made his exit. "It's a very different investment at 70 than at 20," he says.

The art of investing, says Lasry, is about seeing opportunities that other managers don't. "Everybody sees the same situations, but there are only a few who end up investing and even fewer of those who do well." Lasry did especially well in Asia, where he was one of the first to invest in distressed debt. Seeing clearly what other managers did not, he made his move into the region shortly after the Asian economic crisis of 1997 and 1998, a calamity brought on by years of easy borrowing and spending that eventually led to defaults, tumbling currencies, and International Monetary Fund bailouts. "We concluded that there were a lot of things that were underpriced," says Lasry. "Many believed the risks were too high. Very few went there and spent time looking at the companies. If you did, what you saw were world-class companies trading at low multiples. It seemed illogical. And sooner or later, logic wins out." The problem, of course, is that prices can remain illogical for a considerable time, which is difficult for those who can't afford to wait. The turnaround in this case didn't happen in a year or two, but the returns were ultimately pretty large. For example, Avenue bought the debt of PT Indocement Tunggal Prakarsa Tbk, Indonesia's second-largest cement company, for $0.50 on the dollar, and it appreciated to par.

Realizing that in distressed investing, having time on your side is a huge benefit, Lasry had made the decision early on—in 1998—to create funds that lock up investor capital for several years. His so-called institutional funds account for about 65 percent of his hedge fund money. The funds have five- to seven-year lockups, and Avenue doesn't draw on the cash investors have pledged until it's time to purchase the distressed securities.

"Now the challenge is finding another market where you're a little bit early," says Lasry. "I still think things are cheap out there, but not as cheap as they were in 2004." Still, the Avenue Asia Investments Fund has been the most profitable of Lasry's offerings, with an average return of 13.75 percent through July 2007 from its start in 1999. Malcolm Robinson, who joined Avenue in 1999, manages the Asian investments. He had been chief investment officer for the Richmond Parly Investment Company, a Hong Kong firm investing in private and public equity and distressed debt of Asian companies. Before that, he was a portfolio manager for Pacific Group in Hong Kong, a firm once partially owned by Julian Robertson's Tiger Management.

There are two keys to building a successful hedge fund business, says Lasry: "First, you have to have good returns. It's not complicated." And how do you increase the likelihood of producing good returns? That's key No. 2: "You hire smart people who are talented." And you hire more of them than you need for the job. A plan that relies on hiring a start-up crew, then adding to staff as the firm grows, is not going to work, says Lasry. "You have to view it as a business. If you don't, you could get hurt. When I was building Avenue, I looked to see which firms did very well and why. The reason for their success was that they had built the infrastructure and built an environment where people wanted to be."

But staff size doesn't guarantee a thing. "I look at these things in very simple terms. Lots of people have grandiose ideas. They say, 'I built a phenomenal firm. I've got one hundred fifty people. We have the best infrastructure and technology.' Whoopee. How much money did you make me?" So the question comes down to attracting talent. Lasry looks for job candidates who are self-assured. "The person who comes across as confident has a greater likelihood of being hired here," he says. He tells a story of a fellow who came in for a job interview after spending three years traveling around the world.

"Sounds like you had a blast," Lasry told him. "But I think it indicates a lack of commitment."

The candidate thought differently: "I think you're dead wrong. I wanted to learn about people. I wanted to find out what goes on in the world. If I'm going to make investments around the world, I need to know how people think. If you find that irrelevant, you have no idea what you're talking about." That was enough to convince Lasry. He liked not only the young man's confidence but also his willingness to express it so forcefully. Lasry hired him.

During another interview, a candidate eyed the chess and backgammon boards in Lasry's office and challenged him to a game of backgammon: "If I win, you have to hire me. If I lose, you don't." Lasry told him the deal wasn't good enough for him.

"Okay, what's the starting pay?" the candidate countered. For a Wharton MBA, Avenue paid $125,000 plus a $75,000 bonus. "If you win, I'll work for half price," the candidate responded, taking the interview in a whole new direction. "I wasn't even considering hiring the guy," Lasry says, "and now I'm in a discussion about his starting pay." The candidate lost the game, but ended up with a job—at the full starting salary.

In staffing, it's critical to have the right people in the right roles. Lasry says there is a huge difference between an analyst and a portfolio manager and that he knows early on who will make the jump. "The manager will come into your office and say, 'Absolutely. You've got to buy it; there's no question.' The analyst will say, 'Here's the reason you should, and here's the reason you shouldn't.' They will never, ever give an opinion."

Lasry agrees that some things about portfolio management can be learned, but he believes a lot of what it takes to succeed is innate. That may explain why—despite Bonderman's considerable influence on him—he doesn't put much energy into mentoring in his own shop. "I don't think it's my role. I think my job is to figure out how to make money, to figure out how we grow, and when and where we invest."

When it comes to assessing the top talent, Lasry gets right to the heart of the matter. "The great thing about the markets, and about what we do, is that there is a very easy scorecard: If you're right, you do well." He cites one manager who does remarkably well and with whom he invests money: Craig Effron, who runs Scoggin

Capital Management, in New York, which invests in companies going through corporate events like mergers and restructuring. "That is someone who is good at what he does," says Lasry. "Year in and year out, he makes you money."

Out of Trouble

Lasry's $7 billion Avenue International Fund lost 25 percent in 2008—about average that year for hedge funds that trade the securities of troubled companies. Lasry and his fellow distressed players got hit in every sector of the distressed market in which they played. Bank loans, as measured by the Standard & Poor's leveraged loan index (LCD) Index, fell to 63 cents on the dollar in December, down from more than 90 cents in June. High-yield bonds fell 26 percent during the course of the year, compared with investment-grade bonds, which slid just 6.8 percent.

Some of Avenue's individual holdings also went awry. The firm owned debt of the newspaper publisher Tribune Co., which abruptly filed for bankruptcy at the end of the year, on the back of weak earnings, a downgrade in its bonds by Standard & Poor's, and an inability to find buyers for its assets. Avenue also had to write down the value of a residential building in Manhattan, which it bought for $98 million in April 2005.

Although disappointed with his losses, Lasry viewed the drop in loan and debt prices in the fourth quarter as an opportunity to snap up securities of high-quality companies at bargain prices. Avenue's purchases included debt in telecommunications companies NextWave Wireless and Level 3 Communications; retailers Macy's, Nordstrom, and Target; and oil and gas companies Chesapeake Energy and Williams Companies.

Among Avenue's largest holdings at the end of the year were second-lien loans in Rite Aid Corp., which were trading at a level that suggested a high likelihood that the drugstore group would default and that the collateral backing the loans wasn't worth enough to cover the debt. Lasry reckoned, however, that the retailer would make enough money to meet its obligations, and that the collateral, including medications and other inventory, was more valuable than the money it owned. In May 2009, Rite Aid said it would refinance its debt, meaning the current debt holders would get paid off in full.

As the number of defaults increase in 2009, Lasry is also looking to "have a seat at the table" as the companies whose debt it owns restructure. In past downturns, Lasry has invested in restructuring companies, and 2009 is no different. In the early part of the year, he was providing debtor-in-possession financing for a number of companies in bankruptcy. Although Lasry had been buying as the price of loans was falling in 2009, he wasn't expecting a quick end to troubles in the credit market. In addition to his purchases, he was also increasing his percentage of shorts, securities he was expecting to fall. "We may be approaching the beginning of the trough, but as we've cautioned before, the trough may be lengthy," he told investors in March, adding he wouldn't be surprised if there was another drop in prices. For that reason he was being conservative—sticking to the bank debt of distressed and stressed companies and the most senior bonds of higher-quality companies and betting that more junior paper might end up becoming worthless. As of September, his Avenue International Fund had climbed 48 percent before fees.

Chapter 5

Craig Effron
A Grip on Risk

IT's BEEN TWO DECADES since Craig Effron traded gold, silver, and crude oil at the New York Mercantile Exchange, but the lessons he learned in ten years in the pits, where decisions are made at a manic pace, still dominate his approach to money management. His $3.25 billion hedge fund, Scoggin Capital Management, buys and sells the stocks and bonds primarily of companies that are merging, spinning off units, or going through financially tough times. Between 1988, the year he started the fund, and August 1, 2007, he produced average annual returns of 18.2 percent a year, after fees and using no borrowed money. He had only one losing year, 2002, when he was down 1.3 percent. His returns are not correlated to the stock market, and 90 percent of the time, his funds make money in the months the Standard & Poor's 500 Index is down. "I'm a risk manager, which I believe is more important these days than being an analyst," says Effron.

That's because Effron's approach hinges on responding to change. The investment world gets smaller every day and faster. Events that seem unconnected drive markets to move in sympathy. When Russia devalued its currency in August 1998, the benchmark U.S. stock index tumbled 13 percent in the following two weeks. In February 2007, when China said it was creating a task force to clamp down on stock market speculation there, the S&P

500 plunged 3.5 percent. Twenty years ago, knowing a company was paramount, and you had the leisure of spending weeks learning about it, Effron says. "Nowadays, cause and effect are much more instantaneous. It's much more like commodities trading."

Everything about Effron has its accent on "now." The day we met in his midtown Manhattan offices, he wore faded jeans ripped at the knees and yellow argyle socks with brown suede loafers. His manner is definitely more akin to "regular guy" than "Ivy League big shot." When his son called to talk about picks for the men's college basketball championships—the tournament was in full swing—his cell phone rang with rapper Eminem's "Lose Yourself."

Although Effron, forty-eight, got his undergraduate degree at the Wharton School at the University of Pennsylvania, he always counted on becoming an attorney. "It's all been happenstance," he says of his career path.

The first of the chance occurrences came in 1981 and was born of a hitch in Effron's plans for a legal career. He had been wait-listed at New York University's law school, and his parents suggested he find a job on Wall Street for a year before reapplying. Not many wanted to work on the Street then—the country was in the middle of a recession—and he readily got a job at brokerage firm E. F. Hutton. Nine months into the gig, having decided that the law no longer interested him, he had dinner with a friend who had been a year ahead of him at Wharton. "Screw E. F. Hutton," his friend said. "You should see what I'm doing. It's really fun." His friend was trading commodities.

Effron took a day off and went down to the Nymex to see how it was done. There he saw young guys shoulder to shoulder in the pits, screaming their buy and sell orders. "It's a football game," says Effron. "You're standing with a bunch of very big guys, all pushing and shoving. It's very Darwinian. It's the purest form of capitalism I know."

Finally, he knew where he wanted to be; all he had to do was make it happen. His first step was to get his dad to come down to the Nymex floor to take a look. His father was skeptical about the idea. He bought oil as part of his business and had heard plenty of stories about traders losing their fortunes in commodities. But Effron, the family's eldest son, eventually persuaded his father to help him. They bought a seat on the exchange, and Effron started his trading career with $30,000 and one key stipulation: If he lost his stake, that was the end of it. He'd be out of business.

They needn't have worried. Effron was a natural. "It's all about feeling the energy in the pit," says Effron. "Is it going up or is it going down? You don't have a clear answer. It's all intuition. You can just tell." Success in the pits requires skills that can't be taught. Because the right choices depend entirely on sensing what's happening among the scrum of traders in the ring, Effron refused to read the papers until after the markets closed. "You didn't want to know what was going on. The more you knew, the worse you did. If you knew there was an oil strike in Nigeria, you'd be thinking all day 'I'm bullish,' when in fact that might not be the driver at all. The real driver might be that Russia was selling 40 million barrels that day and you didn't know about it."

Seeking intellectual stimulation, Effron started dabbling in stocks when commodities trading ended at 2:00 p.m. "You have to be at least somewhat coherent in English to understand how to trade stocks," he laughs. He liked to look for events that would send a stock higher or lower. He might read an article that junk-bond king Michael Milken was providing financing to investor Nelson Peltz to buy company XYZ. Peltz was offering $37, and the company was trading at $37.25. Effron would risk $0.25 on the likelihood that another bidder would come in with a higher offer.

At first buying and selling stocks was a lark for Effron, a hobby. He ran a few separate accounts free of charge for his parents and their friends. His neighbor in the silver ring, Paul Jones, who had gotten his start trading cotton, was the first to encourage Effron to think about stock picking as a business. Jones later went on to start Tudor Investment Corporation, in Greenwich, Connecticut, one of the biggest hedge fund firms in the business. Jones wanted Effron to trade stocks for him but demanded he take a fee for managing the money. "You'll take it more seriously if you do," Jones told him.

That understanding helped bring the future into focus for Effron. "There's a business here, I realized. I can charge people a performance fee and enjoy what I'm doing." He traded both stocks and commodities for a few more years, but by the late 1980s, the pit had grown much more competitive. "When I first started, seventeen out of eight hundred guys had college degrees. By 1990, 90 percent of them did. The average trader's intellectual capacity had dramatically increased," and it was harder to make money for the same amount of risk. The next step became clear. In 1988, with $500,000 from Jones and another $2.5 million from other investors, Effron started Scoggin with his friend Curtis Schenker.

Effron had first met Schenker at Camp Androscoggin in Wayne, Maine, and ran into him again at Wharton, where Schenker was a year ahead of him. The two were no more than acquaintances until after college, when a mutual friend who was supposed to go to Puerto Rico with Effron got sick and gave his ticket to Schenker. "We became best friends that weekend," says Effron. "We hit it off. We had everything in common. It was another happenstance."

Despite his respect for coincidence, Effron doesn't leave his portfolio to the vicissitudes of chance. The most important lesson he learned as a commodities trader was to cut his losses when a position moved against him, and he applies the same rule today. "I am the quickest guy to sell stuff and buy puts," says Effron, referring to a way of betting, through options, on the falling price of a security or index. "I do it more than I should."

That's because he has seen how unforgiving the markets can be. One day, he'd be in touch with a guy whom everyone knew was a millionaire. Two days later, the fellow would be wiped out, having stuck with a trade when the market moved in the opposite direction. Later still, the former millionaire would come calling, looking for a job as a clerk. "I learned at a young age that markets are much bigger than the people working them. You can't outlast a market. These were experienced traders, moving a lot of money," he says of the people driven out of business. "I was twenty-two or twenty-four at the time, and they were thirty-eight. I thought they were the gods of my business. I have nightmares about that. My whole focus for my business is this: I want to be around tomorrow."

In hedge funds, gods come and go, and survival is almost as uncertain as it is in the pits. A loss of, say, 20 percent on the year can put a fund out of business. Hedge fund managers generally have high watermarks, meaning they have to make up their losses before investors will pay them their 20 percent cut of the profits. In the months before the manager makes his investors whole, employees often leave because there is no money for bonuses. Investors, skittish after bad performance, redeem, and the fund goes under.

Effron's bite-the-bullet handling of the WorldCom debacle in 2002 exemplifies his approach to managing risk. His fund was 90 percent invested in distressed debt, and Scoggin had been making money until June 25, the day WorldCom, the second largest U.S. long-distance phone provider, announced it would restate earnings after misreporting $3.9 billion in expenses. The next day World Com bond prices fell as low as $0.14 from a high of $0.78 the day before. Many investors had been bullish on the bonds because their analysis suggested they were trading below the value of the underlying assets of the company. "We had been long WorldCom, and everything else we were long went down," including Qwest Communications and cable operators Comcast Corporation and Charter Communications. "The minute the WorldCom news hit, we sold whatever had a bid that wasn't ridiculously stupid," says Effron. He continued to sell over the next month and a half, until the bonds got to prices that were so inexpensive he felt the downside was minimal, but he imposed a moratorium on buying, telling his traders: "If the world ends here, we don't want to be out of business." Ultimately, Scoggin lost 8 percent peak to trough, its largest drawdown ever.

The fund was flat for the year, and Effron went from August to October without buying any bonds. He did buy puts on the S&P 500, a good call given that the index tumbled almost 8 percent in July. "We made a lot of money back on the shorts," says Effron. When Scoggin started buying debt again, it initially stuck to the safer play of senior debt. In 2003, the fund made 40 percent.

Many managers like to talk about conviction, the gumption to stay put when other investors are jamming the exits, and although Effron isn't averse to staking as much as 10 percent of his portfolio in one trade, he'll sell a position, even one he likes, if the market isn't going his way. "I think having no conviction is how you want to be," says Effron. "When the market is ugly, I'm not buying stuff. I'm probably selling it. I can buy it back tomorrow." Transaction costs have come down so much, he says, that he can buy a million shares at a cost of just $5,000. He tries to hold positions for at least a year because that lowers his investors' tax bill, but that's less of a concern for him than losing money. "I'll sell things out when I feel the market is ornery. I feel liberated. You get a clearer vision of what's going on when you don't have an axe to grind."

Investing more than 10 percent of capital in any one company is something Effron won't do, and he generally prefers to limit positions to 5 percent to 7 percent. Historically, his portfolio is 20 percent to 70 percent net long, with an average of about 40 percent net long. "That's a bit deceiving because when the market gets mean, we can get to zero very quickly by selling longs and buying puts," says Effron. "When we're concerned about the markets, we're 20 percent net long. We're big players of options. I love options, because I understand what I'm risking."

Effron also will buy puts on positions if he's uncomfortable. The day I was in his office, he had bought April 40 puts on Qualcomm, the world's second-largest maker of mobile telephone chips, for $0.30, meaning he locked in a price of $40 for Qualcomm shares between his purchase date—March 14—and their expiration date in April. The shares had climbed to $43.21, but he was happy to have the insurance, given that the benchmark index had plunged 4 percent in the previous two weeks. "If the world ends next month, we get out at $40," says Effron. "I throw away $0.30 all the time. It's all about staying in business."

As protection against a big market tumble, Effron likes owning puts on the S&P 500. When the S&P 500 moves around with greater volatility, making options more expensive, he uses futures or Spiders, exchange-traded funds, to protect his downside. Although he does sometimes wager on stocks he expects to fall, he doesn't short individual stocks as a hedge against his long positions. There is nothing worse, he says, than being short fifteen stocks on a day when the S&P 500 tumbles 2 percent, and not having one of your fifteen shorts lose ground. The day before our interview, the S&P 500 had dropped 2 percent, yet Scoggin lost only 15 basis points because Effron owned puts on the S&P.

Effron has other ways to position the portfolio conservatively. Ninety percent of Scoggin's debt in 2007, for example, was in senior paper because Effron felt that debt farther down the capital structure wasn't paying enough. The so-called junior paper of distressed companies once traded at around $0.60 or $0.70 on $1.00 whereas the senior debt traded at around $0.90. In mid-2007, senior paper might trade at $1.02 and junior paper at $0.92. "It's too expensive to short, but we're waiting for stuff to happen," he says. "You'll see the spread go out 20 or 30 points."

The decisions made with regard to the subprime loan sector also illustrate just how willing Effron is to change his mind. Companies that offered mortgages to home buyers with poor credit ratings got crushed as late payments and defaults on these loans rose to a four-year high in the last quarter of 2006, and more than two dozen mortgage lenders had closed down or sold their businesses since the start of 2006.

In the latter part of 2005, Effron had bought puts on the ABX Subprime Mortgage Index, betting the index would tumble. In his judgment, the subprime mortgages were in danger because housing prices were falling, people were overleveraged, and if they lost their jobs or interest rates rose, default rates would increase. But for six months, the index didn't plunge as expected. "I went in to my guys and said: 'This trade sucks. This thing never moves no matter what happens. I don't like it.'" Effron got out of the position in February 2006. A year later, the index plummeted.

He had been short mortgage lenders New Century Financial Corporation and Accredited Home Lenders Holdings for about three months before the tumble, bets he made by buying puts on the stocks. Accredited Home Lenders, which traded at close to $37 in October 2006, fell $10 before Effron exited, missing most of the slide as the stock continued all the way down below $4.

Like a lot of successful managers, Effron says his main flaw is leaving profits on the table. "I sell too soon. We have targets and we abide by them. A lot of guys, they get to a target and then they raise it 10 percent. I like to say, 'Stocks don't know you own them. You can sell them and they don't care.'"

Effron's game plan has always depended on moving to new strategies or geographic regions once a space gets crowded, or the investments no longer work. When Scoggin first started, Effron and Schenker traded in companies that were the targets of leveraged buyouts and mergers. Michael Milken, head of the Beverly Hills, California, office of Drexel Burnham Lambert, helped create the junk-bond market that sent investors and companies on a decade-long buying spree. It was a very easy way to make money, at least until October 13, 1989, when the pilots' union and management of UAL Corporation, parent of United Airlines, called off their $300-a-share bid of the airline because they couldn't get financing. UAL shares plummeted more than $56 once trading resumed, and the Dow Jones Industrial Average fell almost 7 percent. Scoggin had been up about 50 percent so far that year, but market turmoil during the next few days wiped out 20 percentage points of its profit. Effron knew the days of merger arbitrage were over for the time being.

Still, there was a silver lining. Many hedge funds had made leveraged bets on UAL, and some had gone out of business or were forced to scale back, putting good analysts—which Scoggin couldn't have afforded to hire a year earlier—out on the streets. The firm picked up a distressed-bond analyst who led Scoggin into a new investment game. The junk-bond market had also crashed, and there were scads of cheap corporate bonds to pick through. "We learned quickly," says Effron. "A lot of names we traded in the mid-1980s as leveraged buyouts were coming back as bankruptcies." Scoggin traded distressed debt until about 1995, when that game got too crowded. By then the firm had discovered the next course in the feast Effron calls idiot-proof investing: spinoffs.

Lots of companies, including AT&T, 3M, and H&R Block were spinning off units. Many of their stockholders were mom-and-pop investors who dumped the shares in the new companies. They wanted to own AT&T, a well-known telephone company, not some technology company called Lucent about which they knew nothing. "For a year or two, no one knew this phenomenon existed," says Effron. "We were buying all these companies at half multiples." Later, he bought shares of Freescale Semiconductor, which Motorola spun off for $13 a share in July 2004. Freescale Semiconductor was subsequently bought out by a group of investors led by Blackstone Group in December 2006 for $40 a share.

Effron still trades the stocks of merging companies and will sometimes even buy shares on the mere speculation of a merger. In the summer of 2006, there was chatter that sneaker retailer Foot Locker would get bought out. The company was selling at $22 a share, which Effron said was cheap relative to its earnings, and it rose to above $27 on the possibility it would be sold. The talk was unfounded, and the stock dropped back to $22 by the end of the year. Scoggin sold at $24.

Over the years, Scoggin has made money betting on the outcome of litigation, be it asbestos, cigarettes, or lead paint. In 2007, Effron was wagering that Qualcomm would win in a patent dispute with Finnish mobile-phone maker Nokia. Effron never shies away from playing outside his usual sandbox, and his search for gains has led him to buy Chinese equities, Russian vouchers, commercial real estate, and the government debt of Zaire. "A lot of people who have an analytical mind-set don't go there—where the risk is; it's outside their thinking. I *want* to go where the risk is, but I want to understand it," says Effron. "I'll watch a dog piss for a dime if it will go to $0.20. There's no reason to put yourself in a box."

His foray into real estate happened in 1998 when he got a call from his college roommate, Glen Siegel, who runs the New York real estate investment company Belvedere Capital. Siegel knew Leona Helmsley, who decided after her husband Harry died that she wanted to sell some of the less-than-prime office buildings for $100 million. She came to Siegel to find a buyer, and Siegel was soon on the horn to his old friend. "I'm only on the sixth building and it's already at $100 million, and there are eighteen buildings," he told Effron. "If we don't act quickly, she'll put it out to auction." They had one week to do due diligence. Siegel put up $10 million. Effron put up $45 million, and Angelo, Gordon & Company, a large New York hedge fund, invested the balance. They figured they were getting the real estate for about half price.

Within two years, they had sold most of the properties for $250 million, more than doubling their money on the deal. By 2007, the buildings were probably worth $900 million. They never considered making it a longer-term trade. There was recession risk, and because the buildings were "B" properties, they would lose their value faster than premier properties if bad times hit.

Effron watches for opportunities outside the usual boundaries regionally and otherwise. About 20 percent of the portfolio is outside the United States, primarily in Europe and mostly in the stocks of merging companies and in spinoffs, particularly in Sweden. "What we've been able to do is to find the place where people aren't willing to go, and go there and learn it quickly," he says. "I can't tell you there are a lot of great undiscovered opportunities out there." But there have been some. To get a piece of the action in Russian vouchers in 1995, he sent someone to Russia to buy them. In 1992, President Boris Yeltsin had given every citizen a voucher worth 10,000 rubles that could be used to buy state-owned companies when they were sold to the public in the next several years. Many people sold the vouchers because they needed the money immediately or because they didn't understand the whole concept of shareholding. Early on, the vouchers changed hands for as low as 3,000 rubles. "That was a good gig," laughs Effron.

Equally unusual was Effron's purchase in 2003 of the debt of Zaire, now the Democratic Republic of Congo, from the Bank of Brazil, which had lent money to the African nation to build a power plant. It was a 20-year loan, and the bank had seen no money from Congo for 19 years and 11 months, so the Brazilians decided to sell the $150 million debt for $0.05 on $1.00, or $7.5 million, just to get it off the books. Four years and $11 million in legal bills later, Effron collected $70 million from the Congolese government.

To get its money, Scoggin had to sue Congo in courts from Paris to Luxembourg to Dallas, and once the firm had won (they were victorious in 98 percent of the cases), it had to uncover pockets of money so it could get paid. When the government of Congo realized that Scoggin was not only serious but also making inroads in going after some cash held in France, the Congolese Finance Ministry sent a seven-person delegation to Scoggin's offices, where they made offers and counteroffers until they settled on $70 million. "The rate of return was 20 percent a year, not that high, but it was kind of fun," says Effron. Scoggin is now getting calls from other lenders who want to sell their debt because the Congo was considered the hardest country to collect from, given its minimal assets and wide-spread corruption. "Even the Congo is calling us to settle its other debts, offering us 10 percent of the take." That deal is on.

Effron's Chinese investments resulted from a vacation he and his wife took with another couple in 2005. "When I got to China, I realized immediately that we were in America 1910," says Effron. "Today in America everyone hates everyone. There is so much negativity. In China, it is all positive. I don't know how it will play out, but this place is for real."

He returned from his trip, wanting to figure out a way to invest in China. All the while, the stock market there was rising and Effron feared he was missing an opportunity. He posted a notice at Harvard Business School, seeking someone to travel to China to work for Scoggin there. He got sixty-five responses, narrowed it down to three people, and finally chose a woman born in western China, Emily Dong. She worked for Scoggin in New York for nine months and then headed for Hong Kong.

Effron's plan for investing in China is simple: He's focusing on the western provinces, closer to Tibet. Most foreigners concentrate on Shanghai and Beijing. "Dong grew up there," says Effron. "She meets companies that have been around twenty or thirty years trading at two times cash flow, but they are small—$500 million to $1 billion." In 2007, Scoggin bought some Chinese stocks. Effron made a profit and sold them in the summer as global stock markets became more volatile. He's chosen not to invest in debt. "That requires a whole level of sophistication and connections to banks that we don't have." It took a year for Scoggin to get a certificate that allows the firm to trade so-called A shares (shares of Chinese stocks that trade in Shanghai and Shenzhen) so he's buying A shares and H shares (shares of Chinese companies that trade in Hong Kong). "I don't want to tell you we have the magic potion," says Effron. "Dong's done better than indexes, and the wind is at our backs. I'm hoping I have a few years to make money in China."

Effron or Schenker approve every position in Scoggin's portfolio; they figure out how to construct the trade (whether to use options, for example) and how big to make the bets. Effron and Schenker are the largest investors in the fund, together accounting for 10 percent of assets. Scoggin has been closed to new investors for five or six years, in part because Effron figures that if he establishes long-term relationships with his clients, they will be less likely to jump ship in the event of a loss.

That's a different approach than his friend Marc Lasry's (see Chapter 4). "Marc raises money all the time. It's a great model. It is much more management-fee driven and ours is much more incentive-fee driven," says Effron. Effron's goal is to produce annual returns of between 15 percent to 20 percent a year, rather than the 8 percent to 12 percent that larger funds target. Effron met Lasry in 1990, when Lasry was a bank debt broker and Effron was buying bank debt for the two-year-old Scoggin. They became friendly over the years and today Effron counts Lasry as a close friend and nearly family—Effron's brother married Lasry's sister-in-law.

Scoggin's investment ideas come from the news, and the ten investment professionals who work at the firm read papers from around the world and synthesize any interesting tidbits into e-mails. Analysts don't wait for a formal meeting to pitch ideas. "Everyone knows my attention span is three minutes, so if it doesn't hit me right away, it means I'm not going to put it on the sheet." Effron will sometimes use news articles to help him decide when to go the other way on a trade; it's a tool he calls the *Wall Street Journal* test. If journalists are writing about an investment idea or trend, it's usually the time to do the exact opposite. "They tend to be late, because the guys they're talking to are late."

Late may be better than never in some jobs, but not in Effron's.

AFTER THE CRISIS

Why Size Matters

Scoggin Capital's four funds lost 26 percent in 2008, in large part because Effron bought distressed debt too early. "Our biggest mistake was to start buying senior bank debt in September and October," he says.

Effron's portfolio had been conservatively positioned when Lehman Brothers went bankrupt in September 2008, with about half of the funds' assets in cash. Effron figured that the markets would rebound quickly, as they did in 1998 and again in 2002. So he reduced bets that would make money if the prices of bonds fell, and started buying the senior bank debt.

As it turned out, a rapid turnaround wasn't in the cards. Investors started liquidating those very same securities he'd just bought in an effort to raise cash, sending the prices of the loans he'd purchased to nearly 60 cents on the dollar, down from the 70-cent-to-80-cent level at which he'd bought them. And for the first time since he began managing the funds, Scoggin also marked down the debt and equity of private investments in the portfolio, including auto and home lender GMAC, which later received $13.5 billion in federal funds, and carmaker Chrysler, which filed for bankruptcy in early 2009.

Unlike some of his competitors, Effron still thinks that there is room in a portfolio for illiquid investments, but he has told his clients he won't buy any more of them until his current positions, about 10 percent to 12 percent of assets, are sold. That means he won't be making such purchases again until the middle of 2010. "When you see things that are good you have to do them," he says, explaining why he would continue to trade in hard-to-sell assets. "There are things that are lay-ups and some guys won't do them anymore," which he expects will create even more opportunities for him.

Scoggin lost about 18 percent of assets to redemptions in 2008, meaning it started 2009 with about $2 billion, down from more than $3 billion in 2007. Overall, Effron says, having fewer assets in the hedge fund industry is a good thing. "As funds got bigger, we all started doing things we might not have done if we were running, say, $500 million instead of $3 billion," he says. "Guys ventured outside of their sandbox because they had excess capital." He reckons that's why, overall, the largest funds did worse than the smaller funds in 2008.

Challenges relating to fund size taught Effron the biggest lessons of the crisis. "The hedge fund model doesn't translate into mutual fund–size funds" of tens of billions of dollars. "You have to be nimble and you need to operate under the radar." Size was the main reason that funds lost money in 2008, he says. "No one could get out of positions."

So far, 2009 hasn't brought more hard lessons. As of October 1, 2009, Scoggin's funds were up an average of 36 percent and Effron calls his equity portfolio "fairly uninteresting," though he expects that there will be a pick-up in merger activity and that he'll be increasing his bets in stocks because of that. His credit book is focused on companies in distress or in bankruptcy.

Scoggin has also slimmed down its operation. The firm has twelve analysts, down from 18 in early 2008, and it closed its office in China in April 2009. "We did well there, but we made no investments in China in 2008," Effron says.

The motto for 2009 has been back to basics, says Effron, who's happy to focus on the kind of investments at which he's always excelled and delighted to be one of the funds still standing. "I'm re-energized. There are things going on—a slew of bankruptcies and defaults." For funds that have a track record, says Effron, the next two to four years will be great.

Chapter 6

Lee Ainslie
A Stock Picker, Pure and Hardly Simple

LEE AINSLIE LOOKS younger than forty-three. He's got boyish good looks and the hint of a Southern drawl from a childhood spent in Virginia, where his father was an English teacher, and later headmaster, at two private schools. The day I talked with Ainslie, he was dressed up—at least by hedge fund manager standards—wearing a gray pinstripe suit, a blue button-down shirt, and a silk tie. His office, outfitted with a table and chairs for frequent small meetings, overlooks the seven-member trading desk and a large television screen tuned to CNBC at the far end.

Ainslie, who has been constructing stock portfolios since he was a teen, runs Maverick Capital, one of the largest pure stock hedge funds in operation today, with assets of $9.7 billion and serving about one thousand investors. Ainslie's equity hedge fund, like his taste in clothing, is traditional; indeed, it's among the more traditional around. Ainslie buys stocks in companies whose shares he expects to go up more than the market, and he sells short any shares he expects to lag. That's it. He doesn't take private equity positions; he doesn't dabble in bonds, currencies, or commodities; and he doesn't use options to hedge.

What he does is serve investors well. The firm's flagship Maverick Fund has never had a losing year and posted an average annual return of nearly 17 percent between March 1995 and July 2007, according to investor documents. That compares with a return of 11 percent during that period for the benchmark Standard & Poor's 500 Index. The fund's volatility, or the swing in its performance, is about half as large as that of the benchmark index.

Trained by master stock picker Julian Robertson, Ainslie says his success results from sticking to his long-short strategy. He believes that market timing is a futile game. So he adheres to his investment approach even when markets get ugly.

The markets looked especially homely in 2003 and again in 2005, when Ainslie's fund underperformed the S&P 500 and lagged the average return of long-short equity hedge funds. During those years, it was the stocks he shorted—that is, wagers on companies whose stocks he expected to tumble—that dragged on his performance. Instead of falling, these stocks jumped. Low interest rates and ease of borrowing made things tough for short sellers, who traditionally borrow shares and then sell them in the hopes that they can buy them back later at a cheaper price. Lots of money sloshing around the financial markets led investors to take on more risk so they bought the stocks of lower-quality companies—in some cases, the very same shares that Ainslie was betting would plummet.

In these trying years, as other fund managers capitulated and bet increasing amounts of cash on stocks they expected to rally, Ainslie refused to abandon the practice of short selling. He remembers two letters from investors sent to him in 1999, another year when his bets on falling shares cut into performance. The investors complained, telling him that when stocks aren't going anywhere but up, it's time to throw in the towel on shorting. "Our response was to explain that we are a truly hedged fund," says Ainslie. "The odds of my adding value consistently by trying to time the market are very slim. At the time of maximum pain, you need to maintain your discipline."

By and large, the discipline works. In 2000, the fund was up about 29 percent, while the market was down 9 percent, and it made money in 2001 and 2002 as the S&P 500 continued to tumble. In 2006, Ainslie began making money again on stocks he was shorting, and relative performance improved. In 2007, as stocks took a nasty dive in February and early March, and again in July and early

August, he trounced the benchmark index and most other stock hedge funds.

Ainslie started managing a paper portfolio when he was fourteen and a member of an investment club at Virginia Episcopal School in Lynchburg, Virginia, where his father was headmaster. He didn't have the cash to buy the real thing until later, but the seed was planted. In college, he imagined he would be an architect or a doctor, and he began taking courses for both until he realized the impracticality of his double-barreled plan. In the end, he left the University of Virginia with a degree in systems engineering. He took a job with accounting firm Peat Marwick for two years and worked for the firm's national director of information technology consulting before heading off to the University of North Carolina's business school. While at UNC, he met alumnus Julian Robertson, who offered Ainslie a job at his hedge fund, Tiger Management, when he graduated. Ainslie immediately gave up any ideas of going to an investment bank or consulting firm. "Stock picking had been a hobby for a long, long time," says Ainslie. "Julian was going to pay me to do what I would have done for free for fun. Other than joining the NBA, there wasn't anything I'd rather have been doing."

When Ainslie arrived at Tiger in 1990, the firm had only eight investment professionals, including Robertson, and they were managing about $700 million. Initially, all the analysts were generalists. Over time, analysts were assigned areas of expertise, and Ainslie was assigned the technology beat.

Robertson made all final investment decisions: which stocks went into the portfolio, how big each position should be, and when it should be entered and exited. The analysts' job was to sell Robertson on their ideas, both long and short. As he reviewed prospective investments, "Julian was very focused on the quality of the management team—their abilities, their background, and their desire to create shareholder value," says Ainslie. "He has always had an intuitive understanding of the key drivers and pressure points of a business. He was quick to home in on the key variables and made sure we had a thorough understanding of those factors."

Robertson also cared about integrity and reputation, both within his own firm and at the companies in which he invested. In the money-management business, an investor can pick up the phone, call a broker, and spend a billion dollars. There is no other business that operates that way, so trust is critical. With each company targeted for investment, Robertson focused on the ethics of corporate managers, their intelligence, and their integrity, both personal and in regard to their dedication to improving shareholder value. Consequently, Tiger analysts spent much time studying company executives as well as the company's financials. Robertson looked for well-run companies whose stocks did not reflect their earnings power or the value of their underlying assets. For shorts, he looked for the exact opposite—bad companies with bad management that were overvalued.

Barely three years after Ainslie joined Tiger, Texas billionaire and entrepreneur Sam Wyly approached him to propose he run a money-management business Wyly wanted to start. He had learned about Ainslie from Richard Hanlon, who served with the Texan as a director on the board of arts-and-crafts retailer Michaels Stores. Hanlon was also a senior executive at Legent Corporation, a software company that was a large Tiger holding and for which Ainslie was the analyst.

Happy at Tiger, Ainslie wasn't interested at first. Yet he knew that someday he wanted to run his own firm, and Wyly was offering a well-funded start-up with lots of infrastructure. "So I decided— prematurely—to go ahead and pursue this opportunity." He was twenty-nine years old.

Ainslie left Tiger in August 1993 and opened Maverick on October 1, the day before his wedding. Initially, he was managing a stock portfolio, and Wyly was trading a macro book—everything from junk bonds to emerging-market debt and currencies. Ainslie's stock-picking style flourished in 1994, which proved to be a difficult year for many investors because the Fed unexpectedly raised interest rates, catching many market participants off guard. Ainslie and Wyly decided to sell the nonequity positions and make stocks Maverick's sole focus. Ainslie took over the whole portfolio on March 1, 1995. Two years later, he bought out Wyly.

As Ainslie began attracting assets and adding investment staff, he created a business model that differs slightly from those of most large funds, which generally fall into two categories. One is the Julian Robertson approach, in which one or two guys run the show and make virtually all the investment decisions. The other, the model preferred by Paul Jones's Tudor Investment Corporation and Steven A. Cohen's SAC Capital, is to have various desks, each more or less autonomous, making investment decisions for their own books. A leader at the helm of the firm takes care of risk management and asset allocation.

Maverick's model is a hybrid of the two. The firm has six industry sector heads, most of whom are more or less the same age as Ainslie. They are the experts in their respective industries: consumer; health care; cyclical; retail; financial; and telecommunications, media, and technology. Ainslie talks to them throughout the day about new and current stocks in the portfolio. With that input, Ainslie ultimately has the final say. "It really is a team culture," says Ainslie. "The sector heads are very experienced and talented individuals. I spend the majority of my day talking to them because they know so much more about each of their stocks than I could ever hope to. We're all peers."

In 2007, the tenure of sector heads at Maverick averaged seven years, each with investment or industry experience averaging more than fifteen years. Every team has five to seven analysts typically covering twenty-five to thirty positions. The industry sector teams are supported by the accounting, emerging markets, and quantitative teams. With fifty-four investment and trading professionals in all, the ratio of investment positions to staff is three to one.

At the end of every day, Ainslie or Steve Galbraith, the former chief equity strategist at Morgan Stanley, who joined the firm in 2004, goes through the list of 160 to 180 stocks, and they come up with a plan of action based on their judgments and their conversations with the sector heads. Together, they decide whether to add to or reduce a position, buy new ones, or close one out. They might suggest trigger points, like selling shares of one company at 29, or buying more of another if it falls to 53. "The plan of action reflects our view of those debates," says Ainslie, "but it should also reflect the views of the sector heads."

When Ainslie reviews the overall plan, he's thinking about the size of every position. Robertson taught him to test his conviction by asking himself if the stock is a buy or a sell. A hold isn't an option. "This is how I've come to think of it over the years: Either this security deserves incremental capital at the current price point or it doesn't—in which case, let's sell it and put the money to work in a security that deserves that incremental capital."

Maverick doesn't use preassigned price targets. The world changes, Ainslie says, and his sector heads and their teams are continually reevaluating their positions. Sometimes, it makes sense to exit or reduce a bet even if they expect there's still profit to be made because they see a better moneymaking opportunity elsewhere. Maverick isn't a trading fund so they're willing to wait for the price they want before they buy or sell, meaning that not every order in the plan is placed the very next day.

Sector heads review the suggested trades each morning, and Ainslie expects them to be vocal if they don't agree. Their feedback may be something as minor as "Let's sell at 29.25, instead of 29," or as significant as "we should be selling, not buying." When there's a difference of opinion, Ainslie discusses the issues with everyone involved. He doesn't make unilateral decisions. He believes that matching the industry knowledge of the sector head with his judgment about the stock market and portfolio construction makes for a better result than having either party work solo. "Whether we're making investment decisions or business decisions, I rely on the abilities and talents of each of the partners. I think we each feel that collectively, we have been and will be able to produce results far superior to those that any of us could produce on our own," says Ainslie.

The sector heads agree. Steven Kapp, who has been running the health-care sector at Maverick since 1997, says the system works extremely well. He and his team of six analysts produce investment ideas on the long and the short side in companies ranging from biotechnology to drugmakers to managed care. With input from his team, Kapp decides which stocks are the best moneymakers in his arena and should be included in the portfolio. He also makes the calls on when it's time to reduce or add to a position and when it's time to sell. "I'm doing a mini version of what Lee is doing with the overall portfolio. We have a lot of autonomy and that's one of the great advantages of our system."

Ainslie's job, as he sees it, is to balance all the input from the different sector heads to make sure the best ideas get the right amount of capital.

• • •

Ainslie and his partners are true stock pickers. They aim to profit on both their longs and shorts. They don't short stocks just to serve as a hedge, nor do they use other hedging strategies like buying puts on the S&P 500, which will make money if the index falls. Instead, to mitigate a macroeconomic risk, like a move in interest rates or a spike in the price of oil, they try to balance their longs and shorts within each region—Maverick invests in Asia, Latin America, and Europe as well as the United States—and within each industry.

Maverick's core fund, however, is biased toward the long side. First and foremost, that's because the market tends to go up. The majority of investors—mutual funds, pension funds, and individuals—are buying stocks based on the assumption that they will move higher. Shorting stocks also makes you unpopular with management teams, and Ainslie and his sector heads like to have strong relationships with corporate executives. Finally, the very mechanics of shorting can make it difficult to produce big gains. The upside is limited to a 100 percent return, yet the potential losses are limitless. Plus, the more successful the short position is, the smaller it becomes as the stock price drops further and further; whereas, if you find a good stock to go long, you can own it year after year after year.

Although Maverick's net long position can range from 25 percent to 75 percent, historically it's been about 49 percent, with 148 percent of the capital in stocks they expect to climb and about 99 percent in stocks they expect to tumble. The gross exposure, which includes borrowed money, has traditionally ranged between 190 and 280 percent of net assets.

Ainslie says that in the case of a market plunge, the way Maverick uses leverage makes for a safer, more balanced portfolio. If he is 150 percent long and 100 percent short, he's 50 percent net long and his ratio of long to shorts is 1.5 to 1. If he chose to be 50 percent net long without leverage, he could wager 75 percent of assets on stocks he expected to climb and 25 percent on stocks he expected to drop. His ratio of longs to shorts would be 3 to 1. Say, for example, the stock market falls 15 percent. If Maverick has done a decent job of stock picking, the portfolio's longs are down only 10 percent and its shorts have plunged by 20 percent. The portfolio using leverage would be up 5 percent. For every $100 of net assets, it would have lost $15 on the long side but gained $20 on the short side. Without leverage, the fund would be down 2.5 percent, having lost $7.50 on the long side and making only $5 on the short side.

More assets under management means Maverick owns more of each position. "We're very thoughtful about liquidity," says Ainslie, who estimates that on average, the fund could liquidate more than 75 percent of its holdings in a week of trading, without significantly moving the stock price. Its median market cap midway through 2007 was about $9 billion.

As 2003 dawned, Ainslie and the sector heads anticipated they would have a difficult time making money on the short side, and they hashed out the problem at one of their weekly staff meetings in April. Interest rates were at 1.25 percent, and some were speculating that the Fed would lower them to 1 percent because of slowing growth and the war in Iraq. "It was evident to us that liquidity was being unleashed from many different sources," says Ainslie. With more money readily available to borrow, the market would probably continue to be strong and lower-quality stocks would benefit most.

So Ainslie and his team took a good look at their short book. They covered, or bought back, any stocks for which the catalyst they expected to cause a drop in price might not play out for a year or more. They also got rid of any stocks they had wagered would fall primarily because they were too expensive, since the market probably wouldn't care as much about valuation. "If the stocks had a fundamental issue that would be apparent to the market within the year, we kept them," says Ainslie. "Despite this insight and a great deal of effort to respond to conditions, our shorts outperformed the market."

The appetite for risk among stock jocks was just too strong. In 2003, for example, the S&P 500 stocks in the bottom quintile of estimated earnings revisions—most of which were revised downward—ended the year outperforming the shares in the top quartile. "That's an extraordinarily difficult environment to short," says Ainslie.

Maverick's short portfolio didn't end up making money in the next two years either. They decided to bring down the number of stocks the fund owned to roughly 170 from a peak of 240. "We wanted to make sure we were taking full advantage of our very best ideas and to make sure each short was an investment that we expected to be profitable and not meant simply to serve as a hedge," says Ainslie. "When you go through a prolonged period of losing money on the short side, you tend to become much more defensive, and we started to think more about where we would not lose money, instead of where we would make money."

So in the beginning of 2006, Ainslie reinforced his discipline of keeping capital focused on the best ideas and ensuring that every single short was an investment, not a hedge. It started to work. "We added significant value on the short side in 2006," he says.

When the short side is going his way, Ainslie tries to squeeze the most money out of them. "In certain situations, it's really important on the short side to have the courage to maintain if not increase the position size," he says. A classic example was Kmart in 2001. In May of that year, Maverick was short almost 20 million shares of the discount retailer primarily because the company's loss of market share to competitors Wal-Mart and Target was accelerating. The stock closed that month at $11.28. In the summer of 2001, a Maverick analyst visited Kmart and met its treasurer and head of investor relations. The Kmart executives laid out their strategy. They planned to undersell Wal-Mart. The analysts were shocked. Wal-Mart was bigger and had a lower cost structure. It could bury Kmart in such an assault.

In August, Kmart reported that its gross margins had increased in the second quarter, even as it had lowered prices. More stunning was that Wal-Mart and Target had reported a drop in gross margins. Further research revealed that Kmart was accounting for rebates from vendors immediately rather than as products were sold, an attempt to make current earnings look rosier. Maverick increased its short position to about 27 million shares in August, when the stock was trading at around $10. By October, it was trading at $6 and Maverick added another million shares to its wager. In January 2002, the company filed for bankruptcy. The shares fell as low as $0.70. After an internal review, Kmart changed the way it accounted for rebates.

Ainslie also follows Robertson's advice when ferreting out stocks to buy: look for great management. "We go to great lengths to evaluate a management team's ability to think strategically and their desire to maximize shareholder value," he says. Generally, they also look at how they're using free cash flow, how they're structuring their balance sheet, and how they're interacting with Maverick.

Some of Ainslie's biggest mistakes have come from not heeding that advice. In 1995, he was long NeoStar Retail Group, then the largest retailer of video games. Ainslie forecast that the video games market was about to grow a lot faster, with Sony set to launch its first PlayStation game console. Ainslie figured NeoStar was well suited to take advantage of the explosion in the industry. That was true, but the company went bankrupt. "We didn't ride it all the way down," says Ainslie, "but we rode it closer than I care to remember."

Management was the key to the failure. Ainslie had concerns about the quality of NeoStar's management team, and how it was structured, but he calculated that the macroeconomic opportunity was so strong, it would more than compensate for their deficiencies. It didn't. The stumble reinforced a lesson about conviction: You have to be constantly attuned to any discrepancy between your view and what the rest of the world is thinking. And you have to keep studying that discrepancy, especially as the stock moves in the wrong direction. "That was a case in which the rest of the world was right, and we were wrong," says Ainslie.

Ainslie and his team are firm believers in finding out as much as they can about a company. In particular, they want to understand how sustainable earnings growth is and how much free cash flow the company will continue to produce and for how long. Maverick analysts spend much time talking to competitors, suppliers, and customers, as well as to corporate executives. The analysts and sector heads think strategically about the business and the industry, looking out two or three years, identifying the winners and the losers.

To illustrate the importance of in-depth study, Ainslie points to Maverick's investment in Lexmark International. In 2005, the U.S. No. 2 printer maker in the world by sales was Maverick's biggest loser for the year and, in fact, its biggest single stock loss for any year in the fund's history. Yet the next year, it was the fund's biggest winner. The disastrous losses had caused the Maverick analysts to dig even deeper to know the business better. That scrutiny allowed them to see things other investors missed.

In 2005, Maverick accumulated shares of Lexmark as the stock was falling; by the end of the third quarter, the fund owned 7.89 million shares and Lexmark was its largest position. The stock ended the year down a sickening 46.8 percent. There were several reasons for the decline, but one of the more interesting was a result of some sales to Dell Computer. "This was an instance where things didn't work in reality as well as they appeared to on paper," says Ainslie.

Lexmark had developed a very low-cost printer. As it did with most of its printers, the company sold it at a loss because Lexmark's moneymaker is its printer supplies, which at the time accounted for about 59 percent of total revenue. Indeed, the printer was so cheap that Dell included it as part of a package at no cost to the consumer. With Dell essentially giving away a large number of printers, Lexmark was expecting a huge increase in cartridge sales.

There was, however, an unforeseen catch. It seems many people threw the Lexmark printers in the trash because they already owned better ones. So Lexmark was losing money on the printers and not selling as many additional cartridges as forecast. Since sales of replacement cartridges for new printers generally don't happen for months, it took a while for Lexmark to realize that the increased business wasn't materializing and more time for Lexmark to work out a solution with Dell.

In the aftermath of Lexmark's stumble, Maverick built a better relationship with the management team and improved its ability to track various pieces of the business. Just when other investors were giving up on Lexmark in late 2005, Maverick was buying shares. By the end of the year, it owned almost 9 million of them. In January 2006, the company announced a dramatic restructuring, adding new products and cutting 825 jobs, and the board agreed to add $1 billion to its stock-buyback program, a move Maverick had strongly encouraged. The stock climbed 63 percent that year.

Although Ainslie has stuck with his classic long-short hedge fund model, he's continually looking to improve Maverick's investment process. To that end, he hired Galbraith in 2003. Ainslie realized that in trying to manage the portfolio and the firm simultaneously, he wasn't doing either job as well as he would have liked, so he sought out help. "We looked for somebody who could bring strengths that I don't have on the investment side and who could also be helpful on the business side," says Ainslie. "When we drew up the list of people to interview, it was a very short one."

Galbraith had been at Morgan Stanley for four years as chief investment officer; before that, he'd been a partner at Sanford Bernstein. Galbraith brings a more macro orientation to the table. "He's always done a very good job of taking those macro considerations and boiling them down to the real world and explaining how they will relate to individual stocks," says Ainslie. Galbraith's experiences in finance differ greatly from Ainslie's. "Those relationships and those experiences are very helpful as we think about the business."

Indeed, Galbraith was one of the partners who assisted Ainslie in the decision to open four new funds at Maverick in early 2005. Maverick's main funds—its flagship and another that uses borrowed money to double the size of the investments and is now Maverick's largest fund—have been closed to most new investors since 1998. Maverick added a long-only fund; a long-enhanced fund, which is 150 percent long and 50 percent short; a market-neutral fund, which is 100 percent long and 100 percent short; and a leveraged market-neutral fund, which is 200 percent long and 200 percent short. The new funds don't require additional decision making on Maverick's part. They contain the same stocks as the core portfolios, just in different quantities. How they're allocated to each fund is purely a back-office function. Investors can commit their money for one to five years, with reduced fees for the longer lockups.

These latest offerings help diversify the revenue stream. In 2002, when the S&P 500 was down 22 percent, the Maverick Fund was up 2 percent, which didn't produce a huge amount in fees. Had the leveraged market-neutral fund existed then, it would have been up 14 percent.

Galbraith has helped to mentor Maverick's junior analysts through a program called the "small-cap effort," which makes 2 percent to 4 percent of assets available for small-cap ideas generated by the forty or so analysts. Neither the sector heads nor Ainslie intervenes in these investment decisions. An analyst pitches his or her ideas to Galbraith, and if he approves, they're made part of the portfolio. The program offers analysts a way to learn from their successes and mistakes and also gives Ainslie and the sector heads the chance to see how the analysts perform independently and which staffers might have potential as portfolio managers over the long term.

Ainslie believes that as fewer funds control the lion's share of the money—at the end of 2006, the top one hundred funds in the industry controlled about two-thirds of assets—the new breed of superstars who grow up in big firms will eventually take the reins of groups like Maverick, rather than quitting to go off on their own. "The next generation of really talented hedge fund managers are not running some new fund they started when they were in their twenties; they're working at firms like Maverick," says Ainslie. "At our firm, there are at least a dozen individuals who certainly have the potential to take my place someday. Part of our job will be to train them and retain them."

That's the kind of potential Ainslie sees realized in Roberto Mignone (see Chapter 13), who started Bridger Management in New York seven years ago when he was twenty-nine, and Bernay Box (see Chapter 7), who runs Bonanza Capital in Dallas.

"Roberto is very thorough, very thoughtful, very levelheaded, and has a high degree of integrity," says Ainslie. Mignone also has an indirect Tiger connection. Before starting Bridger, he was an analyst at Blue Ridge Capital, a firm founded by Tiger alumnus John Griffin.

"Bernay Box has the same qualities," says Ainslie. Box, forty-five, was a portfolio manager at First Republic Asset Management in Dallas until 1992, when he began managing separate accounts for his clients and later opened a small fund of funds. Box was an early investor in Maverick and became friendly with Ainslie over the years. In 2002, Box decided to start his own hedge fund. "He made the brave decision to shut down those successful businesses and start all over from scratch, and his numbers have been quite strong ever since."

Maverick invests with both managers through Maverick Stable, its fund of funds, which farms out money to other hedge funds. Maverick started this fund of funds in July 2002, primarily to allow employees to diversify their personal assets, since Maverick investment professionals aren't allowed to trade for their own accounts and virtually all of their net worth is invested in Maverick's funds. The fund of funds is now open to outside clients, although the lion's share of assets still belongs to insiders.

It's not surprising that Mignone and Box appeal to Ainslie. Like him, they're both research-intensive stock pickers.

Optimism on the Rise

Ainslie's flagship Maverick Fund dropped 26.7 percent in 2008, his first annual loss since he began managing the fund in 1995. Virtually all of the damage occurred between August 26 and October 7, among the most volatile weeks of a tumultuous year. Within that brief period, regulators banned the short sale of almost 1,000 stocks, the volatility of share prices intensified, Lehman Brothers declared bankruptcy, and hedge funds and other investors around the world rushed to exit the markets.

Starting in July, Maverick was already raising its cash levels and reducing the amount of money that it was putting into the markets. By early October, the fund had 160 percent of net assets invested, the lowest in the firm's history, and down from about 260 percent in late July. Even so, Ainslie told investors that he should have moved more swiftly. "By mid-August Maverick's total gross exposure had been reduced by only 9 percent from the levels of late July," he said. "Had we reduced our gross exposure in a rushed and frantic fashion, our performance during that difficult six-week period would have been dramatically better."

Ainslie told clients his team was too focused on company research. And though their views turned out to be right after the dust settled, the team failed to consider just how much havoc would be caused by the mad rush of so many investors cashing in simultaneously.

From a business standpoint, Maverick fared better than many of its competitors. While some funds lost as much as 50 percent of their assets from client withdrawals, Maverick's clients pulled less than 10 percent from its funds. As of March 31, 2009, firm-wide assets stood at $9.8 billion, about $100 million more than they were in mid-2007.

Ainslie credits the low level of redemptions to more than 80 percent of Maverick's assets being from clients who have been with the firm for more than five years. Some investors have opted to be locked in for three years or five years in exchange for lower fees. Only 7 percent of Maverick's client base was made up of fund of hedge funds, which tend to be the most skittish investors because they generally let their own clients exit their funds every quarter.

Maverick's largest fund can't charge performance fees until it recoups its 2008 losses. That will take a return of about 36 percent. Maverick was able to charge fees on four of its six funds in 2009, bringing money in to pay personnel and expenses. Over the years, Ainslie has built a reserve fund large enough to cover one year's expenses, including all salaries, bonuses, and overhead. He's never needed to use it and doesn't expect to in 2009.

Through September 2009, the fund returned 22 percent, as Ainslie increased net and gross exposures to levels closer to historic norms from his more conservative stance in the spring. "The risk of instability in the financial system has dramatically declined," Ainslie says. He has more confidence about buying stocks he sees as trading too cheaply and about selling shares he thinks are too dear.

Chapter 7

Bernay Box
The Big Time in Small Caps

BERNAY BOX, by his own account, is not a particularly patient man. He met the woman who became his wife in the first or second week of his freshman year at Baylor University and by April, they had eloped. They had their first child fourteen months later. "I have a very clear understanding of who I am," says Box, "and I just like to get stuff done."

Which he does, and quite well, but not because he hurries things along. Box might be the type to move quickly in some areas of his life, but when it comes to investing, he's the soul of patience, and that, he says, is his edge.

Box, forty-five, runs Bonanza Capital in Dallas and he looks for the small-cap stock that will at least double, if not soar fourfold or fivefold, over a three-year period. For shorts, he wants stocks that lose all their value within a year to eighteen months. For that kind of return, you need to be willing to wait. "Our main competitive advantage is we have a very long time frame, and that creates a much higher probability of our being right," says Box.

With his eight-member investing team, Box oversees $510 million. In July 2007, they had ninety-two stocks they were betting would jump in price and the rest they were wagering would tumble. Box started the firm on March 1, 1999, and the fund has returned about 16.3 percent a year on average after fees. He's had one losing year, 2002, when the fund was down 4 percent compared with the Russell 2000 Index of small-cap stocks, which plunged 21 percent. Although he continues to take money from current clients, his fund is closed to new investors. He aims over the long haul to return 20 percent annually to investors, after fees.

The décor of the offices of Bonanza is simple but handsome. The reception area has a leather woven rug, with one glass table in the middle supporting a huge vase of lilies. The long handles on the glass doors are covered in leather. Wearing khakis and a blue blazer the day I met him, Box has the kind of good looks and easy manner one associates with a high school quarterback.

Just as Bonanza is 1,400 miles away from the epicenter of hedge fund land—New York and its leafy suburbs—Box's world of small-cap investing is far afield from that of his peers who wager on the rise and fall of larger companies. To find a winner among fledgling enterprises, you need to focus even more on the future of the business, and while some quantitative analysis of cash flows and company valuations is important, the main driver is whether the business works, he says. "You really have to look to the next two to three years and ask yourself is that product something that the people will actually buy," says Box. You also have to evaluate the management team, understand its motivations, and assess its ability not only to understand what its customers want but also to deliver the goods.

Understanding these matters seems to come naturally to Box. He learned about business models almost from the cradle. He is the fifth child of a serial entrepreneur, and over the years his father, Boyce, invested in real estate, oil and gas, mobile home park development, restaurants, hotels, gold mining, apparel companies, and insurance. "He always wanted to start new things," says Box.

So do the people who run the companies Box considers for investment. Observing his father helped Box understand what it takes to make a business work—and what can and will go wrong. He recalls his father's dealings in the oil and gas industry in the early 1980s. Between 1978 and 1981, the price of crude oil rose as high as $40 a barrel from $14, spurred by lower production in the Middle East because of the Iranian revolution and Iran-Iraq war. Domestic producers came online as prices rose, and they made good money until the Saudis increased their output, pushing oil back down to $10 a barrel by 1986. "It made me realize that all businesses, all industries, are cyclical," says Box. "There has never been a scenario where the trees grow to the sky."

To fill in any gaps in what he'd learned at his father's knee, Box enrolled in 1980 to study business at Baylor, the state's oldest university, in Waco, Texas. After his wife Robin became pregnant, he left school for a year and a half to work for his father in several businesses, including a gold and silver mining operation, but he eventually graduated in 1986, by then the father of two.

Box was fascinated by the stock market, and his hero during his college days was Ivan Boesky, who had amassed hundreds of millions of dollars as an arbitrageur betting on the stocks of merging companies. "I wanted to figure out a way to be like Ivan Boesky," he says—that is, until Boesky got arrested in 1986 for insider trading. That event turned off Box to the idea of looking for a job in merger arbitrage.

Instead, degree in hand, Box went to work for a small investment bank in Dallas called Rauscher Pierce, now part of RBC Dain Rauscher, which focused on small stocks. "I liked the idea of finding companies that are under the radar," he says. What he didn't like was being a salesman, and after about a year and a half he left to become a portfolio manager at First Republic Asset Management, one of the largest asset-management companies in Dallas at the time.

The bank was a great training ground, but the pay was low compared with what other money-management jobs offered. Even if Box was promoted to chief investment officer, he would still be making a fraction of what investment professionals who started their own firms would make. And like his father, he had the itch to run his own show. His thirtieth birthday was approaching quickly and he had a wife, two kids, and a mortgage, but he was determined to take a chance. He knew that if the worst happened, if he failed completely, he could always get another job.

With the backing of Shad Rowe, who runs Dallas-based hedge fund Greenbrier Partners, Box struck out on his own in 1992, managing separate accounts for wealthy individuals. He later set up a small fund of funds that invested in hedge funds including Lee Ainslie's Maverick Capital.

A student of business models, Box saw after a few years that running separate accounts was not the optimal approach for an investment firm. The business wasn't scalable. The more accounts you had, the bigger your back office had to be and the more communication you had to have with clients. Generally, when you did a trade, the customer would call you and ask you why you bought or sold that stock, and you'd have the same discussion over and over again. As his business grew, it became less and less about investing, which he loved, and more and more about administration, which he didn't. "My wife noticed this disturbing trend of my being in a bad mood all the time," he says. He realized he needed to change tacks.

About that time, three hedge fund managers, Jim Smith, Houston Hall, and Jimmy Gallivan, from whom he sublet office space, invited him to a meeting with a broker, Montgomery Securities. Montgomery, which was later bought by Bank of America, was marketing its prime brokerage business, a fairly new business at the time, to hedge funds. Prime brokerage services may include custodial and administrative tasks as well as lending stocks for shorting purposes and money to increase the size of the wagers. All the information can be sent and received over the Internet. A light went on for Box. He could start his own hedge fund and let Montgomery take care of the administrative work so he could finally concentrate on investing.

He worked on a business plan for several months and told his clients he was going to start a stock fund that would buy small-cap stocks and sell them short. He had lots of details still to be worked out, but one thing was clear: Box wanted his company's name to start with the letter B. In naming his children—Baxter and Bailee—Box had followed a family tradition. His father, whom he considered his best friend, was named Boyce, and Boyce had named him Bernay. Recalling the days when he worked for his father in mining, he thought of the word *bonanza*. The meaning fit: an ore body very rich in value. "*Bonanza* to me represented the small nuggets of value that I was mining every day," says Box.

Coming up with a name for the new venture took a lot less time than raising money for it. "I was so naïve," says Box. He figured that a third, perhaps even half, of the assets from his original clients would follow him into his hedge fund and that he'd start with $20 million or so. Ultimately, he had to launch Bonanza with $2 million. What he hadn't quite realized was how big a change this new fund was for his clients. With separate accounts, they could take their money out at any time and they knew every position they held. They paid Box a 1 percent management fee. Now, he was asking them to pay an extra 15 percent of any profit he made and telling them they could withdraw money only once a quarter with thirty days' notice. They wouldn't know all the positions in their portfolio; in fact, they'd have to be satisfied with a quarterly performance letter and an annual audit. What's worse, the new fund was structured as a limited partnership, a dirty word in Texas after the 1980s, when plenty of investors got swindled by scammers taking advantage of the booms in the oil and real estate markets to sell fraudulent private partnerships. "Looking back, I was probably fortunate to get $2 million," says Box with a laugh.

The first few years were grueling. "I started alone with an assistant, a Bloomberg terminal, a telephone, and a crappy little desk," he says. It was a twenty-four-hour-a-day, seven-day-a-week job. He'd manage the portfolio Monday through Friday from 6 a.m. to 9 p.m. and work Saturdays and half days on Sunday doing the back-office chores not covered by the prime broker and other business-related projects. Fortunately, he lived three blocks from the office.

The start-up had its challenges, but he was back doing the kind of investing and detailed research he enjoys. "I never understood the model in which a portfolio manager in Boston or New York or San Francisco calls an analyst, who is probably in New York, and asks him what's going on in the asphalt business in Phoenix, Arizona. Why doesn't the guy just get on a plane and go to Phoenix and talk to a bunch of asphalt companies?" says Box. Likewise, if you want to know what's going on in the oil and gas business in the Gulf of Mexico, you need to go down there and see for yourself. "That's how you keep your thumb on the pulse of what's happening with a business."

Most of Bonanza's investment ideas come from its own research, through what Box jokingly calls the "Hansel and Gretel approach." Box and his team follow the bread crumbs. They talk to one management team, who tells them about a big order from a customer. From there, they find out that the customer was in a position to place that big order because it was doing a lot more business with a third company. Bonanza follows the money.

Once he's invested, Box generally gets close to management, although he understands the pitfalls of becoming too chummy. "You definitely want to understand them and know what their motivations and strengths and weaknesses are, but you don't want to get so close that you lose your objectivity," says Box. Entrepreneurs tend to be overly optimistic—they have to be—until they lose that customer they never imagined losing or face a competitor on a product that was supposed to have the market all to itself. "They tend to put off telling you certain things because they don't want to disappoint you. They don't want you to get upset with them: you own a million shares of their stock and they don't want you to sell it."

When Box suspects company management is straying from the path, he approaches issues gingerly. He likes to ensure he'll always have communication with management by behaving well. "We never walk into a meeting or write letters to management teams telling them what a bunch of idiots they are," says Box. "We may think that, but being disrespectful, being obnoxious, being a know-it-all is really a good way not to be invited back to their office or get a phone call returned."

Even when Bonanza is short a company and even when he and his analysts think the management is lying or cheating, they won't get on the phone and scream or get them in a conference room and accuse them of cooking the books. "It's disrespectful and not civil and you cut your information flow off if you act that way," says Box. "If you're an unpleasant investor and fire off 13Ds to the SEC, talking about how the CEO wears nylon panties under his suit and accusing them of all kinds of crazy stuff, the communication is going to be pretty muted," he says, referring to Securities and Exchange Commission filings that activist investors sometimes make when they own large stakes of a company.

Ultimately, the money talks. If Box and his team don't like a company or disagree with management, they'll sell the shares, or if the company's prospects are really abominable, they'll short them.

Although Box wants to know everything he can about what management is up to, he's not particularly concerned with what other investors think. He tends to be a contrarian, and he doesn't like to chat with other analysts or investors. "I don't talk to that many people because doing so might skew my thinking," he says. "I want to be very objective and very unemotional. I think it really helps us to be here in Dallas rather than in New York, where that noise can sometimes overcome your thought process."

It's not unusual for Box to buy companies in industries that everyone else hates, as in 2001 and 2002, when he was buying energy stocks, and in 2002 and 2003, when he took a liking to small airlines. He often gets his short ideas from watching for the hot new thing that everybody has to own, the stock that you're an idiot if you don't buy. "I like to go to the party to see who's drunk," says Box. "And I like to go to fires to see what's coming out of the ashes."

Box's contrarian tendencies were evident when he invested in Deckers Outdoor Corporation, which makes Teva sandals and Uggs, the ubiquitous sheepskin-lined boots that everyone from Hollywood stars to junior high schoolgirls wear. It was 2001, and analysts were pessimistic about the stock, given that the company had missed earnings estimates for a quarter or two. The stock fell from around $5 to as low as $3.40, which Bonanza saw as encouraging: earnings were down because demand was so high that the company had run out of sheepskin.

Everyone in the Bonanza office, or rather their wives and kids, had tried and approved the product. When Ugg slippers came out, Box bought a pair and was hooked. Deckers's CEO had plans for all sorts of new designs and products, so Box and his analysts were confident the growth would continue. But it took time. The stock didn't jump above the $5 level until April 2003. By the end of 2004, it was trading at $48.

Box fell for another obscure venture in late 1999 or early 2000, when he bought Hansen's Natural, which made good-for-you beverages like smoothies, juices, and natural soda. Brett Hendrickson, who has since come to work for Bonanza, was then a salesman at a securities firm and pitched Box the idea. Box met with management and liked what he saw. The company had a good brand, and its distribution was expanding from health food stores in Southern California into northern California and Arizona. What's more, its management was thinking ahead. The energy drink market was taking off, and Hansen's chief executive, Rodney Sacks, had the idea of developing its own entrant, a beverage called "Monster Energy," which he launched in 2002. Most analysts believed Monster couldn't compete against Coke and Pepsi, which had energy drinks in development as well.

When Box first bought shares of Hansen, they were trading around $4 and the company had a market cap of about $40 million, meaning it took Bonanza a couple of weeks just to buy enough stock to have a meaningful position. Again, Box was content to wait. Sales of energy drinks exploded in 2003, and Monster Energy became the No. 2 best seller, behind Red Bull. In the first half of 2004, the stock was trading in the midteens, and Bonanza sold.

Such happy times put an altogether different spin on the wisdom of waiting. They raise the question of whether to get out or stay in. Hansen was trading at twenty to twenty-five times the next year's projected cash flow. "When a stock gets to our target price, unless we can really justify significant upside from there, we have to start scaling out," says Box.

As sometimes happens, Box ended up leaving money on the table with the Hansen wager. "I had no idea that in the next two or three years the Monster brand would continue to grow and that the valuation really wouldn't matter to institutions," says Box. Indeed, the stock went up more than five times within the next twelve months after he sold it, but one of Box's main tenets is that when other investors cease to care about how expensive a stock gets, he backs away. He knows the inevitable tumble will be just as dramatic and swift as the rise. "The market gods rule. We don't understand what makes all the animal spirits wake up one day and decide to sell all at once."

The decision on when to sell sometimes comes down to patience. Looking back on some of his biggest hits, Box wishes he hadn't sold his entire position, because the businesses were good and he underestimated either the market potential or the ability of management to keep the earnings growing. "Sometimes you can be too pessimistic or not optimistic enough."

When it comes to fads, however, nothing much has come along to change Box's mind. His basic belief in long-term, enduring business models keeps him away from them. He had the chance to buy a big stake in True Religion Brand Jeans when the stock was at $0.80. He passed because he was afraid that jeans selling at $150 wouldn't fly for very long. "Of course, we were dead wrong," says Box. The stock went up more than twenty times in the next two years. Yet he sticks to his antifad discipline because his overall rule is to have time on his side, not working against him.

With small-cap stocks, however, waiting can be painful. The long investment periods Box prefers can bring greater risk because small caps tend to be more volatile than large caps. To counter that, he has developed several practices to cut the damage of a position moving against him. For one, he owns a lot of stocks across a broad number of sectors. And although he doesn't use options to hedge moves of individual stocks, he will trade in his positions, adding to or taking away, say, 10 percent or 15 percent of his stake if he expects a piece of news or an earnings report that might cause the price of shares to fall when he wants them to rise or vice versa.

He might also box a position, meaning he'll temporarily sell some shares short of a stock he's expecting to take a hit but rise over time, or he might buy shares of a stock he is shorting. He doesn't worry about hedging overall market risk, such as buying puts on the Russell 2000 Index. "Guessing what the market's going to do or hypothesizing about the market being overvalued or undervalued is not what we're good at," says Box.

For added protection, Box introduced position size limits after a frustrating experience shorting a stock in 1999. A company called Metricom had caught his attention as a good short, so he borrowed the shares and sold them, believing the stock would tumble and he could buy them back later at a cheaper price. The company was selling wireless Internet access—a precursor to Wi-Fi—and it had mounted ricochet radios on light poles in cities across the country. The company was using a lot of cash, and Box didn't think the business model would work. It was too expensive to make and install the radios and there were too few customers. Box started shorting the stock in mid-June, when it was trading between $10 and $11.

But Metricom had its believers. Microsoft cofounder Paul Allen was a majority owner in the company through his investment arm, Vulcan Ventures. And WorldCom at that time was looking for ways to grow its business. So it decided to match a $300 million investment Allen was putting into Metricom. The cash injections came only about a week after Bonanza had put on its short. By July 2, the stock was trading close to $30. After four or five nights of fitful sleep, Box decided to buy back his shares, at between $40 and $50 each. There was no point, Box saw, in being dead right. "At some point the need to survive has to override anything that you think you know."

Box watched the stock climb to $103, all the while continuing his research. He saw that the subscriber counts were not going up, so he shorted it again when it was trading between $80 and $70 and rode it into bankruptcy in July 2001.

In the sickening days when the stock had jumped, it had become an almost 10 percent position for him. From then on, he decided that his short positions would generally be 1 percent to 2 percent of the portfolio, with a maximum of 4 percent, and his long positions would be 2 percent to 3 percent, with a maximum of 6 percent. He immediately trims any position that spreads out of those ranges.

The biggest challenge for Box is making sure the size of each position makes sense in the context of the entire portfolio. Ideally, the best ideas get the most capital, but once a stock has risen 50 percent and become the biggest position, it's undoubtedly not the biggest money-maker anymore, because it's already jumped so much. "My job and my biggest problem—the issue that I deal with every day—is making sure that I properly work with my team to understand their conviction levels about particular companies and to understand the companies' valuations," says Box. "I have to make sure that I have the capital allocated to the right names in the right proportions."

To do that, Box weighs all the information—the company's business model, the risks it faces, management's experience, how easy it is to trade the stock—and decides whether a stock should be a 2 percent, 3 percent, or 4 percent position. If conditions at the company improve, he'll buy more shares, as long as it still has the potential to at least double in value. If a stock is close to its target, and he doesn't expect it to move higher, he starts reducing his position so that he can free the money to invest in another trade with greater moneymaking potential.

To make sure he's up to date on all the information his analysts unearth, everyone feeds any data on a company—whether they're new earnings forecasts or a chat with a company executive or a competitor—into a database. Once Box decides on the size of the positions and the price target at which he wants to do the trade, he passes the information on to Cody Reynolds, Bonanza's trader, to execute. He gives Reynolds some leeway so that opportunities aren't missed. "If you make a target decision and your limits are $0.20 or

$0.40 away from where the market is, you need to give your trader the ability to use his discretion. He has a better feel for what the short-term movements are in the markets," says Box.

Reynolds and the other senior members of the team—analysts Brian Ladin and Brett Hendrickson, and Amanda York, who takes care of business not related to investments—are all "smart, hungry, with a good work ethic," says Box. All went to non–Ivy League yet highly ranked schools and none of them, including Box, has an MBA. "I'm not saying that not having an MBA is a positive. What I am saying is most of our team are self-taught, with a bootstrap mentality. They acquired their skills through experience and through the school of hard knocks."

A learning-by-doing approach is particularly important in small-cap investing, says Box, because the analysis tends to be less academic than it is in large-cap plays. "We believe the efficient market hypothesis is a bunch of crap," says Box, by way of example, referring to the notion that prices of a stock reflect all the available information.

To ensure that prospective employees fit into the Bonanza culture, Box has even taken them along on research trips before he hires them. He recalls his trip with Ladin, who joined Bonanza in 2002. "There are four or five management meetings a day, you take [the candidate] out to dinner and maybe you serve him too much wine. You're out late, and then get him up at six o'clock the next morning. You put him in some crappy hotel, driving a crappy rental car, and do that for a week. Over that four- or five-day period, you're going to get a very good idea of what his thoughts are."

Ladin did more than survive. "He had a high energy level, he's very, very smart, very diligent. He was always down in the lobby waiting for me. He was good at talking to management, and he knew what we needed to ask. Brett [Hendrickson] is the same way."

Box, who speaks from time to time at his alma mater, says his advice to students who want to get into the hedge fund game is to develop skills that make them really good at what they do and different from anybody else. Then, having done that, he says, don't worry about what anybody else thinks. "You've got to play your game," he says. "You have a skill set, a mentality, a background, a genetic makeup to do things a certain way. Develop those skills and do it that way." And keep learning. "Constantly develop your craft and get better at it."

His final word on investing? "Keep your eye on where the ball's going, not where it's at."

Moving On

Box faced some unhappy choices in 2008. By June 30, his flagship Bonanza Master Fund had tumbled almost 23 percent for the year. On top of the losses—his worst ever—Box anticipated that many investors would be pulling their money from his fund as the industry faced a wave of redemptions.

His dilemma was shared by an unprecedented number of managers in 2008: What do you do if a large percentage of clients rush for the exits? Box had three choices. He could either refuse to give back some or all of their money, let the clients exit the fund and leave the remaining clients with a concentrated portfolio, or liquidate everything and close the fund.

Some of Box's largest holdings were quite profitable in the first seven months of the year. His stake in independent oil company Contango Oil & Gas Co., which had started the year worth $13 million, climbed 68 percent. He owned less than 2 percent of the company, which would make it easy to dump the shares if he needed cash.

His biggest position at that start of 2008, a $30 million stake in a company called Thinkorswim Group Inc., plummeted 54 percent during that same period, after the online brokerage and investment-education company disclosed a Securities and Exchange Commission probe over statements made by presenters at its investment seminars. (In January 2009, TD Ameritrade agreed to acquire the company for $606 million, or about $9 a share. Box had paid $2.)

Another sizeable stake, a $13 million position in Telular Corp., which makes technology that lets traditional phones communicate over wireless networks, dropped 57 percent. Bonanza was its biggest holder.

In the beginning of August, Box decided to close his funds.

"Bonanza's investment time horizon has always been long-term— two to three years—and this patience has historically given us a competitive advantage," Box wrote in the letter announcing his decision to clients. "However, given our year-to-date performance, investing for the long term is impossible if our investors want liquidity in the next three to six months.

"In the current market environment, I am no longer able to 'play my game.' This is all somewhat ironic to me given that the opportunities I see in the marketplace are probably some of the best in my twenty-plus years in the investing business."

Most important, Box wanted to make a decision that was right for all his investors, he says. "I didn't want to have the me-first mentality that had become pervasive in the industry," he says, referring to managers who kept people from redeeming and continued to run the fund and earn management fees. "I wanted to do what was in the best interest of the fund and the investors."

His decision was also influenced by his own experiences managing a growing business. Assets had jumped to more than $500 million—large for a small-cap fund. "I had become a little frustrated with the challenges," he says. "It started to become much more management intensive than investment intensive."

By October 1, 2008, Box had given investors 50 percent of their money back. By January 2009, he'd returned more than 90 percent.

For now, Box is managing his own money and has changed his investment focus to take advantage of today's environment. "When I started, back in the 1990s, I focused on small caps because there was a huge value discrepancy," meaning that the stocks were cheap because no one paid attention to them.

Today, he says, it's the large and mid-cap stocks that are selling at bargain prices, while the small-cap companies are relatively expensive given that their prospects are much more questionable in difficult economic times, in part because their business are U.S.-focused.

He's also less likely to bet on stock prices falling farther, given that the trailing 10-year returns on stock indexes are already at historically low levels. Shorting is also less lucrative today because brokerages are charging more to lend stocks, and once those borrowed shares are sold, the cash proceeds sitting in one's brokerage account earn almost no interest.

Although he's not ready to divulge his future plans, Box, ever the entrepreneur, says he's already planning the next phase of his money-management career.

Chapter 8

Boone Pickens
The Imperturbable Oilman

ONE REASON BOONE PICKENS likes his new job as hedge fund tycoon so much is that it's a lot more lucrative than any work he's done before. "I've made more money since I've turned seventy," says Pickens. That birthday came just a few years after starting his first fund with BP Capital Management in Dallas. In April 2006, when he made out his check to the Internal Revenue Service, his accountant told him that since becoming a septuagenarian he'd paid 90 percent of all the taxes he'd ever forked over to Uncle Sam—surely a considerable sum, given that by 2007 only about 350 people in the country had more wealth than Pickens, according to *Forbes*.

Pickens's tax obligations show no sign of winding down, because even now, at seventy-nine, he plans on making money, something he's always found ways to do. Pickens once ran Mesa Petroleum, the largest independent oil company in the United States. In the 1980s, he was known as one of America's preeminent takeover artists, making unsuccessful—yet moneymaking—bids for the likes of Phillips Petroleum Company and Cities Service Company.

"I get more satisfaction out of this work," he says, sitting in his suite in the Lowell Hotel in Manhattan, where he, his wife Madeleine, and their dog stay when they come to the Big Apple from their home in Dallas. Pickens is a down-home kind of guy, very friendly, given to deadpan joking. In his workout clothes—gray sweatpants, a striped polo shirt, and athletic socks—he's looking spry. CNBC is on mute, and he's ready with the remote for any news on oil or natural gas.

Pickens oversees BP Capital's investments with an eleven-member management team, three of whom—Dick Grant, Ronald Bassett, and Robert Stillwell—have been with him since the Mesa days. His energy stock hedge funds, which invest 90 percent in equities and 10 percent in commodities, averaged returns of about 38 percent a year through mid-2007 since starting in August 2001. His oil and gas commodities fund distributed about $2.8 billion to investors since he started it in 1997. About $1.6 billion of the $4.3 billion BP Capital manages is Pickens's personal fortune. New clients pay a 1.75 percent management fee and 30 percent of any profit.

Pickens's strategy is simple: The team makes forecasts on the direction of oil and natural gas and then makes bets in the futures markets. Based on where they see things going, they also buy energy stocks or sell them short. Pickens doesn't hedge his positions, nor does he trade around them. If the fundamentals haven't changed, he holds tight, even if the market goes against him. "We are fundamental players and we will stay with the position," he says. "We pick up a lot of long-term capital gains on our winners," with most positions on the books for four to twenty-four months. He continually analyzes and reassesses every position to ensure he's right, so he's not one to panic when prices go the wrong way. He controls the size of the trade so that he can stay in the market even if he's early. "You can't overlook the volatility, but you don't let it push you around in the market," he says in his quintessential Pickens parlance. "You don't let any position get your dress over your head."

Born in Holdenville, Oklahoma, Pickens started his career in the oil business in 1951 as a geologist for Phillips Petroleum after graduating from Oklahoma State University with a degree in geology. He founded what would become Mesa in 1956, when he was twenty-eight. After spending decades looking for oil and gas in the ground, he started eyeing undervalued oil and gas companies.

His first buyout, in 1969, was Hugoton Production Company, which owned a huge natural gas field in Kansas. This was followed in the 1980s by a series of bids for companies—including Cities

Service Company, Phillips Petroleum, Gulf Oil Company, and Unocal Corporation—that he never purchased. Instead, the target company would institute a stock buyback or find a white knight to make a counteroffer at a premium to the current stock price. Either way, as a shareholder, Pickens would end up making millions.

In managing Mesa, however, Pickens miscalculated in a plan to buy gas reserves and pay shareholder dividends. He borrowed more than $1 billion, betting that even though natural gas prices were tumbling, they'd soon reverse course and more than cover his debts. That didn't happen soon enough; in the end, he was forced to sell the company to Texas billionaire Richard Rainwater in 1996. "We got out of step at Mesa," says Pickens. "Our timing was off, and it cost us."

More often, however, Pickens's timing has been on the money. He had been trading commodity futures on and off at Mesa since the early 1970s, at first to hedge his exposure to a cattle business. Between 1986 and 1996, he and his Mesa team turned $2 million into $150 million trading oil and gas futures. "I never had a losing year in that period," says Pickens. "That seemed to be where I was doing the best, so I thought why not pursue that?"

The next step made perfect sense: becoming a hedge fund manager. In 1997, he started a commodities fund with six investors and $34 million, a quarter of which was his own. The first few years didn't work out so well. Between the day he launched the fund and the end of 1998, Pickens lost about 90 percent of the money he'd started with. "We didn't have it right," he laughs, sounding like someone who's learned to handle setbacks. This one, too, was temporary. He hasn't posted a losing year since. He distributes the profits annually and generally begins January 1 of each year with $275 million. A larger amount might become unwieldy, he says.

His stock fund also lost money—35.7 percent—in its first full year, 2002, but not since. "I learn from every experience," says Pickens. "When you get your fingers mashed in a door, you don't go back to that door."

Knowing what *not* to do is important, but Pickens's edge comes from being in the oil and gas business for more than half a century, both as an operator and a trader. "I think I'm one of the few guys who has both the business experience and the commodities experience," he says. That combination allows him to see things other traders don't. In 2003, oil futures a few years out were trading at $20 to $25 a barrel. Given how much it cost to find and pull oil out of the ground, Pickens was convinced that those prices were absurdly cheap. That started him on a multiyear buying spree of oil futures four or five years into the future. Oil eventually jumped to nearly $80 a barrel in July 2006, and the bets turned out to be huge winners.

Veteran or not, Pickens doesn't shy away from the hard work required for results, and he spends a good deal of time watching the markets. "Especially when you get to be my age, you have to make sure you stay current," he says. "Don't step out of the picture and then try to get back in." When he's away from the office, it's not unusual for him to call his team ten times a day.

Pickens is a proponent of the controversial theory known as "peak oil," which proposes that global oil production is at or near its apex. And so his positions in the market tend to be long rather than short. "[My feelings on oil production have] had a lot of influence on the money I've made and some of the money I've lost," says Pickens.

In 2007, his belief in the peak oil theory wasn't helping in his bets on crude. "I'm a loser in the oil market and a winner in the gas market," says Pickens. The stock fund was up 6 percent as of mid-2007, and the commodities fund was down 21 percent. The trouble came in January, when oil fell from close to $60 a barrel at the start of the year to around $50 midmonth after Saudi Arabia said it wouldn't cut production, and stockpiles in the United States rose. "We took a $10 hit on oil," says Pickens, who in June 2007 was forecasting that oil prices would average $70 a barrel in 2007, barring an economic slowdown. "I'm not counting on a recession, but I'm a lot more concerned about it today than I was two months ago." His economic consultants originally fore-cast economic growth at 2.5 percent in 2007 and later lowered it to 1.75 percent. He's a bit nervous they may continue to cut his estimates, although he'd prefer to have his bad news all at once. "I don't want to be gummed to death by a rubber duck," he says. "I'd rather be eaten by a man-eating tiger."

Although his eye never leaves the big picture, Pickens will sometimes make shorter-term trades when he sees how the wind is blowing. In the first four months of 2007, Pickens and his team were long, then short, then long natural gas, and made money on every leg. But, don't confuse what he does with day trading, a practice he says is akin to rolling the dice in Las Vegas. "If you hang around long enough there, they will take your money."

Pickens also structures trades to make the most money with the least amount of capital. In August 2002, he made a fairly large bet on natural gas. "We were stretching the rubber band pretty far," he says. For futures set to expire in 2003, 2004, and 2005, he and his team put on the following trade: They bought a $4 call, sold a $5 call, and sold a $3 put. In other words, they were betting that for those years, natural gas futures—then trading at around $3.50—would rise above $4, but not above $5, and that they wouldn't fall below $3. Pickens earned money selling the two options, more than covering the cost of buying the third. Of his penchant for making large bets when he's convinced the trend is going his way, he says, "As long as they're giving it to us, we've got to keep taking."

But why not make the bet outright, one of his team members wondered at the time; why use options? "We've got to stay safe on the thing," says Pickens, figuring that with the use of calls and puts he was putting up less capital to make the trade and earning income at the same time.

The bets at BP Capital are always directional. Pickens isn't a so-called spread player, wagering on the price difference of, say, a contract that expires in the beginning of the winter and one that expires as the weather is warming up—known as a calendar trade. Spread trades generally aren't very lucrative unless a lot of leverage is used or there's an unusual weather event, like Hurricane Katrina or Rita in 2005. "The kind of money I'm in there for, you can't do it with spreads," says Pickens.

To help decrease swings in prices, he tends to buy futures that expire as many as four or five years out, which tend to fluctuate less wildly in price from day to day.

Although Pickens and his investment committee mostly agree on which investment moves to make, they don't always agree on when to make them. "I generally want to do something faster than they do," he says. Impatience has characterized him for his entire career. In 1997, convinced that natural gas could be turned into a serious transportation fuel, he paid $1.3 million for a company, now called Clean Energy, which had two natural gas fuel stations at the international airports in Phoenix and Los Angeles. Today, it has 170 stations, and Pickens sold the company to the public in May 2007, with a market capitalization of $750 million. It was a win, although he had expected something big would happen within three years of the purchase. "Most of my ideas work," says Pickens, "but the timing gets screwed up every once in a while."

Pickens has tried all different ways to lessen his tendency to jump into things too early. Sometimes, he just walks away for a day before making a decision. Although he has not conquered the urge altogether, he's making progress. "I'm not getting worse," he laughs. And his eagerness does have an advantage. He is rarely late on a wager. "I don't let things go by. Usually, we are in on most of the plays."

Although he monitors bets closely, he isn't one for Monday morning quarterbacking of individual wagers as long as the portfolio is making a profit overall. For the commodities fund from 2004 to 2006, those numbers were good: $418 million in profits in 2006, $1.26 million in 2005, and $432 million in 2004, all on beginning assets of $275 million. The fund struggled in the first half of 2007, losing $140 million of its original $420 million in January, before reducing the loss to $89 million by midyear.

When trading commodities, Pickens shies away from having an exit price in mind. He remembers buying natural gas when it was trading at $3, which had been a "gut up and go" decision that wasn't easy to make. When it rose to $4, it was clear he should buy more. Ironically, the second decision to buy was much easier, even though the price was higher. "That's because I knew a lot more about the market at $4 than I knew at $3," he says.

The secret to Pickens's success in his funds may well be his team approach, a management method he's fostered since his Mesa days when he worked with the twenty- and thirty-year-olds referred to as "Boone's boys." An athlete in competitive sports in high school, Pickens thinks of investing as a sport—albeit a serious one—and his investment committee as his team. "We look at the year ahead as if we were a football team with twelve games. This year we lost in January, came back in February. Looks like we are up in March, so the first quarter is 2 and 1," says Pickens. "Everything is like a game and a team. We don't have titles; we play positions."

Pickens is definitely calling the plays, and his game plan is conviction, backed by continual research and analysis. He remembers one hellish day in 2003, when the fund lost $60 million on a natural gas trade. He came into the conference room that afternoon and looked around the table. "Guys, your faces are so long, it would take two barbers to shave you," he told them, and moved right into the key questions: Have the fundamentals changed? The response was immediate; everyone got into the discussion. None of them believed that anything was different. "Would you guys be interested in doubling our position?" he asked. They were, they did, and they were right.

Pickens is quite aware that it can be painful to stick to a trade when it's losing money, even when you're confident that it will be a winner tomorrow or the next day. "Sometimes, it gets so bad you hate it. It's like a dog chewing on a rancid bone. It doesn't really like it, its lips go back, but it stays in there and chews on it," he says, curling his lips to mimic the disgust.

He thinks of his team as made up of juniors and seniors—namely, his advisers from Mesa—and sophomores and freshman—his two traders Michael Ross and David Meaney and his equity analysts Alex Szewczyk and Brian Bradshaw. The younger four range in age from thirty-one to thirty-three. "Our team is very close," says Pickens. "I don't think anyone ever feels that he doesn't have support. We've worked together a long time. We've had no change in personnel. It's like a good basketball team. You don't have to actually see them to pass them the ball. You know where they will be on the court."

Much of the closeness results from how often they communicate. They talk frequently, meeting at least once a day, sometimes more. The stock guys understand everything about the commodities trades, and vice versa. Pickens says he never understood why the exploration and production teams at Phillips always attended separate meetings; when he ran Mesa, the gatherings were all-inclusive. "'We're in there together, and this is the goal line,' I'd say. I got better results with that. Here, it's the same way. We have a great amount of respect for each other, and that's evident at meetings."

Generally attended by ten to twelve people, the meetings have no agenda and the discussion can range from oil wells in Saudi Arabia to politics to baseball, and from rumors in the oil and gas markets to weather conditions and how they will affect natural gas prices. Team members discuss current positions as well as new trading ideas and performance, and together they decide whether to buy or sell. They want every issue of importance put on the table, and they encourage—and expect—everyone to contribute to the debate. Generally, the team comes to a consensus. Pickens finds his role is to push the team to take on more risk when the situation warrants it. Invariably, he'll be the one to ask, "Does everyone want to take bigger positions?"

The first meeting can be as early as breakfast. Pickens works out every day at 6:30 a.m., and by 7:00, he and the team will decide whether they will eat together, either at the Hilton or at the office in North Dallas. In either case, they'll be at their desks by 8:30. There's sometimes a lunch meeting, which might start at 11:30. That gathering takes place in a large conference room dominated by a huge oval table and twelve leather chairs. Supersized Bloomberg screens dominate the far wall. These discussions can last an hour or two if the markets are hectic. Usually, there's a meeting after the market close, starting at 4:00 or 4:30 and sometimes going until 6:00 p.m. When the occasion requires it, Pickens will arrange for one of his consultants—he uses about ten experts in areas including economics, weather, and foreign policy—to join the meeting in person or participate by telephone.

The team also gathers for a two-hour dinner once a month in Dallas. A topic may be assigned—perhaps someone has been to a conference or industry convention and will talk about that for ten or twenty minutes. "The wives don't complain," says Pickens. "I'm not sending husbands home late. It's all strictly business."

Pickens's vast personal wealth seems to be surpassed only by his imagination and the ideas he comes up with for increasing it. He's currently trying to sell water to Dallas. His ranch, where he first bought land in 1971 and which now takes up 50,000 acres, sits on a part of the Ogallala Aquifer, which extends from Texas to South Dakota, making it the largest aquifer in North America. Because of the land's rolling hills, the water can't be used for irrigating the ranch and surrounding properties, so Pickens wants to sell half the water and draw the aquifer down 50 percent.

He's also interested in wind power, and he's looking into using turbines to produce 4,000 megawatts of energy across 200,000 acres in the Texas panhandle. And after swearing off oil and gas exploration and production, he's been drawn back to that game as well. "After you've had so much experience, you don't have to look at a deal long to know whether or not it's a good one," says Pickens, explaining his reasons for getting pulled into these transactions again. Sometimes, his personal projects catch the attention of the other members of his staff, and they invest with him.

A longtime backer of Republican politicians, Pickens has decked the foyer of his office in Dallas with no less than twenty photos, many of them autographed, of himself with such GOP luminaries as former President Ronald Reagan and Nancy Reagan, former President George Bush, and President George W. Bush. In the 2008 presidential elections, he's backing former New York City Mayor Rudolph Giuliani.

Closer to home, Pickens is betting on his own team, which he says is the best he's ever built. "I don't manage people; I lead people," he says. "I don't sit at the head of the table; I prefer another chair." In the Dallas conference room, his is the chair to the left of the head, the one with the great view of the screens.

"This team will have so much experience and have such good results. When I'm gone, these are going to be the best guys on the street," says Pickens.

Gone doesn't seem to be coming any time soon.

AFTER THE CRISIS

A Focus on the Future

In 2008, Pickens was forecasting that oil would climb to $150 a barrel. As of early July, with crude hovering around $145, he seemed to be right on the money—until the price turned on a dime and went into a free fall as the global economy weakened. BP Capital, which managed about $4 billion at the start of the year, erased about $1 billion of that amount in a matter of weeks. Pickens's commodities fund, which buys and sells oil and natural gas futures and uses borrowed money to make those wagers, dropped

84 percent by the end of August and plummeted 98 percent by the end of the year.

The firm's larger fund—which trades mostly energy stocks but also has about 10 percent in oil and natural gas—plummeted 30 percent in the same period and ended the year down 62 percent. Given the poor performance, Pickens decided to go to cash and told investors they could pull their money out of the funds if they wanted. Many clients took him up on his offer, to the tune of 65 percent of the assets in the energy stock fund. No investors withdrew from the commodities fund, which had begun the year with about $600 million. "The move to allow investors to redeem was a voluntary one because we recognized the economic hardship our investors were experiencing in this market," said BP spokesman Jay Rosser at the time of the announcement.

In 2009, Pickens slowly began to put the remaining money back to work, and he had not veered from his view that oil prices would rise over the long term because producers would raise prices and the overall supply of the commodity was falling.

He has forecasted that oil prices, which by late May were trading around $60, would climb to $75 a barrel before the end of 2009. Within three years, he expects that oil will match 2008's record $147 a barrel as producers fail to increase output. "I can tell you that OPEC has got to have more money for their oil, and they are going to cut supply and by the end of the year, you'll be back up to $75," he said. He estimated in July 2009 that by 2013 we're going to see a decline in production, and in 10 years, oil will be at $300 a barrel.

Pickens has also been spending time and $60 million developing a national energy plan. He's urging automakers to make cars that run on natural gas, "which we have coming out of our ears." Without such a switch, he says, the United States will be spending $2 trillion a year importing oil.

He's also asking the U.S. government to improve the power grid to accommodate more wind and solar power, so that the nation, which gets almost 70 percent of its oil from outside the United States, can cut its dependence on foreign producers.

His hedge funds are back on track. Through June of 2009, his oil-and-gas fund gained 79 percent, and the equities fund climbed 14 percent.

Chapter 9

Brian Bradshaw, David Meaney, Michael Ross, and Alex Szewczyk

A Place at the Table

CONFIDENCE AND CONVICTION. Those are the most important lessons the four thirty-somethings who work for Boone Pickens's $4 billion BP Capital have learned from the seventy-nine-year-old oil tycoon turned takeover artist turned hedge fund billionaire. "He doesn't get rattled by the day-to-day price movements," says David Meaney, thirty-one, who joined the Dallas-based hedge fund in 2005 and is one of the firm's two traders. Pickens spends his time assessing and reassessing the situation to ensure he's right, says Meaney, but "he has an uncanny ability to see through the noise."

Turning down the volume means staying focused, and equities analyst Alex Szewczyk, thirty-three, says working with Pickens has shown him that keeping your eye on the ball is essential. "Don't be distracted by every tick of every stock price or commodity price," he says. "Have a fundamental view."

Szewczyk's focus has been clear from the start. When he graduated from the Southern Methodist University Edwin L. Cox School of Business in 2001, he didn't want to go to a dot-com like all his other classmates. He wanted to be an analyst at a private equity firm or a hedge fund. Then he heard that Pickens was starting a stock fund, and he knew that's where he wanted to be. He wanted "to work for a legend who had been doing this for a long time." It took Szewczyk three months just to set up an interview, he says. "Every time I'd finally get one, he'd cancel it on me." But Szewczyk's perseverance got him the job.

The ability to hang in there is prized at the firm. Michael Ross, thirty-one, who joined Pickens's shop as a commodities trader in 2001, says Pickens can squeeze a lot of profit out of the trade when it's going his way. "When he knows he has the market in his hand, what he does is amazing. He's good at catching that trend and riding it. I wish I had that instinct," says Ross, who is a fast-talking New Yorker in a team dominated by Southerners. "If he thinks the market is going higher, or lower, and every day he gets more evidence of that, he'll put his money up to play." Ross says he's acquired his share of sangfroid from his boss.

Ross's first encounter with Pickens was in the office of Ross's father, who was founder and chief executive of an energy consulting business in New York called PIRA Energy Group. Ross had just quit a job at Marcstone Capital Management in New York, where he was trading foreign currency and European equities, and it was his first day working for his dad. Pickens asked him if he'd be the head trader for an equity fund, and Ross said yes, so Pickens invited him down to Dallas to meet the other members of the staff.

Over the next few months, they talked a number of times, and finally the discussion turned to money. Ross told him the salary he wanted. "Pickens said, 'I can't give you that,'" says Ross. "I said, 'Fine, I'll trade.' Boone loves that story. I took the lower salary and moved to Dallas."

For every member of the BP Capital team, getting on it took determination. That's especially the case with Meaney. He had been trading since his senior year in college. Before joining BP Capital, he had worked for two securities firms as a trader for about seven years. He wanted to make the move to the buy side, and he wanted to work for an energy hedge fund, and he wanted that hedge fund to be Pickens's. "That was my goal," he says. So he sent a résumé over and heard back from Ross a couple of weeks later. Ross told him that they had been looking for someone for a while, but that there was no rush. They would wait until they found the right fit.

"I was going to make sure I was the right fit," says Meaney. That was during the late spring or early summer of 2005, and the oil market was jumping. Meaney called or messaged Ross every couple of days "so he couldn't put me on the back burner," says Meaney. "I was very persistent." Meaney's experience to date hadn't been in the oil or natural gas markets, but that didn't seem to be an obstacle. "Ross told me Boone liked people with clean slates," he says. And he told Ross he was a fast learner. Meaney came into the office several times to talk to Ross and to meet the other members of the team.

Only for the last interview, which lasted half an hour, did he sit down with Pickens. "I told him about myself. He told me the way things work at BP Capital. It was a discussion. It didn't feel like an interview. He was trying to get a sense of who I was, and obviously I got a sense of him," says Meaney. A few days later, he was offered the job. "It was somewhat of a pay cut, but this was where I wanted to be, and I knew there would be nothing better than to learn from the guys in this office."

And that's what he's done. "Every day is a learning process," says Meaney. "The best thing about working here is observing and listening, because Pickens has such a wealth of experience and he looks at things differently. Certain people just have a different view of things, and that's what makes them successful."

In the case of Pickens, that view must surely have come from having seen so much over the years. Brian Bradshaw, thirty-one, equities analyst for the BP Capital Equity Fund, puts it this way: "He is stone-faced when it comes to market moves and decisions. He really has ice in his veins." If they make millions one day, Pickens says, "Good day." And if they lose millions the next, he says, "Bad day." They'll never hear "What the hell just happened? What are we going to do?" Bradshaw believes the ability to stay cool distinguishes people who are good at managing money. "If you let the market shake your confidence, if you let it dictate what is a good idea and what is a bad idea, then you end up making mistakes," he says. "If you trade off what the market is doing, you will always be behind."

It's obvious from spending even a brief time with this team that Pickens has created a close-knit group whose members respect one another. Attire at the office is casual, polo shirts rather than suits; the mood is almost familial. The team's cohesiveness may well result from Pickens's own behavior. He trusts these guys. "One of the things that's remarkable about working here is the autonomy that he gives you and the freedom he gives you," says Bradshaw, who started at BP Capital in 2003. "He gives relatively young guys a lot of room to make decisions and try to make money."

Pickens's trust is evident in the very fact that all the buy and sell decisions are put on the table at the daily investment committee meetings, and generally the group comes to a consensus about what action to take. "He lends a lot of weight to all our opinions," says Meaney. Bradshaw tells the story of an oil stock they owned in 2005 for a company called Spinnaker Exploration Company. They'd owned the shares for some time, and Pickens thought it was time to sell. Szewczyk, Ross, and Bradshaw all disagreed. Fortunately, Pickens went along with the group. Over the next two weeks the stock jumped $10 and then, soon after that, Norsk Hydro, Norway's second-largest oil company, agreed to buy Spinnaker for $65.50 a share, a 34 percent premium over its previous close.

It works the other way as well. In early 2007, the funds were long natural gas, and after several discussions the team decided that prices weren't going to run much higher. The winter was nearly over, and the cold weather was about to break. Everyone agreed it was getting close to the time to exit; the only question that remained was when. Bradshaw suggested selling half the position right away. The others agreed, and they phoned Pickens, who was at his ranch that day. "I wouldn't be thinking that. Tell me why," said Pickens. The team laid out the argument. "I hear you, but give it a couple more days. I think there's room left in it," he told them. They followed his advice, and when natural gas went up $0.80 the next day, they sold. "He has great instincts" honed by an enormous amount of experience, says Bradshaw. After all, Pickens has been trading natural gas since there was a contract for it on the New York Mercantile Exchange.

Every member of the twelve-person investment team is conversant with the fundamentals of the oil and gas industries and with the macroeconomic, political, and weather trends that influence them. Szewczyk and Bradshaw focus on analyzing companies for the $2.3 billion equity hedge funds. They don't move in and out of large positions without a discussion with the rest of the team. Ninety percent of the money in the firm's three identical stock funds is invested in about forty equities. These funds include stocks Szewczyk and Bradshaw expect to climb and those they expect to tumble. Ten percent of the assets are in commodities that mirror the positions in Pickens's commodities fund. As is the case with the commodities portfolio, the trades are based on fundamental analysis. Szewczyk and Bradshaw don't increase or decrease their positions unless the big picture changes, and they don't use options to hedge.

The fund trades stocks in a broad range of companies within the energy sector, including those that deal with exploration and production, petrochemicals, coal, tankers, alternative energy, refining, energy-intensive manufacturing, power and utilities, and oil-field services. The stock picks flow from the group's analysis of the direction of oil and natural gas prices, both near term and over the next few years. After they've established an idea of where prices are moving, they put on a position that represents that view. "If we think crude oil will trade up for the next six months, the next question is how that will affect equity markets," says Bradshaw. If the price of oil is rising, that could be good news for ExxonMobil Corporation stock. Or maybe it's just a short-term spike, and Exxon won't be able to capitalize on it, but smaller producers who sell oil on the spot market every day will benefit. At the same time, the team might decide to short airlines because fuel costs are rising and that hurts their profits.

Managing a sector fund is different from running a large portfolio of diversified stocks. In the midst of a roaring bull market for oil and gas, Pickens's crew probably won't end up with a lot of shorts. "If oil is going from $35 to $70, you can't really be short and expect to make money," says Bradshaw.

The funds' investment horizons are generally six to twelve months, and they don't have a target return. "We're more focused on taking what the market gives us," says Bradshaw. Because Szewczyk and Bradshaw trade only in one sector, they don't have the luxury of, say, limiting their investment choices to stocks they expect to rise by a certain percent. In 2005, for example, when oil climbed from $42 to nearly $70 a barrel, the funds' stock and commodities positions rocketed, returning 88 percent. The following year it was a lot harder to make money. The price of natural gas fell from $14 per British thermal units (Btu) to $4 per Btu, and oil started and ended the year in the $60 range, although it went as high as $78 a barrel midyear. There were some energy stocks that were up 20 percent and some that fell, and overall the fund returned 19.6 percent. Szewczyk and Bradshaw made about 5 percent on stocks they shorted—that is, the stocks were borrowed and then sold in the hopes of buying them back at a cheaper price. There weren't many 88 percent gains to be found.

Szewczyk and Bradshaw generally have some idea of how much a particular stock might rise, or fall, and when the stock gets close to the target price, the investment committee will discuss whether to stay in or move on. If they decide to stay, they adjust the target upward. That approach differs somewhat from the approach taken with the commodities fund, for which Pickens eschews price targets because circumstances are always changing.

More hedge funds are in business now than ever before, but that doesn't make the odds of getting a job at one of them terribly good. The Pickens team has some thoughts on how to reduce them.

Managing expectations may be key. "Offer a lot and don't ask for a lot," says Szewczyk. He says he sold Pickens on hiring him because he was prepared to take on any task. The message Szewczyk sent was this: "I'll do anything. I'll work as many hours as you need. I'll do it for free."

Humility helps. You won't be running the fund the first day. "You have to be open-minded about what your initial responsibilities are," says Bradshaw. "The funds out there right now don't need you. That may sound harsh, but it's true. You have to be willing to do whatever it takes to get in the door and prove yourself. Good things will happen, but you have to be willing to be humble on day one."

The Boone Boys landed their jobs at Pickens's shop in part by being persistent and taking the longer-term view that even if it wasn't the highest-paying job they could get today, it would more than pay off in the future. The long view, they've learned, applies to investing as well. "I used to run around here like a monkey," says Ross with a laugh. "They'd say, 'Calm down, kid.' They used to call me Junior." Ross says Pickens has also taught him a lot about life, but asked for details, he smiles and says, "That's personal."

AFTER THE CRISIS
_____

Expecting the Unexpected

For Bradshaw and his colleagues at BP Capital, the biggest lesson they learned in 2008 was to move on. "One thing Mr. Pickens is good at is focusing on the now and going forward, and that's what we've done," he says. "We left last year behind us."

The energy stock and commodities fund Bradshaw helps manage with Szewczyk had about $450 million as of May 2009, an asset level lower than any the fund had seen in four or five years. It had started 2008 with about $2 billion, but that was before the fund lost 30 percent through August and the managers made the decision to go to cash. By the end of the year, the fund lost 62 percent and investors representing 65 percent of the rest asked for their money back. "We were definitely taken by surprise by the magnitude and speed that energy commodities sold off" in 2008, says Bradshaw. "The supply side for oil still poised some problems, but that got fixed temporarily because of demand," he says.

Oil fell from a high of $145 a barrel in July 2008 to $34 by December, as the global economy slowed. Pickens and his crew had been forecasting that oil would rise to $150 a barrel because the supply is dwindling. They revised that forecast, expecting oil would rise to $75 by the end of 2009, and by June it had nearly reached that level before falling to about $60 a barrel in mid-July.

Bradshaw says 2009 is going much better. Boone's Boys—Pickens's team of analysts and traders—continue to invest the way they always have at BP Capital, by analyzing market and company fundamentals to decide what to buy and sell. That has led them to own many of the same stocks in April 2009 they held in mid-2008, but in quantities that are much smaller given their reduced assets.

As of June 2008, for example, the fund's largest holding, according to a regulatory filing, was a $184 million stake in Occidental Petroleum Corp. Its second-biggest position was $170 million worth of shares of Transocean Ltd. As of the first quarter of 2009, Transocean, the world's largest offshore driller, was the fund's largest stock position, yet it held only $26 million worth of shares. Occidental, the fourth-largest U.S. oil company, was an $11 million stake.

The fund returned about 14 percent through June of 2009, still a long way from its so-called high-water mark, its peak net asset value before the losses began. The firm won't collect its 20 percent performance fee until it has recouped those losses for investors, which is why BP Capital was making a concerted effort in 2009 to raise money from new investors, who would be paying all the fees.

"The one thing that's unique about Mr. Pickens is that he's been in the energy business for years and it's a highly cyclical business," says Bradshaw. "If you change the way you look at the world when markets go up and down, you get out of step. He tries to be consistent."

Chapter 10

Josh Friedman and Mitch Julis
Doyens of Debt

JOSH FRIEDMAN AND MITCH JULIS have been friends since their days at Harvard University, where they both pursued dual graduate degrees in law and business. Almost thirty years have passed since their meeting in Aldrich Hall, where the two attended first-year business school classes, and almost two decades have gone by since they began running the now $17 billion Canyon Partners in Los Angeles. For most of the 1980s, Friedman, fifty-one, and Julis, fifty-two, worked for junk-bond king Michael Milken at Drexel Burnham Lambert in Los Angeles. Those years honed their understanding of debt markets, and that in-depth knowledge, combined with seventeen years of investing experience since, they say, gives them their edge in multistrategy investing, an all-inclusive approach to money management that allows Canyon to make money through a wide range of investment styles—everything from stocks to convertible bonds to bank, high-yield, and distressed debt. "Multistrats," as these funds are called, attract institutional investors because the managers have the flexibility to move into whichever strategies are making money and out of any that aren't. In mid-2007, these funds accounted for 15 percent of the $1.7 trillion in hedge funds, and they pulled in more money from clients in 2006 and 2007 than any other style, except for long-short equity funds.

"Our firm is built on a culture of extremely careful and thorough credit and valuation analysis, and we have a pervasive presence in every debt-oriented market there is," says Friedman. While Canyon invests several billion dollars in equities, most of its multistrat competitors focus far more on stocks—some well over 50 percent of their assets. Friedman and Julis concentrate more on bonds and bank debt.

Canyon's conference room overlooks Wilshire Boulevard in Beverly Hills, and as I talked with Julis and Friedman there, it became clear in only a few minutes that they have tremendous respect for each other and for their complementary skills. Friedman, with short curly hair, a compact build, and glasses, was running off on a business trip and wore a dark suit befitting his role as the firm's public face. Julis, who looks like a clean-shaven, younger version of comic actor Jerry Stiller, was wearing a tan cardigan and beige slacks that gave him an avuncular air. His passion is research, and he keeps his focus there. When he talks about investing, his tone is more characteristic of an academic than a Wall Street trader.

Since the end of 1998, when Julis and Friedman ceased trading emerging-market debt, they've trounced both the debt and equity indexes, producing an average gain of almost 13.5 percent a year, compared to a 3.6 percent annualized return for the benchmark stock index and about 10 percent for multistrat funds, on average. They produced returns averaging about 12 percent a year since their flagship Canyon Value Realization Fund started on November 1, 1993. That compares to a 10.6 percent for the Standard & Poor's 500 Index.

To explain their approach, the managers' 2006 year-end letter to clients used the language of baseball—Julis spent his early childhood in the Bronx and is a Yankees fan; Friedman grew up fifteen miles outside of Boston and roots for the Red Sox. Quoting George Will's *Men at Work*, they reminded investors that baseball "involves constant attention to the law of cumulation, which is: A lot of little things add up, through 162 games, 1,458 innings, to big differences. A 162-game season is, like life, an exercise in cumulation." That keep-plugging working style captures Friedman and Julis's philosophy on managing money. It's about getting on base often and hitting singles or doubles, rather than setting out to hit a home run every time and risking a lot more strikeouts. "We tend to run a relatively low-volatility, well-diversified book, probably too diversified, in my opinion, but that's who we are," says Friedman. At the end of 2006, about two-thirds of their investments were in an array of debt instruments. They rarely use borrowed money to boost returns.

Their focus on research and company analysis is supported by their years of experience in the markets, in which they have built an encyclopedic knowledge of companies and industries and strong relationships with Wall Street, private equity, and buyout firms. The network they've developed over the years allows them to participate in the sort of special situation loans that many other hedge funds don't get to see. In mid-2007, such transactions represented less than 10 percent of Canyon's assets. Yet the characteristics of these deals—providing companies with creative solutions to often complex financial problems and giving private equity firms quick access to cash to complete buyouts or restructure the debt of their portfolio companies—illustrate how Canyon sometimes spots ways to make money that other funds miss. Many of these deals come to Canyon through investment banks, which often take a piece of them as well. "In the current crowded arena, we seek out these situations and as a result we end up being the recipients of a lot of those investment opportunities that are shared with a somewhat more select group of partners," says Friedman.

In 2006, for example, Canyon worked with Goldman Sachs to provide a loan to private equity firms Carlyle Group and Providence Equity Partners for their acquisition of Swedish cable television operator Com Hem. Because Canyon knows the industry well, it could do the analysis quickly and decided it was a good deal to pursue. "These transactions require a certain size, certain relationships, a certain amount of embedded knowledge, and a certain mentality about being a good partner," says Friedman.

Valuable as their relationships may be, Friedman and Julis's returns result far more from what they know than who they know. Big believers in in-depth research, they look for situations in which a company's stock or bonds are selling cheaply but are poised to move higher because of some announced event. Maybe the company is going to get acquired. Perhaps it's restructuring its debt. Since they started Canyon they've been paying particularly close attention to the gaming, media, telecom, energy and utilities, and financial services industries, and they continually recycle their knowledge and experience with companies and industries. "You get to know a company extraordinarily well because you've traded its securities for many, many years and you've become acquainted with the management teams as well as the management teams of the competitors and the customers and the buyers and the suppliers," says Friedman. "I guess there are certain benefits of age in the investment business."

To help develop a full picture of a company or its industry, Canyon occasionally hires attorneys or consultants or may even chat with private equity or leveraged buyout executives, who generally have a less biased view than corporate honchos. Canyon analysts and portfolio managers concentrate on a few key questions in their research: Does the company have staying power? How much cash does it generate? Does it have a competitive advantage? Is management creating—or destroying—value? What is the company's cost of capital? What is its growth rate? How much is it plowing back into the business and what return is it getting on invested capital?

Once those questions are answered, Canyon portfolio managers and analysts figure out the best way to put on the position, be it through stocks, bonds, bank debt, or some combination. In late 2006, for example, when private equity firms Apollo Management and TPG announced they would buy Harrah's Entertainment, the world's biggest casino operator, for $17.1 billion, most merger arbitrage investors, who deal in the shares of companies going through buyouts and mergers, bought the stock. Canyon sold the stock instead and bought the company's convertible bonds. These bonds also benefited from the rising stock price, although they had been hurt somewhat because the option to convert them into stock had lost value, given the looming takeover for cash. If the transaction had fallen through, the price of the bonds would have slid, but unlike the equity, the failure of the cash takeover would have caused the option to rise in value again. That, combined with the income from the interest payments, would have provided downside protection.

Likewise, Canyon bought the bonds of power companies operating in California that were hit by financial troubles beginning in 2000, when wholesale prices spiked and the biggest utilities, including PG&E Corporation and Edison International, weren't allowed to pass on the higher costs to consumers. PG&E's Pacific Gas and Electric Company utility entered bankruptcy after accumulating more than $11 billion in debt. Edison skirted bankruptcy protection by borrowing heavily. "The balance sheets were complicated," says Friedman. So were the regulatory issues and the bankruptcy issues. "Situations like these are very research intensive as opposed to trading intensive, and there was a high payoff to doing really good homework." Canyon took a long-term view of the companies and the industry and saw value. "With expensive and difficult-to-replicate resources and appropriate staying power, the utilities had a chance to provide significant value to their stakeholders," says Friedman.

As the companies worked their way back to financial health, Canyon rode the bonds higher and eventually sold its positions, switching into the companies' shares, whose prices were still in the doldrums because traditional buyers, such as mutual funds, weren't yet snapping up the equity. Canyon calculated that the stocks would eventually attract buyers as the companies got their financial houses in order by selling subsidiaries, closing down units, processing legal claims, and restoring peace with the regulators.

As a value investor, Canyon screens for what it calls "stressed" companies like Edison. Even though such companies don't end up in Chapter 11, mutual funds and other long-only managers tend to bail out at any early signs of difficulties. In the first quarter of 2007, two of Canyon's biggest equity holdings were Williams Companies and El Paso Corporation, both gas pipeline companies with a lot of debt. Williams, the biggest U.S. natural gas pipeline operator, had borrowed money early in the 2000s to expand into fiber optics, a move that caused rating agencies to cut its debt ratings to junk status in 2002. El Paso had borrowed heavily to enter the energy trading business. "These companies were good places to look for value because they fell from mainstream attention after being so close to getting into trouble," says Julis. After extensive research, Canyon bought the debt of both companies and after that investment proved profitable, it bought the companies' stocks, whose prices, again, didn't yet reflect the improving corporate prospects. Finding good value, say Friedman and Julis, is about looking across a wide range of securities.

Another of Canyon's research-intensive investments was Adelphia Communications Corporation, in which it accumulated, at a discount, mechanics' liens from the companies that had laid the cable for Adelphia. The cable company filed for bankruptcy in 2002, and two years later its founder, John Rigas, and his son Timothy Rigas were convicted of conspiracy, securities fraud, and bank fraud. "The work we did in Adelphia was painstaking," says Julis. "It represented tremendous fundamental analysis and also a sensitivity to market dynamics: Who was doing what to whom at different stages of that long, protracted bankruptcy process?"

The research on Adelphia also added to Canyon's knowledge of Time Warner, which eventually bought some of Adelphia's cable assets. "We were able to use the insights into Time Warner and the insights into Adelphia to make investments on those situations and others in the cable space. As an investor, you want to be able to recycle the knowledge you gain," says Julis.

Canyon's success over the years has been consistent. Its only losing year was 1998, when the flagship fund lost approximately 15.75 percent. The trouble came in August, when the fund tumbled after Russia devalued its currency and defaulted on its debt. Canyon had been investing in emerging-market debt and making money for several years before 1998. Julis and Friedman had figured that they could analyze country debt using the same approach they used in analyzing corporate debt. After all, markets tended to be relatively liquid and in the early 1990s, the governments of emerging countries were becoming more fiscally responsible, and the covenants of the debt more standardized.

After the loss, the decision about what to do was simple: "We saw clearly that we really didn't have a competitive advantage in that area," says Friedman. He and Julis sold all the emerging-market debt in the portfolio, even though they knew they were dumping it at the bottom of the market. Notwithstanding the loss that year, they decided to pay hefty bonuses to the research staff, to ensure that employees wouldn't jump ship. "It wasn't their fault, and they had done a good job," says Friedman.

Not everyone felt Canyon had done a good job, Julis remembers with a smile. His mother, whose father had come from Bialystok, a city over which Poland and Russia played tug-of-war, had little sympathy for her son's stumble. "How could you give money to those people?" she asked him. "Don't you remember what they did to your grandfather?"

In crisis situations like the one in August 1998, almost every market moves in tandem, a lesson that Long-Term Capital Management learned in spades when it ended up losing more than 92 percent of its money after Russia's default. Friedman and Julis noted the connections and learned from them: Stick with areas in which you have a competitive advantage, and be cognizant that in a market meltdown there can be correlations among various positions in the portfolio that no one ever expects. Those lessons have led the two to hedge their portfolio when they suspect the markets might be poised to fall.

When I talked to Julis and Friedman in 2007, credit spreads—the differences in yields between the safest and riskiest bonds—were very small by historic standards, and the equity markets were close to the highs of 2000. They were prepared for a possible correction that could hit both bonds and stocks. They had bought puts on the S&P 500 and Russell 2000 indexes, for example, which would gain in value if the stock market plummeted. They purchased credit-default swaps on high-yield and investment-grade bond indexes and on the subprime mortgage index, as well as protection on pieces of mortgage obligations involving subprime loans made to home buyers with poor credit ratings. Credit-default swaps are used to speculate on a company's ability to repay debts, and they rise in value as the company's prospects worsen. All would make money if the indexes took a dive and credit spreads widened. They also invested in a number of credit-default swaps on the investment-grade debt of companies including First Data and Dow Chemical. The First Data position made money in April 2007, after buyout firm KKR said it would buy the world's largest processor of credit card payments, and the credit-default swaps rose in value because the company would be saddled with more debt. In 2007, Friedman and Julis were also holding bonds with an average duration of about three years. When credit spreads were wide, as in 2003, they held longer maturity bonds and the hedges were smaller. Their portfolio positioning and hedges worked. When stocks tumbled and credit spreads widened in the summer of 2007, the flagship fund was down less than 2 percent between July 1 and August 24. It was well positioned to take advantage of the opportunities presented by the market, including buying high-quality bank debt at a discount and the shares of merging companies for which Canyon believed the market had overestimated the risk of the transaction failing to close.

• • •

The difficulties of 1998 also led Friedman and Julis to take steps to protect the company itself in the event of a major financial catastrophe. They began building a complementary business offering collateralized debt obligations (CDOs) and collateralized loan obligations (CLOs), in which they package bonds and loans together, creating new securities. "We decided that it was crucial to build staying power in the organization as well as the portfolio, so we created additional products that had reasons to exist on their own and would provide stability to the firm," says Julis. Canyon now manages about $2.5 billion in CDOs and CLOs, and performance has been in the top 5 percent. The firm oversees another $1.5 billion in real estate investments.

The new business has helped the hedge fund in ways Julis and Friedman had hoped. Each CDO or CLO portfolio contains about one hundred positions, requiring the analysts to gather a lot of information about a lot more companies. Creating these instruments also makes Canyon a more valuable customer for investment banks, from whom it buys the loans and bonds. And interaction with these banks leads to Canyon's hedge fund getting looped into more deals.

Julis and Friedman prize staying power, and it's reflected in the way they manage money and in the way they run their hedge fund firm. Unlike many firms, which lock up their investors for two or three years, Canyon lets its clients withdraw their money every quarter from its offshore fund and once a year from its large fund for domestic investors. They want to be able to give their clients their money back when they ask for it. "We watch that match between assets and liabilities very carefully," by balancing longer-term and shorter-term positions in the portfolio, says Friedman. To support that balance, the fund generally doesn't use leverage and about one-third of its assets is in liquid common stocks and more than a quarter is in bank debt, which is also very easily traded.

Concern for the future of the firm also influences the job candidates Julis and Friedman hire. They look for smart, hardworking individuals who can synthesize information well. "I look at people's raw intellectual talent, but I probably look just as hard at their work ethic and their emotional makeup," says Friedman. "You can make a lot more money by making more phone calls than everybody else than you can by just being brilliant." Once the phone calls are made, however, the analysts must be able to boil down the information to the essential ingredients and explain what they see that the rest of the market doesn't. "Warren Buffett is famous for his extraordinary investment acumen as well as his ability to communicate his ideas in a clear, direct, and honest way. That's something we should all aspire to," says Friedman.

Friedman and Julis also look for candidates with emotional intelligence—how well an analyst or portfolio manager interacts with investors at other firms, Wall Street brokers, and corporate management teams, and how skilled they are at reading the players sitting across the table. "At the end of the day, you're playing in a probability game in which judgments about people matter," Friedman says.

The investment professionals at Canyon have these skills to varying degrees, and everyone plays to his strengths. "Some people are on the phone all day long, others are reading all day long and then speaking to consultants and industry players," Friedman says.

Regardless of how they ultimately spend most of their time, being able to see the big picture is what makes for superior performance. "Some of the best people that we've ever hired were not necessarily people who made a beeline for Wall Street," says Friedman. "I think people who go straight to college where they major in business and then rush out to the trading world often lack the needed judgment and maturity and intellectual curiosity. Sometimes people who have studied more broadly end up being terrific investors with a lot more perspective and ideally a value system that reinforces that."

Friedman and Julis have put a good deal of time into building their business. Julis likes to say that at Canyon they both manage money and manage the business of managing money. Toward that end, they have built a large back office, with more than half the firm's professionals devoted to operations and a highly sophisticated set of systems and risk controls.

Canyon has four portfolio managers in addition to Julis and Friedman. Three are responsible for industry coverage, including media, telecom, retail, health care, airlines, energy and utilities, and financial institutions. One concentrates on convertible bonds. More than thirty analysts work for the senior members of the staff. Julis and Friedman are involved in the discussions about all the potential positions once the portfolio manager and his team have fully vetted the ideas.

Friedman tends to have more relationships with leveraged buyout, private equity, and Wall Street firms. He focuses more on any private deals Canyon gets involved in and spends time on business and client issues. Julis's relationships tend to be with the top mutual fund managers, and he pays more attention to what's going on in academia, to apply the latest theories on investing and portfolio management. Julis sets up training in areas like forensic accounting for the firm's investment professionals, and he's the engine behind the research process. "Mitch asks endless questions of our analysts to force them to use certain types of rigorous modeling techniques and somewhat intellectual approaches to valuation that force a certain rigor and thoroughness on the process," says Friedman. In terms of investments, Julis is more interested in traditional value investing—finding companies trading cheaply relative to cash flow and other financial yardsticks—and in complex financial restructurings.

Their educational backgrounds and work experience explain much about the roles that each man plays at Canyon today. Friedman went to Harvard as an undergraduate, where he studied physics, and then to Oxford on a Marshall Scholarship, before returning to Harvard for his advanced degrees. His father, whose own father died very young and who didn't get to return to college after World War II, had always promoted the Harvard-education hat trick for his son, saying his most successful cousin had followed that route. Although he advised his son to go to law school, he also counseled him not to practice law and never to work for unpleasant people, although he gave the advice in more colorful terms, Friedman says.

Julis went to Princeton University as an undergraduate before heading to Harvard, where he graduated in 1981. His first job was at the law firm Wachtell, Lipton, Rosen & Katz, where he worked as a creditors' rights attorney. He also took to writing articles, including one for *Los Angeles* magazine, in which he discussed how performers, including comedian Jerry Lewis, creatively used the bankruptcy code. In 1983, Julis received a job offer from Drexel to work in the firm's distressed-investing area. Graduating from Harvard a year after Julis, Friedman joined the mergers and acquisitions group at Goldman Sachs out of school and worked there until 1984, when Julis called him and told him about a job at Drexel serving as an interface between corporate finance and the high-yield-bond department.

At first, Friedman couldn't imagine leaving a top-tier investment bank like Goldman, but he came out to Los Angeles for a visit and discovered that Drexel was a hotbed of financial creativity. Michael Milken helped fuel the mergers and acquisitions boom of the 1980s with junk-bond financing, at least until the market crashed in 1989. "It's hard for me to imagine a better place to have learned the business," Friedman says.

"Mike had terrific relationships with smart entrepreneurs, and he added value by listening carefully and responding creatively," says Friedman. In doing transactions of their own, Julis and Friedman have also found the best and brightest make the most successful business partners. "We've always found that the best deals you can do are with people with whom you have a good relationship and who are also smart and capital-market savvy. If we can add value by being creative and inventive and solving the problem for them, we can create excellent investment returns on a risk-adjusted basis."

Julis agrees that Milken's talent was creating networks of smart people, something he still does today through his annual Milken Institute conferences. "The man continues to bring people together— Nobel Laureates, people from business, scientists, whomever—to learn about the world. He basically looks at finance as a window into how the world works and then figures out points of leverage where he can try to make a difference."

When Drexel folded, Julis and Friedman found themselves at loose ends. Not knowing exactly what direction they would take but certain that they wanted to work for themselves, they opened Canyon in 1990 with another Drexel executive, Chris Evensen, who has since left the firm. At first, they provided a number of different investment-banking and asset-management services, including running managed accounts of distressed debt for individuals and a bankruptcy and restructuring advisory business for clients that included News Corporation and Zale Corporation, the largest U.S. jewelry retailer at the time. Realizing soon enough that running a boutique advisory firm wasn't the most attractive option, they eventually decided on managing money.

And successful it's been, though Julis and Friedman laugh about what Friedman's wealth might have looked like had he stayed at Goldman Sachs through its initial public offering (IPO) in 1999, which made each partner an average of $63.6 million, with senior executives receiving more than three times that amount. The two tell the story of one of Friedman's friends from Goldman Sachs—and a Canyon investor—who likes to joke about Friedman's decampment to the West Coast: "Josh thought he could make a lot of money and we forgot to tell him about the IPO." Julis doesn't skip a beat: "Which created incredible guilt for me that I brought him out here," he says, tongue in cheek. He's serious, however, when he says that Canyon has survived because of their friendship. "There's a lot of overlap, but there are also significant differences that make the relationship work," he says. "The heart of the organization really lies in our relationship. We've tried to take the checks and balances, the complementarities, and have them resonate throughout the organization. We try to emphasize people working together and to respect differences." That tone, he says, fosters creativity and makes one less likely to be blindsided by unforeseen events.

Perhaps their respect for teamwork is why they have both invested their personal money with another duo: Jeff Schachter and Burton Weinstein (see Chapter 11), who run Cedarview Capital Management, a New York hedge fund started in 2004. "I think Burton is a great portfolio manager and analyst, and Jeff is a great strategic thinker and trader," says Julis. "They just started up, and they've shown good returns, and I think they use leverage pretty intelligently against corporate fixed income. And they try to slice and dice their portfolio and manage the risk."

It's not surprising that Julis and Friedman are familiar with the work of Schachter and Weinstein, since they've both been in the high-yield debt market for more than a decade. "They have good relationships," adds Friedman. "They spend a great deal of time and attention on being in the trading flow and focusing on who's doing what to whom and reading those signals quite well. They have a very good window."

These are the same things Julis and Friedman value in their own shop: knowing the market well and having the insight to see opportunities that others might not.

AFTER THE CRISIS

No Worm for the Early Bird

In 2008, Friedman and Julis had 30 percent of their flagship Canyon Value Realization Fund invested in senior secured first-lien loans, considered the safest category of corporate debt because holders get paid back first in the event of a bankruptcy.

They weren't using leverage. They had wagers on derivatives that would make money if the credit markets fell, were holding less than 20 percent of the portfolio in stocks, and were betting on a worsening housing market. In short, they were expecting bad times ahead for credit markets and for the overall economy. Despite the conservative stance, the fund lost 29 percent for the year, with most of that drop occurring between September and November.

In the wake of the Lehman Brothers bankruptcy and the government takeover of insurer AIG—both in September—banks rushed to sell positions to increase their capital, and hedge funds dumped securities to prepare for client redemptions at the end of the year. In the credit markets, loans were the hardest hit because they were the easiest to sell. Average loan prices dropped from 88 cents at the end of August to 62 cents at the end of the year, a move so out of the ordinary that writer James Grant, founder of *Grant's Interest Rate Observer*, described it as "a black swan with three heads and a propeller."

Julis and Friedman say in hindsight that they entered the bank-debt market too early, buying loans in late 2007 and early 2008, when prices had hit historic lows.

Canyon's hedges—indexes of credit-default swaps, which serve as a form of insurance against defaults and which rise in value as debt prices drop—provided less protection then the two men expected. Although the derivatives did rise in value, the gain wasn't nearly enough to compensate for the plummeting loan prices.

As the credit crisis worsened, some investors who had the option to pull money from the flagship fund quarterly asked to exit. Canyon designated 41 percent of the portfolio as temporarily off limits to withdrawals, putting that portion in a so-called side-pocket in order to avoid having to sell at distressed prices.

Julis and Friedman took advantage of the credit market rally in the spring of 2009 to get money back to their investors as quickly as possible by selling some assets and moving others back into the liquid portion of the fund as turbulence in the markets subsided. By September, departing investors had gotten back more than 95 percent of their money. Canyon recouped all its 2008 losses in under nine months and through the end of the third quarter, the flagship fund had climbed about 46 percent. In 2009, Canyon concentrated on distressed debt and securities backed by residential mortgages. As in previous years, Friedman and Julis have gravitated toward research-intensive investments that traditional money managers generally avoid such as companies going through bankruptcy or experiencing other corporate events. The choice has paid off. The loan market experienced its strongest single-quarter performance in history in the first quarter, and Canyon's flagship fund, which had about a quarter of its portfolio in bank debt, was up 17.5 percent through mid-May.

The Canyon executives have made some tweaks in their portfolio following their 2008 losses. They switched some of their hedges from credit-default swap (CDS) indexes to CDSs on investment-grade companies because they estimated the value of the individual swaps would stand to increase more if credit markets go south again. In the loan market, they have shortened the timeframe of their investments, buying high-quality paper closer to maturity, or looking for an event that will cause a price jump well before the loans come due.

Overall, they are more cognizant of the "macro stresses," such as government policy changes or technical market moves, that might send the prices of their individual positions in an unexpected direction. "This is a unique time," Friedman and Julis told investors at the start of the year, "one which requires great caution, but which also may present some once-in-a-generation opportunities."

Chapter 11

Jeffrey Schachter and Burton Weinstein
Leaving Little to Chance

IT TOOK a remarkable person to inspire Jeff Schachter to finally take the leap and leave his secure Wall Street job to open Cedarview Capital Management with his partner Burton Weinstein. It took rapper LL Cool J.

Schachter, forty-two, doesn't call to mind your average B-boy. He has a slight build, reddish hair, and lives in the New Jersey suburbs with his wife and six children. He had never even heard of the legendary rapper when he met him on a plane in July 2003, just when he and Weinstein were agonizing over whether to launch their own hedge fund.

Schachter was traveling in first class, returning from his father's seventieth birthday celebration in Los Angeles. An affable sort, Schachter introduced himself to the handsome, athletic black man sitting next to him. His neighbor, who was wearing a white T-shirt and basketball shorts, said his name was Todd Smith and that he was in the music business, making records under the name LL Cool J.

"Oh, is that the name of your band?" Schachter asked.

Schachter clearly wasn't hip to hip-hop, but LL was completely conversant in the language of Schachter's world of bonds. "I invest only in AAA munis. I look at duration and I don't reach for yield," he told Schachter. In the course of the flight, they discovered they were both reading the same book, *Think and Grow Rich*, by Napoleon Hill, a 1937 classic that lays out thirteen steps for achieving success based on interviews with the likes of Henry Ford, Thomas Edison, and Charles Schwab. Later in the flight, LL pulled out from his carry-on bag a copy of Benjamin Graham and David Dodd's *Security Analysis*, the bible of value investing.

The two men exchanged cards, and Schachter called the rap artist a few weeks later, proposing that he and Weinstein take him to dinner. LL suggested the fancy kosher restaurant Box Tree, in midtown Manhattan.

Although they sat in a quiet corner, the foursome (LL had brought along his assistant) attracted a bit of attention as they discussed a range of topics from hedge funds to philanthropy. It was understandable. "You have two Jewish-looking guys sitting with two rappers," says Schachter. The scene was intriguing enough to catch the eye of the gentleman at a neighboring table, who was an acquaintance of the managers-to-be and a member of a wealthy family that invests more than $1 billion in hedge funds. That gentleman, who invested in Cedarview Capital from day one, is now one of its largest clients.

Schachter found LL's determination inspiring. The rapper had managed to become a huge star against great odds. As a young child growing up in Queens, New York, LL witnessed his father shoot and seriously injure his mother and grandfather. Later, his mother's boyfriend abused him. Yet LL went on to make his first CD, *Radio*, when he was seventeen years old. It went platinum the next year. Since then he's released hit record after hit record, become an actor, and even launched his own clothing line. "He was very persistent, and that's what it's all about," says Schachter, who was delighted to have met and courted a celebrity, especially one from such an alien world.

Weinstein felt the same way: "I remember telling Jeff: If you can get LL Cool J out for dinner, we can raise a lot of money together." And they did. Weinstein and Schachter spent the next year building their business, and they opened their doors in August 2004 with $50 million. As of July 2007, they were managing about $600 million.

Cedarview bills itself as a credit fund, investing primarily in bank debt, junk (or high-yield) bonds, distressed securities, and equities. The managers pitch the fund as producing steady returns with a target of 10 percent to 13 percent annually after their 1.5 percent management fee and 20 percent incentive fees are deducted.

Schachter and Weinstein, forty-four, who has dark hair and is taller than his partner, say their edge comes from the processes they've developed since opening the fund. Nothing they do is willy-nilly. The two have employed a coach who helps them with business and trading issues. They've developed interactive databases: one to keep track of investment ideas and another to log research calls. Everyone on staff—including four analysts and a trader—writes reports called *"Thoughts of the Week,"* based on the reading they do each weekend. The partners meet every Friday to analyze the decisions they've made in the previous five days, critiquing any mistakes to prevent them from happening again. "We aren't taking anything for granted," says Schachter. "That's the crazy part of this business. We realize it could all go away in a few months. We are creating systems that work and we built them from the ground up. There are lots of checks and balances."

They developed many of the processes after a disappointing 2005, their first full year of operation, when Cedarview ended the year up 8 percent. Although the outcome was better than the average performance of high-yield hedge funds, it fell below their target. Their problems, they decided, were threefold: they didn't cut losses quickly enough, they took profits too early, and they missed opportunities.

Schachter, who has the kind of photographic memory that enables instantaneous recall of dates and details, easily remembered a trade that exemplified some of their problems that year. On May 4, 2005, corporate bonds tumbled, and so did Vertis, which sells direct marketing services. Schachter and Weinstein knew the company well. Earlier in the year, they had bought the company's bonds at 106 and watched them plummet to 80 before finally cutting their losses. Vertis bonds were trading at 57 that day, a price that both men *knew* was too low. Already burned once by the Vertis investment, they were gun-shy and couldn't bring themselves to make the purchase. The bonds rebounded as expected.

Stop-Losses. With such disappointments in mind, Schachter and Weinstein sat down in a conference room—two hours a day for a week—to figure out ways to avoid making such mistakes again. First, they instituted stop-losses—price points at which they would automatically sell if a security fell to that level (or in the case of a short, rose to that level). Lots of hedge fund managers eschew the use of stops, insisting that too often these triggers force them out of a position at the exact moment they should be hanging on. Yet Weinstein and Schachter find that these safety nets have been key to keeping their mandate of producing steady returns.

The two decided that they would not allow any one position to cause more than a 20-basis-point loss. With that limit in mind, they set the stops based on a number of factors including the potential risk of the security and its historical price movements. A bank loan, for example, might have a tighter stop than a distressed bond because, as a relatively safe investment, the loan's price shouldn't move wildly. Likewise if a bond has generally traded in a range, it's bad news if it suddenly drops a lot lower. Once a stop-loss is reached, they never lower it. If, however, a stock or bond rallies, they will reassess the position and raise the stop accordingly if they decide to stay in.

Having these limits in place has helped them trade in and out of investments as the prices and circumstances change. Take, for example, MedQuest, a company that makes imaging equipment for taking CAT scans, mammograms, and other diagnostic medical procedures. The bond prices slipped from 96 to 90, which was the stop-loss, in early 2006 after legislation passed aimed at capping Medicare payments for such tests. Cedarview sold its MedQuest bonds at 90. The bonds tumbled as low as the mid-70s, at which point Weinstein and Schachter bought them back. After the bonds rose a few points, they got out. They both say that without the stop-losses in place, they would not have sold at 90, and would have lost a lot more money as the bonds plunged. With that loss weighing on them, they wouldn't have had the courage to buy them at their lows. "Not having the emotional baggage of holding on to the bonds all the way down makes it a lot easier to reload," says Weinstein. "It gave us a fresh perspective."

The stop-losses have also kept them from taking profits too quickly. Weinstein and Schachter bought senior secured bonds of Evergreen International Aviation, an air cargo company, in 2006, when they were trading around 83, and set a stop-loss at 80. The bonds rallied to 91, at which point they raised the stop-loss to 89 and increased their position from 2 percent to 3.5 percent, expecting that management would tender the bonds so they could refinance under less restrictive conditions. Evergreen bought back the bonds at 108. "The stop-losses kept us in the game and let us increase our position," says Weinstein.

In the early days, Schachter and Weinstein wouldn't put a position into the portfolio unless they both agreed on it. Now, if one of them likes a trade, it goes in. Each takes comfort in knowing the stop-loss will keep any losses to a minimum. "We're taking losses, letting profits run, getting rid of the fear factor, and putting on the bet. It takes away the emotion," says Schachter. "There's a precept that says, 'You don't lose money taking a profit.' We don't believe that. We say, 'You lose profits taking a profit.'"

Leaving a Trail. Schachter and Weinstein say part of what went wrong in 2005 was missing moneymaking ideas that didn't make it into the portfolio before a big price move. They set out to improve communication with analysts and built two interactive databases they hoped would solve these problems. The first repository is an idea log in which they enter every trading idea. The log details the rationale for the investment, its potential risks, ways to hedge, and an estimate of how much the trade might make. The log allows the two managers and their four analysts to see what research has been completed and what still remains undone, whether it's calling other investors, lenders, legal experts, or company executives or digging elsewhere for more information. Some ideas may stay on the list for three or four months. Weinstein and Schachter meet with the analysts every Tuesday and Thursday to discuss these works in progress.

The second data tracker is a conversation log, which keeps records of who talked to whom about what security. Every time any one of the investment staff enters notes into the database, an e-mail goes out to all parties, signaling the arrival of new information. The conversation log allows the analysts and portfolio managers to build a huge list of contacts, as well as to keep track of company executives' comments from quarter to quarter to ensure their messages are consistent.

The log keeps the portfolio managers and analysts from repeating the same work unnecessarily. When the bonds of Stanadyne, a company that makes fuel injection pumps for diesel engines, climbed from 50 into the low 60s, the partners considered getting out.

Schachter turned to the conversation log to review a discussion he'd had with a sell-side analyst who had given him compelling reasons that the bonds would go higher. After taking a look at the argument, they decided to hang on. The bonds rose to $0.82 on the dollar. Without the log, Schachter would have spent time looking through notes, trying to remember exactly who had said what, perhaps having to call the analyst all over again.

The prospect of maintaining the logs seemed onerous at first, but both men say that everyone follows the procedures because they understand that a remedy was needed.

Generating Ideas. Both partners also believe in homework. On weekends, the investment staff has to read *Barron's* and the weekend editions of the *Financial Times* and the *Wall Street Journal.* Various weekly reports from brokerage firms and other sources are also assigned. Everyone sends trade ideas based on their reading, whether they're about some new exchange-traded fund to use as a hedge or a company to buy or sell short.

As they read, they also keep in mind the firm's catchphrase WECBA (short for *What else can be affected?*): What happens if Iran captures fifteen British sailors, as happened in April 2007? How will that affect the fund's holdings? Schachter and Weinstein even had a WECBA ink stamp made, which everyone must use to mark the pages of their notebooks, which are separate from the logs. The firm imposes a $5 fine if a page doesn't have a stamp.

The partners talk about the weekly ideas on Monday mornings, and they go over stop-losses on Monday afternoons. Setting Friday as the day to critique decisions came at the prompting of a rabbi, who suggested the workweek shouldn't be interrupted with conversations about things that went wrong. "So Friday morning we discuss all the issues, and we then move on," says Schachter. They keep records of these meetings, and every week they review what they discussed twelve months earlier to ensure they aren't making the same mistakes again. "We are constantly working on our errors," says Schachter. "We're going to keep working and improving ourselves so that we're as close to perfect as we can be. We don't believe in being complacent."

The fixes worked. In 2006, the fund jumped 17.3 percent, and through June 2007, it was up another 9 percent. Beginning the second week in July, a spate of bad news came out that sent credit markets reeling. Ratings agencies lowered the credit ratings on bonds backed by subprime mortgages. Chrysler said it was forced to raise its proposed interest rates on $6 billion in loans it was seeking for its finance unit, and banks working with buyout firm Kohlberg Kravis Roberts & Company postponed a deadline to finance the acquisition of U.K. pharmacist Alliance Boots, Europe's biggest leveraged buyout. In the last days of July, the fund lost 3 percent, as credit spreads widened. In August, the losses continued as stocks, which made up 10 percent of Cedarview's portfolio, tumbled after quantitative funds, which use computer models to make buy and sell decisions, unloaded shares to meet margin calls. Cedarview was short the CDX High Yield Index and the LCDX, an index of credit-default swaps on senior secured loans. They rallied instead. As of August 24, the fund was up 3 percent for the year. "We learned that we should take some profits off the table, and that we should be quicker to react to bad news," says Schachter.

Facing up to initial mistakes and growing assets by a factor of ten in three years marks an impressive start, especially considering the potential obstacles the fund faced in the early days: Schachter and Weinstein hadn't known each other that long, they had never worked together, and Schachter had never managed money.

Weinstein and Schachter first met in 2001. Weinstein was a portfolio manager at Aviary Capital Enterprises, the investment office for the Taub family, who made their money with Automatic Data Processing, a payroll processing company founded in 1949 by Henry Taub and Frank Lautenberg, now Democratic Senator from New Jersey. Weinstein was a client of Schachter, an institutional salesman at Samco Capital Markets.

Weinstein started his career as an accountant after graduating from Yeshiva University. Dissatisfied with work as a CPA, he enrolled in the business school at New York University as a first step toward moving into finance. After a decade investing in high-yield and distressed debt, including seven years at the Tisch family–controlled Loews Corporation, and nearly two years at Ezra Merkin's Gabriel Capital Group, he joined the Taub family office in 2000, planning to build a three-year track record and then start a money-management firm with the family's backing.

Schachter's path to finance was more circuitous. After college and law school at the University of California at Berkeley, he headed to Israel where he studied the Talmud for a few years, going to the same yeshiva as Morris Smith. Before moving to Israel, Smith had run Fidelity Investment's Magellan Fund, then the biggest mutual fund in the world, for two years following Peter Lynch's retirement. When Schachter was ready to go back to the states, Smith advised him to consider a job on Wall Street.

In 1995, Schachter joined the brokerage firm Jefferies & Company as a salesman and continued as an institutional salesman in high-yield debt for nine years at various firms. He had always dreamed of having a fund, and in 2002, he talked to Weinstein about setting up shop together. "I was on the sell side, and I felt as if I was adding little value compared to what I could do," says Schachter.

Weinstein, who had just turned forty, felt the time was right. "I thought, if I don't do it now, I'm not going to do it. Jeff helped me get there."

Nowadays, a big hedge fund launch depends in large part on pedigree. Analysts or portfolio managers coming out of big hedge funds like SAC Capital Partners or Tudor Corporation or from big investment banks like Goldman Sachs can count on opening their doors with $1 billion or more. Most other would-be managers struggle to find start-up funds.

When the Taubs decided that for privacy reasons, they didn't want to start a business, Weinstein and Schachter began the slow process of raising money from family and friends. Although neither Schachter nor Weinstein had brand-name jobs, they did have a few aces up their sleeves. Weinstein had a three-year track record from his years investing for the Taubs, and it was a decent one. In two difficult years, 2001 and 2002, when high-yield hedge funds averaged returns of 5 percent annually, his portfolio climbed 8 percent.

The partners raised $15 million from their contacts, but it wasn't enough. They needed at least $50 million to start to cover their overhead, pay employees, and meet their personal income needs, which were substantial, given that Weinstein had five kids, and Schachter was about to have his sixth. They went looking for a seeder.

Hedge fund seeders, or incubators, have sprung up since about 2003 for two reasons: More traders want to form hedge funds and more institutional investors want to invest in them. Unfortunately, pension funds and other institutions aren't likely to invest in a start-up unless the founder is, say, a superstar trader coming out of Goldman Sachs or the former head of Harvard's endowment. Institutional investors want a three-year track record and generally demand serious infrastructure, including a general counsel and a hefty back office. The biggest players include Capital Z, Man Global Strategies, Blackstone Group, and most Wall Street investment banks. Even multistrategy hedge funds like Citadel Investment Group are getting into the game. Competition for capital is so great that young traders working at blue-chip hedge funds may start talking to seeders three to five years before they actually quit their day jobs.

Schachter and Weinstein met with several incubators, and one of the interested parties was Capital Z, which has about twelve hedge fund managers in its stable, managing $11 billion in assets. Capital Z takes a minority stake in the management company, and the proportion of the stake decreases as the fund's assets grow. It also guarantees it will keep its money in for three years, during which time it pays full fees. After extensive due diligence on Weinstein's track record and both partners' references, Capital Z executives agreed to back Cedarview. "They provided a lot of credibility," says Schachter. "They've seeded a number of billion-dollar hedge funds."

With $35 million from Capital Z added to the $15 million they already had, Cedarview opened for business in August 2004, a year after Schachter's fortuitous meeting with LL Cool J. Working in their favor for the start-up, Schachter and Weinstein had great contacts in the industry. All Weinstein's former employers are investors, as is ex-Fidelity manager Morris Smith and the principals of some large high-yield and distressed-debt hedge funds, like Mitch Julis and Josh Friedman of Canyon Partners, and Leon Wagner, chairman of GoldenTree Asset Management.

Aware of the pitfalls of starting a business, the two men took some precautions. For one, they hired a coach to help them understand their own strengths and weaknesses—and each other's. The coach helped them relate to one another and worked with them on the psychological aspects of trading—summoning the courage to take a big bet or having the humility to cut a position when it's wrong. "We've seen too many partnerships disintegrate because they didn't deal with issues early enough. We're building a business, an asset, and we have to protect it," says Schachter. "Everyone needs a coach." Weinstein, who spends 100 percent of his time managing money, speaks to the coach every week for an hour. Schachter, who spends about 70 percent of his time on investments and 30 percent on marketing and administration, sees the coach every other week. Now that the partnership has been around for a few years and their trading processes have made the buy and sell decisions easier, Weinstein's conversations with the coach center on how he can work with and develop the analysts so he can free up more time to generate moneymaking ideas.

Over time, each partner has had to tackle a different set of issues. Schachter says his biggest hurdle was learning to cut his losses. "For me," says Weinstein, "the greatest challenge was parking my ego, because that was my track record, and respecting Jeff's acumen, which I've come to do." Indeed, Weinstein says that Schachter has convinced him that 50 percent of market moves are technical and 50 percent are fundamental, a proposition he initially thought was crazy. Technical factors include anything that might temporarily change the amount of money gravitating toward or moving away from a particular security, whether it's the size of an individual bond issue, who's doing the underwriting, or whether a company is close to reporting earnings—times when many managers back away and wait for the news.

Schachter also pushed Weinstein to take bigger positions. "A missed opportunity bothered him more than it would me," says Weinstein. "Jeff was right." The first stock Weinstein bought, truck rental company U-Haul International rose from 25 to 100. Unfortunately, they owned only 5,000 shares.

Eventually, they added guidelines to ensure their bets are large enough to make a material difference in the portfolio and introduced other rules to ensure that risk is under control. For example, a stock position must be at least a half percent of the portfolio, and they want each bond position to be between 2 percent and 4 percent of assets. They use leverage, although it never exceeds four times their net assets, and the amount they borrow is inversely related to the risk of the securities, meaning they're likely to borrow more money to make bets on bank loans and less for plays on distressed debt. They insist on shorting, that is, having some wagers in their portfolio on stocks or bonds they expect to fall in price. On average, their portfolio has been about 110 percent net long.

Because Schachter and Weinstein focus on individual companies, they use various means to hedge out macroeconomic events—a war, a crackdown on speculation in China, a meltdown in the housing market—that might cause credit spreads (the difference between Treasuries and riskier bonds) to widen. During turbulent times, they might buy calls on the VIX Index, a measure of market volatility, as a way to make money if the prices of stocks fluctuate widely, as they can in uncertain markets. Or they might short an emerging-market exchange-traded fund—a kind of index fund— because when investors become risk averse, they tend to sell emerging-market stocks. These hedges worked in July and August, though they took off the volatility trade too soon and wished they had shorted more of the emerging-market ETFs.

Rules and procedures provide a degree of protection, but they're pointless without the right people. One of the biggest risks for a growing firm is finding that talent. Not surprisingly, Schachter and Weinstein have a process for that as well. They ask every job candidate to submit a handwriting sample and give them what's known as the "Tree Test," in which the applicant draws a tree. Their coach, who is also a graphologist, analyzes the test results. The test offers insights into the applicant's character, integrity, intelligence, and motivations and ensures that the person fits into the team-player culture of Cedarview. "It's scary how accurate it is," says Weinstein.

Schachter and Weinstein temporarily closed the fund in May 2007 at $500 million to make sure everything was running smoothly and that they had enough analysts and other personnel in place. In July, they reopened to new investors. Eventually they plan to add other funds, perhaps one that focuses solely on equity, distressed debt, or loans. Both partners believe the growth potential is huge in these areas. "As long as the numbers are good, there are an unlimited number of investors," says Schachter. Weinstein agrees. "By building the infrastructure, we're preparing for the next leg up."

AFTER THE CRISIS

Smart Accommodations

Cedarview Capital Management founders Schachter and Weinstein entered 2009 with a new business model. Like other distressed funds, which lost 25 percent on average in 2008, the team's investments suffered as the global credit crisis indiscriminately pushed down the price of virtually ever bank loan, junk bond and distressed stock and bond they traded, regardless of the solvency of the borrower.

The tumult of 2008 led them to the realization that the hedge fund world had changed, and they needed to adapt to a client base that had become much more demanding than ever before. Investors across the industry, from family offices to the California Public Employees' Retirement System, the nation's largest public fund, decided to push back after years of what could only be called a seller's market for hedge funds. Angered by huge losses and some mangers' attempts to block redemptions, clients now wanted lower fees, more transparency into what managers were trading, and more lenient exit policies. Many hedge funds, whose assets had plummeted, in some cases by more than 50 percent, were happy to oblige.

So in the beginning of 2009, Cedarview started giving its clients the option of investing through separately managed accounts. In such accounts, the investor owns the assets, they can see exactly what the manager is trading, and they can sell whenever they choose. Fees on the managed accounts are generally lower than the traditional 2 percent of assets and 20 percent of gains, which most hedge funds charge. Cedarview charges 0.75 percent of assets and 15 percent to 20 percent of any profits on any gains above 5 percent for its managed accounts. The accounts can be customized to fit investors' appetite for risk and their investment horizon.

Cedarview's more conservative accounts might buy investment-grade corporate bonds that mature in less than seven years, with yields to maturity of anywhere from 8 percent to 12 percent. The more aggressive accounts might buy senior or senior-secured high-yield bonds of companies that have significant assets to back their debt or which generate lots of cash. Those portfolios target returns of 15 percent or more a year.

In 2009, the same securities that had plummeted the year before rebounded, and in midyear, Cedarview traders were betting that the difference between the yields on bank debt, high-yield and distressed bonds and U.S. Treasuries would continue to narrow for the rest of the year and into 2010, meaning prices would keep rising.

In the first nine months 2009, Cedarview's more-conservative portfolios returned as much as 16 percent, with investments in such bonds as Staples Inc., Wendy's International Inc., and Expedia Inc.

The higher-octane accounts were up as much as 65 percent through the first half of the year, holding such bonds as Ford Motor Credit Co. or Rite Aid Corp.

Chapter 12

Dwight Anderson
The Phoenix Phenomenon

IN 2006, Dwight Anderson pulled off an investment feat not often seen in the hedge fund business. His fund was down 19 percent for the year in May, and within nine months, he'd made back all his losses.

Such stunts are hardly the way events typically unfold after a fund's roof crashes in. In the wake of a major loss, a manager struggles to regain his footing. Shaken, he doesn't have the confidence to make the bets needed to rebound. Poor performance can also spark a wave of analyst and client departures. On occasion, he might decide the setback is irreparable and close up shop.

Not Anderson.

By June 2007, more than a year after the worst loss of his career, Anderson was back on course. His flagship $3.5 billion Ospraie Fund, which invests in all manner of commodities, from oil to gold to copper and grains, as well as basic industry stocks, had returned about 7.8 percent in the first seven months of 2007. That's a 33 percent return from the trough.

The fund's comeback required no alterations in Anderson's investment strategy. He continued doing what he's always done: conducting in-depth research to ascertain supply and demand for the various commodities in which Ospraie trades. On the stock side,

Anderson and his team seek out companies whose shares are under-valued compared to their earnings and other financial measures. In both the futures and the stock markets, Ospraie takes the long view, and the average holding period is more than two years.

The wait can sometimes be painful. "We run a concentrated, long-duration portfolio, so I live constantly with stress," says Anderson. "I would love to be able to buy something today, make a bunch of money and sell it tomorrow. It would be a lot less stressful. I'm always worried that we're wrong."

Mostly, they're not. Anderson's flagship fund at Ospraie Management, which manages $7 billion in assets overall, averaged a return of 15 percent annually between its start in February 2000 and July 2007, compared with a 2 percent annualized return for the Standard & Poor's 500 Index, a 6 percent return for the Lehman Brothers Aggregate Bond Index, and 6 percent for the Reuters/Jefferies CRB Commodity Price Index.

The day I talked with Anderson, in April 2007, he was sitting in the conference room of the firm's offices in midtown Manhattan. Anderson, forty, is six feet three inches tall with sandy hair, and in his glen plaid suit pants and blue shirt complete with Osprey cuff links, he looks like a big kid. His affable and loquacious manner reinforces that impression. He actually says "holy cow."

A history buff, Anderson has decorated the walls of Ospraie's headquarters with antique maps. He's particularly fond of his map of the United States hanging in his office, which dates from the late 1600s and shows California as an island. It reminds him that initial perceptions can change as one's knowledge grows, that one needs to keep digging and exploring to uncover the truth.

In uncovering what went wrong for the fund in April and May 2006, Anderson had no trouble identifying the difficulties. "Every single major position we had—equities, agriculture, energy, precious metals, and base metals—lost money," Anderson says. He was, for example, long mining and oil companies, which fell, and he was short copper and other base metals, which jumped.

The poor returns may have taken clients by surprise, but not because Anderson didn't warn them of the dangers. He has always emphasized to investors that his holding period is long and his positions concentrated and that they should expect the fund to have a bad quarter at some time or other. "We do everything that we can to manage that risk—and I think we're better at it today than we were a year ago—but we have always told people there is that possibility," he says. "But as one of our investors told us afterwards, 'You always told us that, but I never believed you.'"

The challenge Anderson's long-duration strategy presents is what to do in the face of price swings while he's waiting for positions to make money. "I'm still on my learning curve as a portfolio manager when it comes to how to manage the volatility in the price path along the way," says Anderson. "You've got a Point A and a Point C and you know with 96.8 percent certainty, as high as you can have, that C is going to happen. The problem is managing the path to get there."

That was the heart of the problem in 2006, when his biggest losses were in copper.

Anderson was convinced that there would be a deficit in the supply of copper in the first half of the year and that beginning in the latter half of 2006, supply would start to come on board, after which there would be a surplus extending out to 2010. He reasoned that the price of copper had been high enough for long enough, that suppliers were taking more copper out of the ground, and that more of the metal would become available. So, in December 2005, Ospraie was long copper going out six months, after which the fund was shorting the futures for delivery as far out as 2010, expecting the price of copper to fall as supply increased.

But Anderson miscalculated the impact of two forces that had nothing to do with either the demand of copper buyers or with the supply from companies that sell it: Pension funds and other institutional investors were pouring billions of dollars into long-only index funds, pushing up the price of futures contracts of most every commodity, including copper. At the same time, fewer copper producers were selling a smaller amount of futures in order to hedge prices going out two or three years.

Those two forces changed the historic relationship of near-term and future copper prices in a way that had never been seen before, says Anderson. Before 2005, in a bull market of any commodity other than gold, the spot price had always been higher than the three-month price, which was higher than all the other prices in the future—a phenomenon known as "backwardation." Yet in the first three and a half months of 2006, the spot price for copper was falling relative to the three-month futures contracts and contracts two years in the future were higher relative to those for delivery three months in the future. All this was happening even as the events that Anderson predicted were coming to pass—inventories were rising as supply was coming on board.

In the end, Anderson's flagship fund lost nearly 10 percent in April and 8 percent in May from copper and other money-losing positions. He was especially surprised by the behavior of the futures going out to 2008, 2009, and 2010, which had never experienced a price jump of that magnitude. "We sized the position off the worst move we'd ever seen before," he says. "And we were wrong in terms of how much that price could move." Anderson cut the position by two-thirds and made some money as copper prices started falling in the second half of 2006. Indeed, his long-term views on agricultural commodities, energy, and precious metals have also all panned out since mid-2006.

Not surprisingly, Anderson made some changes in how he deals with losses after the 2006 performance bruise. The most important of them is to cut back on losing positions sooner. He has also decided that when the price of a commodity jumps or falls by an unusually dramatic amount, even if it's in the direction he's betting on, he will cut the position, because when the swing is without historic precedent, it's hard to predict the future course. Finally, in the event of a loss, Anderson will add to positions when they start to move his way, taking advantage of his better-than-average skill as an analyst.

Anderson expects the safety measures to boost performance. "We have a high success rate of being correct in the positions we put on, and that would imply higher return levels than we've earned as a firm," he says. "We should be able to make much more money by managing our losses and our winners better."

The changes Anderson introduced since 2006 are nuances to the firm's basic approach, not departures from it: "One of the things I've learned in this business is that there are many different ways to make money, and the style has to fit you, your strengths, and your personality." Anderson traces his core style back to his days as a manufacturing consultant, as well as to his time working for hedge fund legends Julian Robertson (see Chapter 15) and Paul Tudor Jones, who runs Tudor Investment Corporation.

Anderson never imagined in his teens that he'd become a money manager. After high school in northern Westchester, he went to Princeton University and studied history. In the beginning of 1989, during the last semester of his senior year, it dawned on him that he didn't want to go to law school as he'd been planning. Many of the choice jobs in every industry had already been filled, so he scrambled around and found a job in manufacturing consulting. After a brief training program in which he learned the basics of business, he found himself flying around the country going from a food processing company in Oregon to a dairy company in New Jersey and a golf club manufacturer in Texas. "I learned how to evaluate a company's operations, how to evaluate a management team and uncover what they can do to improve their business and what they're doing well."

After less than eighteen months, he decided he wanted to see if he could implement the strategies he was recommending to others, so he took a job with one of his clients, a paper company in upstate New York. Although he found the work rewarding, he began to doubt whether a life in manufacturing was right for him. After all, it meant he'd be living in industrial towns, not the best places to raise a family. When he spoke about his college friends, he noted that the happiest of them were the proprietary traders at Wall Street firms, so he decided that's what he would do. Specifically, he focused on the foreign exchange and commodities markets, because like manufacturing, he would be dealing with tangible things whose prices were driven by world events. Once he began managing money, he discovered that all his training and experience helped him in analyzing the companies in which he invests.

With his sights set on investment management, he applied to business schools and ended up at the University of North Carolina (UNC) in the fall of 1992 thanks to a scholarship funded by UNC graduate Julian Robertson, which paid Anderson's tuition, expenses, and a stipend. After the first year of classes, he went looking for a summer job and had the good fortune to visit a friend at J. Aron & Company, Goldman Sachs's commodities trading unit, the very day that Robert Rubin, then cochairman of the investment bank, had delivered a forceful message to the senior executives at the unit: "You're a bunch of old men. You are not in the Goldman culture.

There are no young people here. You need summer hires, people out of business school."

Later that afternoon, Anderson's friend introduced him to a partner at J. Aron, who saw in the MBA candidate a ready-made answer to Rubin's complaint. Anderson came back for a brief interview and was awarded the three-month gig—even though the investment bank generally didn't assign summer postings to UNC business school students. The new recruit ended up spending a fair amount of time on the coffee, cocoa, and sugar desks.

Cocoa turned out to be an excellent vehicle for learning about commodities trading and arbitrage. Cocoa traded in two markets, one in London and one in New York, in two different currencies. There were also two different grades of cocoa, one from Indonesia and one from the Ivory Coast, and Anderson had to weigh all these differences in figuring out if there was a discrepancy in price that he could exploit.

Anderson did well and Goldman offered him a job after graduation. He never started there, however, because Daniel Och, the man who had been instrumental in hiring him, left Goldman to start his own fund. Anderson decided to join JPMorgan instead, although his tenure there would be short-lived. After only a few weeks on the job, he got a call from Robertson, inviting him to breakfast. Anderson assumed it was a friendly, welcome-to-New York gesture, but upon his arrival at Tiger headquarters, Robertson introduced him to several people at the firm, who proceeded to grill him on the cocoa market. Realization dawned: Robertson wanted to hire him.

A month and several interviews later, Robertson offered him a job, and Anderson—after consulting with a JPMorgan managing director, David Pryde, who told him he'd be crazy not to take it—started at Tiger in October 1994. Three months later, Bob Bishop, Tiger's senior basic industries analyst, left the firm and Anderson became head of the commodities team. He'd been trading commodities for less than a year. "I needed the ignorance of youth to have the confidence to take that job," says Anderson. He was twenty-seven.

Anderson and Robertson made many noteworthy trades together, but the most famous was a bet on a jump in the price of palladium—a position they took because they saw a huge imbalance between the demand in the precious metal and its supply. When Anderson joined Tiger, Robertson already had a small position in palladium, used primarily in catalytic converters, electronics, and dental crowns and bridges, which he had first put on in 1993. Anderson continued to research it and agreed the price should go up given that there was a 2-million-ounce difference between supply and demand of the metal. Even as the trade moved against Tiger in 1995 and 1996, Robertson kept buying, always asking if Anderson's calculations about a deficit of supply were still correct. Anderson visited mines in Siberia and talked with auto companies and dentists. The answer, he said, was yes. Finally, in 1997, the price started rising from around $120 an ounce and reached more than $400 an ounce in May 1998.

What gave him the confidence to hang on? "Sustaining a position that long involves a continued fixation on asking, are you right? And with palladium, the period from when Tiger first got into it in late 1993 until it actually started working in 1997 was four years. To maintain that position, we needed to have other things working in the portfolio during that period." The losses in palladium were balanced by winning bets on grains, copper, and later refining stocks and the so-called crack spread, or the margin earned by refiners for turning crude oil into gasoline and heating fuel.

Through this trade and others like it, Robertson laid the groundwork for Anderson's investment style. He emphasized value investing—buying stocks of good companies at a cheap price—and he focused on a company's management as a key ingredient to success. Robertson also stressed the inevitability of economics—the forces of supply and demand—and promoted extensive and intensive research. Even today, with a team of twenty-three analysts, Anderson still likes to get out and see what's going on firsthand. When I met him in April, his travels for the year already included trips to Omaha, Dallas, Houston, Oklahoma City, and Vicksburg, Mississippi; Saudi Arabia, Qatar, Peru, Argentina, Brazil (twice), Australia, Malaysia, Hong Kong, and Korea. "We know our industries as well or better than anyone else," says Anderson.

Anderson was happy at Tiger, but by 1999 some of his colleagues were leaving to start their own funds, and he too thought it was time to move on and try his hand at managing money. He was eager for the responsibilities of portfolio management, but he didn't want the distractions of running a business quite yet. Looking instead for an opportunity to work within a larger organization that would provide back-office support, he talked to a number of shops he respects, including Steven Cohen's SAC, Louis Bacon's Moore Capital, and Paul Jones's Tudor. He chose Tudor in part because Jones had a strong background in commodities—having started as a trader in the commodities pits—and a reputation as a supportive partner.

A start-up comes with built-in risks. A fund can lose money in any year, but Anderson knew that a loss in the first year would have more serious consequences for the business. The right partnership, therefore, was key. "Having a group of people who know you well, who know the markets well and can deal well with their partners, gives you a sense of confidence in starting off," Anderson says.

Ospraie opened on October 1, 1999, with a seed investment from Tudor. By February 2000, the fund was accepting money from outside investors. As expected, the early days were challenging, with Ospraie down almost 5 percent in the first month of running client money. "When you're starting something, you're usually so tense that you exert dramatically more energy than you should," says Anderson. "Ospraie's start-up was draining physically and emotionally."

By the end of 2003, however, he was on more solid ground, having raised more than a billion dollars, and it was time to spin out completely from the Tudor umbrella. Anderson's assets under management were large enough to cover all his infrastructure costs. Given his longer-term investment horizon, he also preferred to lock up his clients' capital for longer periods than was possible at Tudor. Anderson limits withdrawals to every two years or three years, with a break in fees the longer the money stays in.

Anderson's time with Jones left a lasting impression. "What Paul does best—which I am still trying to learn how to do better— is cutting a position as it's moving against you, increasing it as it's moving with you," he says. "He's one of the best risk managers and profit maximizers in the business."

Since leaving Tudor, which remains one of Ospraie's largest investors, Anderson has taken several steps to expand his business while curtailing growth in his flagship fund, which is closed to new investors. Opening new funds made more sense to Anderson than simply accepting more cash into his main fund, and in the beginning of 2006, he launched the Ospraie Special Opportunities Fund, which invests in private equity deals in the commodities arena. "We're trying to learn from the hedge funds that have gone before us, to be aware of why so few of them actually succeeded once they grew," says Anderson. Part of the reason for the failure to thrive is pure math: The larger the fund, the harder it is to find inefficiencies in the market that are big enough to make an impact on returns.

The reasoning behind the decision to open the Special Opportunities Fund, which now has more than $1.2 billion in assets, was simple: "We had seen too many opportunities come down the pike," says Anderson, everything from agricultural farmland to huge energy properties. Ospraie was forced to pass on these exclusive offers to other firms because Anderson limits such illiquid, private equity investments in the flagship fund to about 5 percent of assets.

As part of his expansion plan, Anderson also sold a 20 percent stake in his firm to Lehman Brothers Holdings in 2005 and used the proceeds, in part, to help launch the Ospraie Wingspan group of funds, which seeds new managers. Wingspan now includes nine managers with about $2 billion in assets. Ospraie provides back-office and administrative functions that include everything from employee benefits administration, marketing, accounting services, legal services, and technology and equipment purchasing. This structure frees the managers to run the investments.

In choosing managers for Wingspan, Anderson looks for integrity—how they treat their partners, employees, clients, and counterparties—as well as talent in money management. He sees Wingspan as a network for sharing information, and he wants to deal with people he respects and enjoys talking to. "Rather than cannibalizing liquidity and creating correlated risk, the relationships raise information flow, which increases each manager's probability of succeeding," he says. "There are synergies among all the different organizations because the different investing styles are generally complementary rather than competitive."

As he adds more funds to the program, Anderson says he might look for slightly less conservative managers. "We would probably be more accepting now of people whose portfolios have greater volatility," he says. "Over time, we're going to try to build more of these focused groups so that, for example, we'll have five different energy traders in

Houston, each having a different style but working in the same market and having that informational flow and dialogue back and forth that helps them complement each other."

Developing Ospraie's Wingspan program has positioned Anderson to take special note of managers whom he considers exceptionally gifted. Among those who've earned his respect in the commodities market is Bruce Ritter (see Chapter 14), who runs Yannix Management. Ritter is older than Anderson by more than a decade and has been involved in commodities since he was a boy growing up on a farm in Oregon. "Bruce has experience and wisdom. I've known him a long time and I've seen his insight, knowledge, and judgment in the agricultural markets. He's exceptional at managing his risk, and he is ruthless in cutting his position if he has any concerns about being wrong." Anderson sees Ritter as among the best in terms of knowledge of the agricultural markets and in having stringent risk control and intelligence on a position. "It's a rare combination," says Anderson.

In the equities arena, the name that stands out for Anderson is Roberto Mignone (see Chapter 13), whom Tiger Cub Lee Ainslie (see Chapter 6) also named as noteworthy. "Roberto has very quietly and patiently built a solid investment partnership during the past seven years. He remains a purist on fundamental stock selection and emphasizes the value of disciplined research and patience in his work. He is also one of the few fund managers left who seeks to generate absolute performance from the short side."

On performance overall, Anderson believes that "wisdom is the accumulated benefit of the mistakes you've made in the past."

Not many would argue with that. Especially when you find someone as good at learning from his missteps as Anderson is.

AFTER THE CRISIS

From the Ashes

In early September 2008, Anderson, who once ran the largest commodity hedge fund firm in the world, sent a letter to investors in his Ospraie Fund, certainly the most painful he'd ever had to write. In it, he told investors he was going to close his flagship fund and return all their money.

The fund, which had managed $2.8 billion just a month earlier, had lost 27 percent in August alone, as energy, mining, and resource stocks tumbled more violently and swiftly than they had at any time in the past two decades. The global economy was slowing, and so was the demand for commodities. To make matters worse, the stocks he expected to tumble rose in value instead. Anderson dumped about 40 percent of his portfolio, even though he was confident that over the long run his analysis would prove correct. By the beginning of September, the fund had plunged 39 percent for the year.

The trouble wasn't limited to money-losing trades. When Anderson started Ospraie Fund more than eight years before, he'd included in his fund documents a somewhat unusual clause stipulating that if the fund ever lost more than 30 percent, investors would be free to pull out immediately, even though under normal circumstances their capital was committed for two or three years at a time. With such significant losses, Anderson suspected that a high percentage of clients would run for the exits, so he decided the fairest course of action would be to close the fund rather than burden a small number of remaining investors with a concentrated portfolio full of positions he couldn't easily sell.

Investors got back 80 percent of their cash by the end of 2008. The remaining 20 percent, in hard-to-sell positions, might take as long as three years to sell, Anderson told investors at the time. "Not only as a portfolio manager, but as one of the largest investors in the Ospraie Fund, I have shared in these losses with you," he wrote in the letter. "After nine years of striving to be a good steward of your capital, I am very sorry for this outcome."

But the winding down of his fund was not the end of Anderson's career.

He continues to manage the $1 billion Special Opportunities Fund, which makes private-equity-type investments. In July 2009, nearly a year after Anderson shuttered his flagship fund, he opened two new funds: one to trade commodities and one to trade commodity-related stocks. Altogether, he started with about $100 million, including separately managed accounts and money of his own and from his employees. "After much reflection and with a number of lessons learned, we see a set of opportunities today that we believe could create significant value for investors in the coming years," the New York-based manager wrote to potential investors when he announced the opening of the new funds.

The new funds allow investors to exit quarterly and require no initial lock-up. He gave returning investors the choice of either paying no performance fee until their 2008 losses are recouped or choosing reduced fees of 1 percent of assets and 10 percent of profits in perpetuity.

Anderson told potential investors that he set up two distinct funds because it would help him manage risk easier and avoid the losses that occurred in 2008. He also said he would eschew illiquid assets. His view of the future is confident: "The opportunities are as compelling as I have seen in my fifteen-plus years of investing in the basic industry space," said Anderson.

Chapter 13

Roberto Mignone
Fruits of Firsthand Knowledge

To UNDERSTAND what drives Roberto Mignone's approach to managing money, you need an appreciation of how ancient Greek and Latin are studied. Mignone's classical, liberal arts education at Harvard taught him lessons that the Street teaches only the hard way: the importance of primary sources, the benefits of being a generalist, the superiority of simple themes, and the advantages of taking the less-traveled path.

Mignone's unlikely route from majoring in Greek and Latin to working in finance ultimately led him to Bridger Management in New York, the $2.1 billion hedge fund he started in July 2000, when he was just shy of his twenty-ninth birthday. "Studying classics is something that doesn't get much credit these days," says Mignone, now thirty-six, although he points out that the grandfather of value investing, Benjamin Graham, was also a student of the classics and one of his favorite hobbies, reputedly, was translating Homer into Latin and Virgil into Greek. "When you study Greek and Latin literature, you have no textbooks. There's a constant push to get your materials from primary sources and learn from them directly," he says. "That discipline has carried over into my career."

The thrill Mignone gets from digging up firsthand information is what makes him an analyst's analyst. "For me, the overwhelming

157

passion is to roll up my sleeves and understand a company," he says. "The portfolio-management aspect, the stock aspect—those are, if you will, necessary evils." What he enjoys most is doing the research, the kind he does at Bridger to find stocks to buy and others to sell short. Even talking about it makes him smile, his slightly gap-toothed grin giving him the look of a kid in a candy store, despite his adult garb of blue pinstripe suit, white shirt, tie, and Gucci loafers.

Mignone is on the hunt for stocks that will double in price over three years and ones that will fall by at least 30 percent. His flagship fund, now closed to new investors, returned 16 percent a year on average from inception through mid-2007, after its 1.5 percent management fee and 20 percent incentive fee. "We're trying to make as much money as we possibly can without doing anything stupid," says Mignone. "In some circumstances, that can mean returns of 40 percent per year; in others, hell, holding cash at 5 percent makes you look like a hero."

The name of Mignone's firm seems fitting for a money manager determined to uncover the unknown. It was inspired by the legacy of Jim Bridger, a nineteenth-century trapper, trader, and guide who explored Montana, Wyoming, and other parts of the West and, according to the memorial marking his grave in Independence, Missouri, also discovered the Great Salt Lake in Utah. Mignone was introduced to the western United States by his wife, Allison, whom he married in 1999. Members of her family have been Montana ranchers for generations. "I wanted to give my wife credit for supporting me in taking on this new venture so early in our marriage," he says of the name choice. Stock picker Steve Mandel—a Tiger Management Cub and his wife's boss at the time—picked Bridger from a list of ten possible candidates. "Since Steve is the most successful manager I've known in the last twenty years, I figured his vote counted more than anybody else's."

The name calls to mind Mignone's readiness to explore new territory not only in investing but also in his own life. Mignone, who was born in the Hell's Kitchen neighborhood of Manhattan and was raised in Yonkers, is the oldest of five children. He went to Fordham Preparatory School, the Jesuit all-boys school in the Bronx, where he first studied the classics. In 1992, after four years at Harvard, he chucked the idea of going to law school and took a job at Deloitte Consulting, where he was posted in Russia for nearly two years working with a U.S. Agency for International Development (USAID) program to set up capital markets there. In 1994, soon after his father was diagnosed with terminal cancer, Mignone moved back to New York and took a job in investment banking at Donaldson, Lufkin & Jenrette (DLJ).

Tony James, now president and CEO of New York buyout firm Blackstone Group, was running merchant banking at the time, and the ratio of junior analysts to senior people was a lot smaller than at other firms. "It was trial by fire, and it was a great experience," says Mignone. The pace, however, was overwhelming. Although he was living at home, he felt as if he had seen his family more often when he was in Moscow.

Deciding the academic life might suit him better—most of his extended family members are either doctors or professors—Mignone left DLJ after six months to enroll in Harvard Business School. He loved it and early on seriously considered pursuing his doctorate. That all changed in January 1996, when a friend, Tiger Management president John Griffin, approached him about the possibility of taking a position as an analyst in a fund he was about to launch. "If you do it well, you'll do as much research as you want, you'll make a tremendous amount of money, and you'll have a tremendous amount of fun," Mignone recalls Griffin telling him. "And you'll get to start a company."

Hedge funds had little appeal for Mignone, since he knew nothing about them, but he liked the entrepreneurial aspect of the venture and the possibility of doing creative and in-depth research. He consulted his faculty adviser, André Perold. "Do it for three years," Perold suggested, "and if you're great at it, believe me, you'll love it and you'll have made the right choice. If you're terrible, come back and do academics. Just don't be mediocre."

After graduation, Mignone packed up and moved back to New York, joining Griffin and Rich Bello, chief financial officer for the new fund, Blue Ridge Capital. Mignone was one of only two members of his eight-hundred-student class to take a job at a hedge fund. "The other guy didn't last four months because he hated it so much," Mignone says. Overall, only five people went into equity investing from Harvard that year. Equities just weren't cool in the mid-1990s. Everyone had read Michael Lewis's *Liar's Poker*, which made clear that the worst job in an investment bank is "equities in Dallas." Today, Mignone estimates he gets 400 résumés a year from Harvard Business School students looking for work.

It didn't take three years for Mignone to realize his professor was right: He was a good analyst, and he loved the work. But by the time three years had passed, he wanted to strike out on his own. The timing seemed fortuitous. Blue Ridge had had a phenomenal year in 1999, so he didn't feel as if he was leaving his partners in the lurch. And his wife was still working for Mandel's Lone Pine Capital, so he knew that even if he bombed, one of them would be bringing home a solid paycheck. Mignone also had two partners in mind, men he'd known a long time and who wanted to join him. One was Blake Goodner, a junior analyst in health care at Tiger, and the other was Michael Tierney, who had been the Morgan Stanley point person for Blue Ridge for its brokerage services.

Having been at Blue Ridge from the beginning, Mignone knew the most essential ingredient for success in a start-up is the chemistry of the team. "I didn't have to guess about the chemistry," he says. "We might have gotten a bad market, we might have made some wrong investment decisions, but we were a team before we even launched." Within a few months, the three were managing $80 million and Mignone was doing what he does best: digging deep into companies being considered for investment, which he says is the only way to develop a view that differs from consensus.

"I view myself first and foremost as an analyst," says Mignone. "The important thing we do as analysts is to come up with a central thesis and then build the evidence to try to prove ourselves wrong." For Mignone, those central ideas should be clear and simple to communicate. A brief sentence should encapsulate the whole story. Mignone once heard a comic capture this idea, when he joked that no one reads anymore because books are too long. The comedian argued that you could sum up any great work of literature in one sentence; the rest is superfluous. The eight-hundred- plus-page *Moby-Dick* boils down to this: "Don't hunt white whales that symbolize nature and will kill you."

This premise recalled for Mignone the lessons of classical literature of his high school and college days. The outcomes of the *Odyssey* and the *Iliad* are forecasted in their very first lines, and almost any Greek tragedy is encapsulated in the last five lines of the chorus. "If you could sum up the masterpieces of all time in a single sentence, you should be able to present a compelling research idea in one sentence, too," says Mignone, "a Hemingway-like sentence."

Less than compelling, in Mignone's opinion, is much of the research published by Wall Street firms. He discovered early in his career that a lot of it is incomplete or just plain wrong. The sell-side analysts often do little more than talk to company executives and take their word for the strength of a business's prospects. Mignone and his team seek out primary sources to verify what they're told by the company's management. They supplement visits to the company itself by going to trade shows and industry conferences and talking to trade journalists and competitors. After doing his own sleuthing, Mignone often finds himself wanting to short a company that Wall Street analysts have touted.

One analysts' darling was SureBeam Corporation, a company that sold ground beef that it had irradiated to kill off bacteria, such as *E. coli* and *salmonella*, and make the meat "safe." Mignone started shorting SureBeam in March 2001, soon after its parent, Titan Corporation, spun out a portion of the unit to the public. SureBeam's zapped beef cost about one cent more per hamburger patty, a price the company was betting consumers would gladly pay to have bacteria-free food. Wall Street analysts put buy recommendations on the stock, and it rose from its $10 initial public offering (IPO) price to $19 by the end of May, as the company reported strong sales in its test markets.

As the position moved against them, Mignone and analyst Joel Ramin dug in, trying to determine whether irradiating hamburger meat would ruin the taste or otherwise make it less appealing and whether shoppers would actually pay a premium for the service. To find the answers to those questions, they visited the company, saw the centers where it irradiated the beef, and drove to upstate New York and Illinois to check out the stores where test marketing was going on.

There, they hit research pay dirt. People were indeed buying the SureBeam meat, just as the company and Wall Street analysts reported. What Wall Street didn't know was that SureBeam was discounting the meat by as much as 20 percent using in-store promotions. With that data in hand, Mignone added to the short in

June, when the stock was trading at around $16, and by the beginning
of October, the stock plummeted to less than $5. "There was basically
no demand for irradiated beef, which seemed obviously predictable to
me," says Mignone.

In September, however, came the unexpected, and Mignone
got blindsided. NBC News, American Media, and a U.S. senator
were sent letters containing anthrax, and scores of other
companies reported receiving suspicious packages containing
white powder. Almost overnight, SureBeam dropped the idea of
food irradiation and brought the business of irradiating mail front
and center. News spread that the U.S. Postal Service was looking
at SureBeam's technology, and by mid-October the government
had placed an initial order to buy eight irradiating machines from
SureBeam, with the option to purchase more, sending the stock
soaring to $15.41 from $4.80 in less than three weeks. Bridger's
50-plus percent average gain had just turned into a 200-plus
percent paper loss from trough to peak, because Mignone had
shorted the shares at an average of $10 and they were now worth
more than $15.

Scrambling to reassess the situation, Mignone and Ramin looked
for some answers. Would the U.S. Postal Service indeed end up buying
machines for every postal distribution center? Would Congress fund
such a venture? Did the technology work? They got on the phone
and started talking to postal inspectors and Congressional aides to
ascertain the government's commitment to such a plan.

The Bridger team had their doubts about how well the
technology would transfer from food to letters. When they visited
the company's test facility in Iowa, three-foot-thick concrete walls
surrounded the machines, and a woman on the team had to sign
a disclaimer verifying that she wasn't pregnant. The worry over
radiation levels made the likelihood of the machines appearing
in postal distribution centers fairly slim, Mignone reckoned. He
and his analysts also learned that the amount of radiation needed
to kill anthrax was substantial enough to turn mail packages into
crispy critters. As Mignone and his team debunked what they called
the "postal story," Bridger continued to add to its short position,
borrowing shares at prices as low as $3 in April 2003. SureBeam
announced its liquidation in January 2004. They shorted the stock
into bankruptcy.

In exploring SureBeam, Mignone had followed a course he learned from John Griffin: When a position moves against you, don't panic; research. Nor did he try to trade around the position. "Over the long run," says Mignone, "it has turned out better to have a position size in mind and stick with it until our research can be proven right or wrong." Once the facts were all in on SureBeam, he shorted even more shares and waited for the inevitable disappointments. By early 2002, the shares were back down around $5.

Research rules at Bridger, whose analysts—the firm has eight in addition to Mignone—do the work of looking for investment themes. All but two are generalists, another nod to Mignone's liberal arts education, in which specialty training takes a backseat to logical and creative thinking. The other two, Blake Goodner and Shaheen Wirk, are health-care specialists. Mignone didn't set out looking for analysts with particular backgrounds; it was talent he was after. "We hire individuals, not roles," says Mignone, "so we look for an analyst who we can feel confident will do the kind of work that we do and will fit in well culturally with us." The aim is simple: He wants people who can come up with great investment ideas.

Because Bridger's model is to hold positions for three years, the hit rate needs to be high and the returns big. Mignone's core positions include roughly thirty long positions, which are each limited to 5 percent of the portfolio initially and never get larger than 10 percent. He has about sixty core short positions, each no bigger than 2 percent at the start. He never allows them to grow bigger than 4 percent. Overall, the gross exposure is 150 to 200 percent, meaning the value of the long and short positions adds up to 1.5 to 2 times the net assets in the fund. The net exposure is between 20 and 60 percent.

Coming up with good ideas takes time, and an analyst who proposes a good moneymaker once a month is doing a great job, says Mignone. Each Friday, the team walks through a potential investment idea. They discuss the evidence they've gathered to support the thesis and brainstorm about what might go wrong and how they might gather additional information to ensure their premise is correct. The analysts' compensation is based on the overall performance of the fund, so there's a strong incentive for people to cooperate. All the research on every position is available to all staff members via an information-sharing software program.

The generalist approach makes for lively discussions, Mignone says. "There's not a lot of: 'I'm an expert, don't question my work.'" Even in specialist areas like biotechnology, the generalists' questions are as penetrating as those from the people who know the health-care industry inside out, says Mignone. That's partly because the generalists' exposure to all manner of industries gives them a fresh perspective. "We absolutely collaborate as peers on research," says Mignone, although he is the only member of the team to decide whether an idea makes it into the portfolio and what size it should be.

When Mignone started Bridger, clients invested because he was a good short seller and a great researcher, and he knew a lot about health care. "When I look at my team today, I can see that I've made myself obsolete in many ways," says Mignone. "Goodner is a better health-care analyst than I ever was, and Joel Ramin is a better short seller. I'm very fortunate because these guys have been with me almost since day one. They've created the culture here as much as I have. We have a shared philosophy."

The strength of Mignone's team has made for strong performance on both rising and falling shares. Between 2000 and the end of 2006, Bridger's shorts and longs produced about equal returns, although the short book is more volatile. In 2003, for example, Bridger's wagers on falling stocks did not make money. That was also the only year Mignone didn't beat the Standard & Poor's 500 Index benchmark. One problem was a dearth of stocks to bet against. The Internet bubble had spent roughly two years deflating, and the worst companies were already out of business. His longs that year averaged returns of 40 percent versus 26 percent for the index, but his short positions on individual stocks (he doesn't short indexes or exchange-traded funds) lost 30 percent.

Shorting in general has gotten dicier since Mignone's early days in the industry because more investors are betting on falling shares than ever before, and many of them don't have a huge amount of know-how or talent, says Mignone. One case in point is a short—a Seattle-based biotechnology company named Dendreon Corporation—that was in Mignone's portfolio since November 2006 and one he figured would be gone by the time this book was published. The company had developed a vaccine, called Provenge, to fight prostate cancer. As the drugmaker was preparing its presentation to be made before an advisory committee for the Food and Drug Administration (FDA) in March 2007, Mignone and his team were doing some preparation of their own. "We looked at the quality of the data and thought it was inconclusive at best and failed to meet any of the standards that the FDA uses to approve a product," says Mignone, who has followed FDA decisions since he started at Blue Ridge. He was sure the advisory committee, whose counsel the government is not obliged to follow but usually does, would reject the drug. Instead, the committee approved it, stating the drug was safe and "substantially effective." The news pushed Dendreon stock from about $5 to $13. Within two weeks, it reached nearly $24.

Further complicating matters, almost one-third of the stock's outstanding shares on the market had been borrowed and sold, indicating that many investors agreed with Mignone's thesis. "When short interest creeps up in a name, the field becomes crowded fast because there's a lot of me-too shorting," says Mignone. "When a little bit of good news comes out on a heavily crowded short, the weak hands tend to panic and get out." Bridger's mistake with Dendreon was in making a consensus play. Although Mignone was quite confident that he was right about the stock—and continued to short it after the advisory committee vote—he hadn't counted on the short-term squeeze as other investors covered their position. "We had very little differentiated edge. It's much more dangerous to be in a heavily crowded short name."

Suspenseful as it was, Mignone was right to hang on. About a month after our interview, in April 2007, the FDA said it needed more information to approve the drug, and the stock fell back to $5. His average cost of shorting the shares before the FDA vote was around $4.50. As of August 2007, the stock was trading at around $7, and Mignone had covered some of the position.

Favored shorts aren't the only positions in the market that are brimming with hedge fund dollars these days. Managers are crowding into the same long positions, too. It seems as if every manager has found the same fifty to one hundred stocks, Mignone says. "That's mathematically impossible. Something has created an order out of what should be a random return," he says. He suspects that analysts sharing ideas accounts for the herd mentality.

Such gabfests are damaging to hedge fund performance, he says. Coming out of business school, he had no network to speak of. He knew few people in the investment community, and the people he did meet generally had a lot more experience and more advanced skills than he did. "So when I interacted with people in the hedge fund community," says Mignone, "I learned from them, and there was a great mentoring system as a result." For his part, Mignone worked hard to uncover valuable data to make it worth their while to talk to him.

He reckons that the number of people you know well in the hedge fund arena is inversely correlated to the amount of time you've spent in the industry. "I have the smallest Rolodex of anyone in my firm, having been here the longest," he says, although much of that difference comes from attrition as older managers leave the business. His junior people have an enormous network because they have fifty, sixty, or seventy friends from their business school classes or from their college classes who are working at fifty or sixty different hedge funds. That means that when they talk to other folks in the industry, they are generally interacting with people who have no more experience than they do. The mentoring process has disappeared, says Mignone. "It's becoming tougher to develop great new talent in the industry because the noise level is so high."

Another bandwagon syndrome—and one that Mignone warns young analysts to stay away from—is jumping on the industry du jour. In 1997 and 1998, when he was at Blue Ridge, he spent a lot of time looking at energy and oil-services companies. "I'd go to these lunches that Wall Street would put together and look around the room and think, my God, this is like looking at the ghost of Christmas future for me," says Mignone. "The average person in the room was a fifty-five-year-old balding white guy with a red nose and a poorly cut suit, and lunch was always prime rib and a potato. The tables were half empty." The luncheon giveaway would be a company decal to stick on your hard hat. During those years, Mignone's wife was a retail and Internet analyst at Lone Pine. At her lunches, everyone was twenty-five and wearing black Armani suits and eating sushi. "The giveaway was an electronic gadget."

Now, of course, oil and gas is where it's at. At an energy conference at the Waldorf-Astoria in the fall of 2005, Mignone had the impression he was the oldest person in the room. "The huge opportunity to make a tremendous amount of money in the energy boom existed partially because not a lot of people with brains and talent were assigned to that space during the energy bust of 1982 to 2002," he says. "We had a twenty-year drought of talent. You don't want to look around the room as a young person and see a crowd around you because it's very difficult to have a long-term sustainable advantage."

Mignone's own career path illustrates the importance of taking your cues from strong mentors rather than from widespread consensus. Without older managers to offer advice and counsel, he suspects that he might not have made the transition from analyst to portfolio manager, a move he says was initially unsettling to him, largely because he was so wedded to in-depth, independent research. As a portfolio manager, he went from having 70 percent to 90 percent of what he thought he needed to know about an investment, down to 40 percent or 50 percent, most of which was information he had not unearthed himself. "You have to learn how to make decisions with less information than what you've found traditionally comfortable, and you have to learn to rely on an analyst to give you that information, so it's no longer primary," says Mignone. "Those are both big challenges." Ironically, over time, he discovered that the smaller amount of information he was compelled to work with was all he really needed to know. The rest was superfluous.

Mignone's need to be able to trust his analysts is part of the reason he doesn't hire people in that role unless he knows them very well. "It takes us years to find people with whom we can have that relationship from the get-go," he says. "That decision is not something you can base on a résumé and five hours of interviews." The analysts Mignone hires are the ones who'd be working in hedge funds even if they weren't the hottest area of investment management. They're passionate about investing rather than just chasing the biggest paycheck. "That's missing, by the way, from a lot of résumés I see. They're nondescript, rather than showing some underlying love and passion for what we do."

Mignone takes a characteristically classicist view of the future of the hedge fund industry. "We wanted to start businesses, we wanted to be our own bosses, we wanted to run a partnership, and we wanted to manage our own capital," he says. "There was no thought about building businesses and monetizing them and institutionalizing them." "Big" is not a destination that especially interests him. In particular, he has no desire to run a much larger fund. "I still believe that asset growth is to the detriment of performance if what you're going to be is a long-short specialist."

He reminds managers starting out that fewer and fewer funds make up the bulk of the industry, so those after hefty paydays had better look to Wall Street. Some back-of-the-envelope calculations prove his point: The top one hundred hedge fund firms managed about 68 percent of all assets at the end of 2006. That means an estimated twenty-three hundred single-manager hedge fund firms ran the remaining $460 billion, or an average of about $200 million each. Given an average hedge fund performance of about 8 percent a year since the beginning of 2000, each firm can count on making roughly $3.2 million from its performance fee, which would most likely be divvied up among a number of partners. The average bonus for a managing director at a New York investment-banking firm in 2006 was $2.8 million.

Young people need to be clear on why they want to work for a hedge fund, says Mignone. "They better be doing it because they love being an entrepreneur or because they have enough personal wealth to be running their own money." Hedge funds are not a sure path to riches. To make his point, Mignone points out that according to University of Chicago economist Steven Levitt in his best-selling book, *Freakonomics*, a crack dealer in Chicago has a 25 percent chance of dying within four years. Roughly one of every two new hedge funds fails within three to five years. "So you've got a better chance of surviving as a crack dealer in Chicago than lasting four years in the hedge fund business."

Granted, the odds would-be managers face are tough, but life goes on after a hedge fund fails, even if it doesn't pay as well.

AFTER THE CRISIS

Repairing the Damage

Mignone, who runs Bridger Capital, with assets of $2.2 billion, says a great investment idea can be summed up in one sentence. He takes the same approach to explaining his Swiftcurrent fund's 20 percent loss in 2008: "Bridger Capital's singular error was to remain far more net long than conditions warranted," he told investors in early 2009.

"The clearest lesson is that when our investment style is so clearly out of synch with the environment, we should bring our exposures down more quickly," he says. Generally, Mignone borrows about 80 cents for every dollar of net assets. His portfolio is traditionally 20 percent to 50 percent net long. Net long refers to total long positions (assets whose value the holder expects to rise), including borrowed money, minus total short positions (assets whose value the holder expects to fall). That positioning has protected him from large market swings in the past, but not in the last part of 2008.

Mignone also erred in sticking with his usual investment horizon. He's had success buying stocks that he expects will double in value over two to three years. He doesn't worry much about the near-term outlook as long as the future looks rosy. In 2008, that "long-run" thinking hurt the portfolio. "This year, our faith in the ability to project long-term opportunities made us more dismissive about the near-term dangers than in hindsight we should have been," Mignone told investors as 2008 was coming to a close. "Our contrarian tendency to buy to the 'sound of cannons' compounded this error in the fall, as being the one buyer standing against a mob of sellers hurt—a lot."

Mignone says that asset growth should come through returns rather than from giant marketing efforts to pull in new clients. He told investors at the end of 2008 that he would replace only capital that left the fund, with priority given to current clients. He saw no net redemptions in 2008, whereas other firms saw an average outflow of 20 percent of assets.

As of mid-May 2009, the swings in U.S. stock prices had abated, returning to pre–Lehman bankruptcy levels, yet Mignone's borrowing was still below where it had been historically and his net long exposure was about 20 percent. He was more mindful of near-term risks and said he was focusing even more on catalysts that will move a stock price up or down.

At the same time, he didn't want to position his portfolio too conservatively. "Candidly, we want to make sure that we haven't constructed a portfolio for the coming year that we *should* have had 8 months ago," he said in early 2009. As of September 30, his flagship fund had climbed 11 percent for the year and assets had grown to $2.4 billion.

The approach was paying off. Swiftcurrent was up about 5 percent as of mid-May, compared with a 1.5 percent gain for the benchmark index. Mignone said he would increase borrowing and net exposure once it became clearer how much bad news was already priced into stocks and how well the government's $787 billion economic stimulus plan was working.

Mignone sees 2009 as a chance for all hedge funds to repair their tarnished reputations. "Long-short equity managers had their *Lord Jim* moment in 2008—when called upon in a moment of danger and crisis to exhibit their courage and skill, they collectively failed," Mignone wrote to his clients in 2009, referring to the Joseph Conrad tale of a British seaman who abandoned a sinking ship, leaving his passengers to fend for themselves.

"I know that we at Bridger feel an obligation to make up for that disappointment; I personally want another chance, like Conrad's Jim, to pass that test."

Chapter 14

Bruce Ritter
Mastering a Changing Market

BRUCE RITTER GREW UP on a two-thousand-acre farm in Bonanza, Oregon. His family raised cattle and grew wheat, barley, and alfalfa, and Ritter did his fair share of hard labor: branding cattle, planting crops, and driving combines. Today, Ritter runs $500 million Yannix Management, named for a small mountain in southern Oregon that one can see from the fields of his family's farm, which his brother now runs. Yannix trades corn, wheat, soybeans, cattle, hogs, and other livestock.

Ritter, fifty-seven, is lanky with dark hair and a calm, professorial air. When he talks shop, he sounds a lot like an academic, tossing out phrases like *price elasticity* and *tail events* (his undergraduate degree from Oregon State is in economics). Yet he sees his edge as coming, in part, from those days on the farm, when he learned firsthand that the price of a commodity drives farmers' behavior. He knows the price at which farmers will decide to plant one crop rather than another, or switch one kind of animal feed for another. It's all about substitution.

Joining a network of funds—called Ospraie Wingspan—seeded by Dwight Anderson's Ospraie Management, Ritter opened Yannix in July 2005. In exchange for undisclosed portions of the 2 percent management fee and the 23 percent of any profits Ritter charges his clients, Ospraie takes care of all the administrative and operational business of the fund once the trades have been placed. Ritter is free to spend 95 percent of his time on investing, which he does from a sparsely furnished office in Wilton, Connecticut, with a five-person investment staff that includes a meteorologist.

Ritter's fascination with agricultural commodities remains undiminished after more than thirty years in the business. "Agriculture affects everything in the world," says Ritter, "and everything in the world affects agriculture." He has a point. If the housing market dries up, that could send beef consumption tumbling as families feel poorer and opt for chicken or pork over steak. Likewise, higher economic growth in China may mean an office worker in Beijing goes to KFC twice a week instead of once. "Understanding where the economic stress points are and which way the political winds are blowing is extremely important. Our markets are a function of economic analysis, politics, and the weather," he says.

Yannix made its debut at a particularly interesting time both for the commodities markets and for Ritter. Launching a hedge fund is considered a younger man's game, with most managers making the move in their late twenties or thirties. Ritter was a few months shy of his fifty-fifth birthday when he decided to go out on his own. He had spent nearly thirty years in both manage-ment and risk-management positions with the commodities trader Louis Dreyfus, and for his last two and a half years, he managed an agricultural commodities fund using the firm's own capital. "I was at a point in my career where I wanted a change," says Ritter. "I wanted a new challenge and this was it."

Ritter had known Dwight Anderson over the years, and he respected him. He also liked the business model at Wingspan, and he figured raising money would be relatively easy, given the huge bull market in commodities. A range of investors—from wealthy individuals to funds that invest in hedge funds—was clamoring to put cash into commodities, once the backwater of finance. Ritter was right about the pent-up demand, and by 2007 he had reached his self-imposed limit on the amount of capital he wanted to manage, given the relatively small size of his markets.

As Yannix started up, Ritter saw seismic shifts taking place in the commodities markets. "They're dynamic markets, and if you look back ten years from now, you're going to see some dramatic changes. We're not all going to survive," says Ritter. "To enter this field, either you have to be naïve or you've got to think your skills are well above average."

The market changes Ritter foresaw are the result of two trends: increased interest in fuel made from corn and other agricultural commodities, and huge inflows into commodities funds from institutional investors. Both have changed the very nature of how commodities trade.

The push to use so-called biofuels like ethanol started in earnest with the passage of the Energy Policy Act of 2005, which requires that 7.5 billion gallons—5 percent—of the nation's annual gasoline consumption come from renewable fuels by 2012. In his State of the Union address in January 2007, President George W. Bush mandated that the United States cut gasoline consumption by 20 percent by 2017, replacing it with biofuels.

Ritter, for one, thinks this push for biofuels is bad public policy. The modest energy savings, he says, are far outweighed by the danger of cutting food supplies around the world, particularly in third world countries. Heavy government subsidies are encouraging the production of ethanol from sugar and corn and the production of biodiesel from soybeans. The trouble, as Ritter sees it, is that the first time there's a major drought or other natural event that reduces supply, governments will be faced with a dreadful dilemma: Do we feed people or fuel cars?

Over time, Ritter says, politicians will understand these dangers, but he doesn't see enlightenment coming overnight. "Politics is a popularity contest," says Ritter. "And today the use of biofuels is popular. It sells well in Des Moines and it sells well in San Francisco. It's not going to sell that well when there's a shortage of meat. And it doesn't sell well today in the developing world." Warning signs are already appearing. The demand for corn by ethanol producers drove the price of the grain up 80 percent between the beginning of 2006 and mid-2007, and that's already causing problems in Mexico, where half of the average citizen's calories come from corn tortillas. The government intervened in early 2007 to ask retailers and food manufacturers to cap corn tortilla prices.

The other major catalyst in the commodities markets is the entrance of institutional investors, who started buying commodities in about 2002 through index funds and other so-called long-only products, which wager exclusively on the rising price of commodities. As prices have steadily risen, more pension funds and other large investors have jumped in, buying into funds run by Goldman Sachs and other large financial services firms. The investors betting on commodities these days are doing so for the long haul because they foresee huge demand coming from China and emerging markets. These huge inflows make the market much less predictable in the short term, although in the longer term, the forces of supply and demand still apply. For example, a forecast for better-than-expected weather in the Great Plains would normally mean greater supply and lower prices. Nowadays that drop in price might be less severe than expected—at least initially—because of the money pouring into commodities funds from the likes of Goldman Sachs buying futures for their index fund investors and pushing prices higher. "The endgame is clear; how you get there is not always clear," says Ritter.

These investment flows in late 2006 threw Ritter a curveball that cost him about 9 percentage points of performance that year. Although his funds ended the year up 11 percent, that's below his long-term target of about 15 percent a year, a return he aims to make without losing more than 5 percent in any given month.

September 2006 was not one of those months. The price of wheat by then had already risen about 30 percent since January because of droughts in the United States and Europe and dry weather in Australia, which led to the perception that the world was going to run out of the grain. Ritter wasn't convinced. He calculated that given the rise in wheat prices, farmers were already feeding their livestock corn or other types of feed so the current supply of wheat would be adequate. The price rise had persuaded growers in Russia and other former Soviet Union countries on the Black Sea to plant more wheat, and that wheat, he figured, would be exported, rather than used domestically.

So Ritter made a wager—what's known in the commodities world as a calendar trade. He bet that the price difference, or spread, between the most active futures contract at the time (due to expire in December 2006) and futures for delivery in July 2007 (the first month of the following year's crop) would increase. Normally, because of storage costs for agricultural commodities, the futures contracts closest to expiration are less expensive than those that expire later. On September 28, the December 2006 futures were trading at about $0.15 less than July 2007 futures.

Later that same day, Australia's sole wheat exporter estimated that the drought would cut wheat production by half, more than anyone was expecting. The news sent December 2006 futures contract trading in Chicago to a nine-year high. The amount of cash from institutional investors that was pouring into commodities at the time created a shortage of futures and exaggerated the price jump, as did the fact that producers were selling a smaller amount of futures to hedge price moves. Over the next eight trading days, the spread between December 2006 futures and July 2007 futures jumped to over $1 as the price of the near-term futures rose above those expiring the following year. Ritter and other investors who had been betting the December futures would drop in price got creamed.

It was the most dramatic price move Ritter had seen in his thirty-plus-year career in that it was not caused by weather, political unrest, or other "normal" events. "I've seen larger absolute price movements, but they were explainable price movements," says Ritter. With stops in place as insurance against such price swings, he eventually was forced to sell his position. Within thirty days, the markets were back to where they had been in late September. "It was a classic case of being right on the economic analysis, right on the long-term consequences of price, but underestimating the volatility of the path." He credits the use of stops with saving him from losing a lot more money. "Anybody who doesn't use stops is going to be out of business at some point. It's not *if*; it's *when*."

The influence of long-term investors on commodities prices has prompted Ritter to change the kind of research he does. Before 2002, he spent most of his time looking at crop production and weather as a means of forecasting prices. That's no longer enough. He must also try to divine how much cash is going into commodities index funds. Nowadays, he says, absent any unusual weather, these flows are the biggest determinant of price in any thirty-day period. Getting such data is difficult, though, because the big banks that run the commodities funds aren't likely to tell the world what they're doing. "If you're Goldman, the last thing you're going to do is tell me that I've got a billion dollars coming in or a billion dollars going out," says Ritter.

As more traders have come into the market, Ritter spends more of his time second-guessing less experienced investors. "The markets have excess information," says Ritter. "There's so much noise that it's very hard to know—but very important to know—which data are most important on any given day. And it also makes a difference, more so than it used to, to understand what other people *think* is important." For example, an economic indicator may be coming out that Ritter has learned from his long experience is meaningless for commodities. Yet, if a group of investors think it's important, it becomes important.

Ritter is also cognizant of his relatively puny size compared to that of other players in the market. "There are a lot of multibillion-dollar hedge funds that have the ability to move money into or out of agriculture very quickly," says Ritter. When they are wagering against him, it's best to get out of the way.

Also worrisome to Ritter is the fallout for his markets should there be a major crisis—if political support for ethanol suddenly dries up, for example, or if the economy unexpectedly slows. A rush of investors all trying to exit at the same time would wreak havoc on prices. This prospect has made Ritter more conservative in his investing, and as of July 2007, he was up about 2 percent for the year. "People that get in easily won't always be able to get out easily," he says.

Although Ritter keeps a vigilant finger on the pulse of investment flows into commodities, he continues to do the same kind of research he's always done, and good weather forecasting is a huge part of whether his investments are successful. Suppose, for example, that an acre of land produces 153 bushels under typical weather conditions. Even relatively small differences in weather can cause that production to vary between, say, 145 bushels and 165 bushels. Most investors don't realize that such differences in yields have a significant effect on prices, Ritter says, and that's why an accurate weather forecast is so important. ·

Complicating that task, however, is the abundance of meteorological data now available. "There's a lot more information out there now, 90 percent of which is irrelevant. And the weather forecaster's job, and my job, is to determine which 10 percent of the input is meaningful and which 90 percent is extraneous."

The judgment needed to sort that data is not unlike what's required in culling for profitable trades. The same attributes that make a good trader also make a good meteorologist, Ritter says. They both take a set of data, analyze it, and make a forecast. A very talented meteorologist is probably right 65 percent of the time, and if the weather map changes, the meteorologist has to change the forecast. "It demands the same objectivity and dispassionate analysis and ability to understand when the situation changes as does trading," says Ritter. Indeed, at Louis Dreyfus, Ritter's knack for uncovering essential information enabled him to take on the kind of calculated risk that Anderson said he was so good at assessing. The market in 2004 was expecting a shortage of soybeans, which caused the spread between the July futures contract and the following November futures contract to widen. "This is one of those classic arbitrage trades which either makes people a lot of money or, from time to time, takes people out of business," says Ritter.

The perception of a soybean shortage in the near term was so great that the price of July futures rose higher than the price of November futures. As with the more recent wheat trade, Ritter thought the perception was all wrong. For starters, there was a surplus of soybeans in South America, notably Brazil and Argentina, and he knew that if the shortage in the United States was severe enough, South American soybeans would make their way north to meet the demand. What's more, Ritter had a good handle on the amount of investment flows coming into the market. He also had forecast that the weather in July was improving—so more soybeans would be produced—and he reckoned that farmers had already cut their demand for soybean meal by substituting corn to feed their livestock.

Confident, Ritter made a bet, increased with borrowed money, that soybean prices would tumble. He made the wager by buying put options whose exercise price was far below where soybeans were currently trading. He figured the plunge would come soon, once the other market participants understood just how much substitution of animal feed had already taken place, and when it did, the price swing would be dramatic. "Markets in their final phase are very vertical," he says. The profits from Ritter's wager were substantial. "That's a case where the experience of understanding historical price relationships and price elasticity served me well. That's our job, to understand that we're at a flex point in the markets."

Doing a money manager's job well, in Ritter's view, takes someone who's creative enough to understand dynamic changes in the market, has the conviction to execute those trades, and has the discipline to understand that when a mistake's been made, it's time to look for the next trade. "You have to know when to hold 'em and know when to fold 'em," says Ritter. "You have to recognize that the amount of capital held by someone across the table from you is very, very large. That means you have to get out of positions quickly—even if you're right. That takes discipline and conviction."

Ritter's conviction that he has the necessary discipline to conserve his investors' capital is strong. But after twenty-one months at the helm of his own firm, he has some concerns. "I have not achieved the returns I would have liked to achieve over time and part of that is the need to adjust to a different market makeup," says Ritter. He does not expect the current market dynamics to last forever, though. He's convinced that something is going to go wrong in the next five to ten years—whether it's an unexpected slowdown in the Chinese economy, a change of heart from the government about the practicality of biofuels, or poor returns from index funds that eventually drive institutional investors away—which will make for a very difficult market situation. Most investors in these markets don't realize the magnitude of this risk, says Ritter. "I want to make sure that I am not caught in it."

Essential as his experience and expertise may be, Ritter knows they can be a handicap if they blind him to new forces in the market. "I think they're a very definite plus over time, but in the short term, they can easily lead you to be right too early," says Ritter. "Being too far ahead of the herd can be as painful as being behind it."

AFTER THE CRISIS

Profits and Predictions

In mid-2007, Ritter predicted that within five years an event would occur that would make trading in agricultural markets extremely treacherous. "I want to make sure I'm not caught in it," he said.

Within a year, the market tumult Ritter had expected came to pass. Not only did he avoid trouble in 2008, he made a 20 percent

return for his investors—the fund's fourth year of positive returns—
and beat the average hedge fund performance by a cool 40 percentage points.

In a year when unprecedented events undermined returns,
Ritter's Yannix Fund benefited from his three decades of experience in
the markets. In the first half of the year, he made the sort of so-called
relative-value trades that are his bread and butter. When markets got
especially choppy toward the end of 2008, he reduced risk and headed
for the sidelines.

One of his money-makers was a trade that he first put on in the
fourth quarter of 2007, based on his view that demand for soybeans,
especially from China, would outstrip demand. At the same time, he
forecast a bumper crop of wheat, which would eventually push down
the price of the grain. So he shorted wheat, which rose from around
$9.66 a bushel in late 2007 to a high of $12.82 in March 2008,
before falling to $7.43 by the end of May. At the same time, soybean
futures rose from $11.68 a bushel in mid-December 2007 to $13.22
a bushel by the end of May.

As the global financial crisis deepened, commodities went into a
free-fall beginning in mid-July, and the Reuters/Jefferies CRB Index
ended the year roughly 50 percent lower. The magnitude of the price
moves picked up in the third quarter to the point where they were
no longer being driven by fundamentals. Ritter cut his positions and
increased his cash levels, as he has done throughout his career when
markets move against him. His use of options, buying puts and calls,
also helped protect the fund against the violent swing in values.

Even though Yannix was among the small number of funds
that profited in 2008, investors asked for 50 percent of their
money back because the fund did not prohibit them from doing
so. Other hedge funds blocked redemptions in 2008 because they
held hard-to-sell assets and wanted to avoid a fire sale. At their
peak in June 2008, Yannix assets stood at more than $600 million.
By early 2009, they had fallen to $270 million, and by May 1, they
had climbed to $400 million. In the first four months of 2009,
the fund lost 5 percent; still, last year's performance is helping to
attract new assets. "This is a difficult investment environment, but
one that we believe will continue to reward performance and risk
management," Ritter says. "Our ability to begin to rebuild assets
indicates investors agree with us."

Chapter 15

Julian Robertson

Encores

JULIAN ROBERTSON, seventy-five, settles into a low, off-white upholstered chair in his office on the top floor of a forty-eight-story building on Park Avenue. From his vantage point, he can look south, all the way down the Hudson River to the mouth of New York Harbor and the Verrazano Bridge. A Picasso painting hangs in the conference room next door. Robertson is not in the mood to discuss his career as a legendary stock picker, and pressed on how he went about teaching his analysts the art of investing, he answers reluctantly. "I didn't teach them anything about how to be good investors," he says, his North Carolinian drawl still strong even after decades of living in New York. "They were extremely capable, wonderful people. They had the qualities. They would have done well anywhere."

I prod him again, and he finally folds. "Okay. I'm being a bit falsely modest," he admits. "I know I was a pretty good teacher. But I think it's been exaggerated." Probably not. And his hedge fund Tiger Management's long-term track record—one of the best in the business—is *certainly* not.

Notwithstanding his reticence to claim a talent for mentoring, Robertson speaks with confidence about the talent he selected for the firm. "What we did well was pick good people." Pick well he did. In the two decades that Robertson ran Tiger Management—earning stellar returns of 25 percent a year—his shop produced a disproportionate number of highly successful hedge fund managers, known affectionately as the "Tiger Cubs." Lee Ainslie (see Chapter 6); Dwight Anderson (see Chapter 12); Stephen Mandel, who runs Lone Pine Capital; John Griffin, of Blue Ridge Capital; and Andreas Halvorsen, of Viking Global Investors, are the best known of the group, each now running a multibillion-dollar hedge fund firm.

After twenty years in business, Robertson's Tiger Management, once the largest hedge fund in the world, closed its doors in 2000, when Robertson was a few months shy of his sixty-eighth birthday. He had decided to return investor capital following eighteen painful months of investment losses and client redemptions that caused assets under management to tumble from $22 billion in August 1998 to $6 billion in March 2000. It was the height of the Internet bubble, and the stock valuations made no sense to Robertson, who always looked for good companies selling cheaply. "There is no point in subjecting our investors to risk in a market which I frankly do not understand," he wrote to his clients.

Shutting down the fund meant losing contact with new ideas and energetic young people, and that scared Robertson. "I didn't want to go from my sixties to Methuselah," he says, referring to the Old Testament's most senior of citizens. So he stayed involved in the hedge fund business by seeding start-up funds. "We had this big floor space, so I took a chance and decided to keep it and put a few people to work in here starting their own funds." Initially, he seeded five young managers, all of whom had been working at Tiger.

Still in the business of identifying talent—and still doing a good job of it—as part of his new venture, Robertson continues to provide seed capital to young managers and now has a stable of twenty-five funds. Twenty-one are housed in his New York offices, with the remaining funds in Sun Valley, Idaho; Chicago; Baton Rouge, Louisiana; and Atlanta. In total, they run $12 billion. In 2006, these funds together produced a return of 23 percent, far above the benchmark index and other stock pickers. The largest of them, both closed to new investors, are run by two members of the original group: Bill Hwang's $4.4 billion Tiger Asia Fund, which returned 15.8 percent through July 2007, and Chase Coleman's $3.9 billion Tiger Global Fund, which was up 28 percent.

Robertson met Hwang when he was an institutional stock salesman at Hyundai Securities, talking to clients like Robertson about Korean equities. Every year, Tiger gave a prize—$50,000 to the philanthropy of the winner's choice—to the person outside of Tiger who had contributed the most to the hedge fund's success. Hwang won and shortly thereafter, in 1995, Robertson hired him.

Coleman joined Tiger in 1997 as a technology analyst, after graduating from Williams College. He helped run a Tiger technology portfolio for eight months before the firm shut down. Under the seeding organization, also called Tiger Management, Coleman launched the Tiger Technology Fund, which now invests in all manner of stocks and has been renamed Tiger Global.

Robertson likes to have smaller funds in the pipeline, with assets anywhere between $50 million to $250 million. "We want to always have a group that's coming along into that sweet spot," he says.

Robertson may not want to talk much about his approach to nurturing talent, but his methods speak for themselves. In his seeding business, Robertson's mentoring skills are evident. He leads a regular meeting with the portfolio managers at which they critique each other's best ideas. Robertson says he tries not to be too vocal. "These guys are running money for people, they have their own philosophies that might very well not fit into mine," he says, "but I will give my two cents' worth."

The best exchanges are when one manager wants to go long a particular stock or sector and another one wants to short it. "Very seldom do people change their minds," says Robertson, although he figures that the other portfolio managers learn from listening to the bullish and bearish cases. The younger managers also seek him out informally to ask his advice, and he sees his age as an advantage, just as it was when he was forty-eight and launched Tiger with a bunch of twenty- and thirty-year-old analysts. "I was so much older than they were. I think they felt they had to listen."

Analysts contributed heavily to the investment process when Robertson was running Tiger, and he reckons they benefited from that role. He realized he could put young people to good use. "Just because they were twenty-five or thirty didn't mean they couldn't make key decisions. And we gave young people the opportunity to do that and they ran with it. That was a big part of their development. They were pretty much in charge of a lot of money." Robertson had ultimate veto power over what went into the portfolio, but in his eyes that didn't lessen his analysts' role. "Bush has ultimate power over the White House, but he better have damn good advisers."

For Robertson, the key to success in this business is very simple, and perhaps that's why he's uncomfortable taking credit for being able to teach it. "All you have to do in hedge funds is perform," he says, referring to net returns. "If you perform, money is going to pour in."

Still, given his stellar track record, Robertson seems the perfect person to ask about the attributes that make for a great manager. He ticks off four of them readily: They need to be smart, honest, hardworking, and competitive. "Competitive people are going to make it happen," he says.

That's not all they have in common though. In his years at the helm of Tiger, Robertson also uncovered another important characteristic shared by a number of talented investors, one likely to surprise many: a desire to do good in the world. "I've seen a lot of people come through here who have a real desire to do something to change the world for the better," says Robertson. He notices the same traits in other top hedge fund managers, pointing to such organizations as the Robin Hood Foundation, founded by hedge fund great Paul Jones and supported by a board chockful of hedge fund operators.

Robertson observed this philanthropic bent after he started the Tiger Foundation in 1990. The goal of the foundation was to support nonprofit organizations working to end poverty in New York. "I started the foundation with the idea of making these good money managers I had into philanthropists as well," he says. The Tiger employees gave money to the foundation and also picked the organizations they wanted to support. They had to agree to work with the nonprofits they recommended for funding.

Robertson now says that successful money managers' desire to improve the world is an "internal craving," much like the competitive spirit they're born with. "The Tiger Foundation was never started with this intention in mind, but I think it attracted people to us." Today, the foundation serves also as a quasi-alumni association for Tiger. Former Tiger employees sit on the board and continue to contribute money to the foundation.

Robertson knows the attributes that make a great money manager, and that understanding is the essential first step. The real challenge is identifying the people who have the goods. To overcome this hurdle,

Robertson wisely realized he needed more than his own instincts; he needed a systematic method for selecting talent.

He saw such a tool as essential because not everyone the firm hired was working out. Many just couldn't cut it. "They didn't have the horsepower to do the job, and I thought it was unfair to them." So in the 1980s, Dr. Aaron Stern, a psychiatrist and senior adviser to Tiger, started developing a test to help the fund find winners. "Gradually, we got a test that really looked for what we were looking for," says Robertson. "And it's been damn successful." He views the test as a tool, not the final word. "It's been a very good basis on which to judge people."

Stern and Robertson would not provide much information about the test, other than to say it endeavors to measure attributes including intelligence, critical thinking, and the ability to fit into a familial setting. The intelligence test consists of eleven subtests that measure such traits as verbal aptitude, perceptual skills, and processing speed using standard IQ test fare. There is also a personality test that helps to ascertain whether a candidate would fit into a culture Robertson described as warm and respectful. The personality portion isn't meant to probe too deeply into a candidate's psyche but rather to screen out personality traits, like narcissistic tendencies, that might cause trouble in a team-oriented workplace.

Tiger keeps all the tests on file, although Robertson has always refused to look at the results for fear they would bias him. Stern, the only person in the Tiger organization who ever sees the tests, has fine-tuned the exam over the years, based on how the best and brightest analysts answered the questions. For example, given their subsequent outstanding performance as managers, "if Ainslie and Anderson both said on their tests that the world was square, we would consider that a correct answer," says Robertson with a grin.

Despite his ongoing support of up-and-coming hedge fund talent, Robertson is not interested in picking the best of the best from the analysts who have passed through Tiger Management. "We had an exceptional bunch of people," Robertson says, "so I don't want to get into the business of saying who is exceptional and who is not." He did agree to share his thoughts on his protégées Ainslie and Anderson, both profiled in this book.

He describes Ainslie as a terrific man. "I have enormous respect for him," he says. "Certainly, he has been one of the most successful so-called Tiger Cubs." He and Ainslie share two educational institutions: Episcopal High School and the University of North Carolina (UNC), where Ainslie went to business school and Robertson earned a bachelor's degree. At Tiger, Ainslie was close to John Griffin, Tiger's president in the 1990s and considered at the time to be Robertson's heir apparent. "Ainslie and Griffin had a very nice group of young people with them," Robertson says. "They helped get more young people in."

Anderson also came out of UNC, where he was at the business school on a fellowship program created by Robertson, who plays no role in choosing the candidates. "Anderson is very smart, did a great job in the commodities business," says Robertson, "and he has done very well since he left here."

Ainslie's and Anderson's success, considerable by any measure, is likely due, at least in part, to the lessons they say they learned from Robertson: the importance of a company's management, how to test one's convictions about an investment, and how to have the courage to squeeze the most profit from a wager on a falling stock. Robertson is not inclined to describe how he mentored the scores of analysts who passed through Tiger, and the reference to Ainslie and Anderson only makes him smile. "I'm delighted they learned those lessons. I won't say where they learned them, but I'm delighted they learned them."

Robertson says both men also have a talent for picking good people. When Anderson left Tiger to manage his own portfolio inside Tudor Investment Corporation, the hedge fund run by Paul Jones, he plucked a young analyst out of Tiger named Jason Capello. "He was particularly good," says Robertson. As of mid-2007, Capello was in the process of setting up his own hedge fund.

Nurturing a new generation of hedge fund managers puts Robertson just outside the thick of things, and I wondered if he misses being in it. He says no. He's glad those days are behind him. "The seeding business has been a lot of fun and very rewarding. The work keeps me among young people with young ideas. The synergy here has attracted more people. I would have given anything to have stumbled on this earlier."

If that sounds as if Robertson likes what he's doing now better than managing money, that's because he does. "When you manage money, it takes over your life. It's a twenty-four-hour-a-day thing," he says. The freedom of his new work allows Robertson to spend more time on other important things in his life. His second grandchild was born the day before we talked, and he had taken the day off to be with the family. "For my time in life, it's a much better situation. You've got to know when to quit. I'm glad I quit when I did."

AFTER THE CRISIS

Crisis? What Crisis?

For Robertson, 2008, the year so many want to forget, may well go down as his best ever. His personal portfolio, which started the year with about $200 million, returned 150 percent amid the worst financial crisis since the Great Depression. What's more, the seventy-seven-year-old beat the pants off of every one of the roughly twenty-five managers he has seeded since 2000, as well as the dozens of other hedge fund operators he trained since opening Tiger Management in 1980.

Robertson, who started off his career as a stock picker, made much of his money in 2008 on so-called macro trades, chasing macroeconomic trends by buying and selling bonds and currencies. It was his ability to assess the big picture that allowed him to win big. His genius was in realizing that the turmoil in the housing and credit markets and the policy decisions of governments would overshadow individual company fundamentals.

In the first five months of 2008, Robertson made money betting that the difference between short- and long-term interest rates in the United States would widen, rightly forecasting that the yield on 2-year Treasuries would fall dramatically while the yield on 10-year bills would rise. He put on a similar wager in Australia. He revisited the same trade again toward the end of the year, during the height of the U.S. banking crisis, which accelerated after Lehman Brothers filed for bankruptcy in mid-September. He also made money in 2009 wagering on currency moves.

Although the Tiger Cubs, as his acolytes are called, were more than aware that economic trouble was brewing, most of them lost money in the last quarter of 2008, in part because they underestimated the impact that exogenous events would have on individual stocks.

The younger managers seemed to have learned from Robertson's 2008 triumph. Take Chase Coleman, for example, who runs Tiger Global, one of the largest funds in Robertson's stable. Coleman entered 2009 with less money invested in the markets and a keener awareness of how economic and political forces could continue to create large swings in stock prices. Coleman's fund lost 26 percent in 2008 and gained 7 percent in the first three months of 2009, all on wagers of shares he expected would fall. He reduced his overall market exposure and made less concentrated bets than he had in previous years to help mitigate losses. "There are many false dawns in bear markets, and we do not want to buy into a scenario of 'less bad' economic data when the majority of the information we monitor continues to suggest contractions in business activity," he told investors at the beginning of 2009. "Stepping back, I continue to believe that the most important theme of this period is the deleveraging of financial and consumer balance sheets. As long as businesses and consumers conserve cash and pay down debt, sustained improvements in economic growth will be challenging."

Robertson's view remained bearish going into 2009, and he continued to wager on falling bond prices in the United States because he expects inflation to skyrocket as a result of the government's efforts to stimulate the economy. High inflation means higher interest rates—and falling bond prices. Robertson forecasts that yields on 10-year Treasuries, which were at 3.3 percent in July 2009, could climb to at least 7 percent, and potentially more than twice that amount over the following three to five years.

Chapter 16

Jim Chanos

Out on the Short-Selling Limb

JIM CHANOS DOES what very few investors on Wall Street dare to do. He bets exclusively on stocks he expects to tumble. Chanos, who started his firm Kynikos Associates in New York in 1985, now runs about $4 billion, making his fund the largest of any dedicated to short selling.

Within five years of the launch of Kynikos—named for the Greek word from which *cynic* is derived—there were close to twenty short sellers, says Harry Strunk, who tracks these managers as the head of consulting firm Aspen Grove Capital Management. The most famous were the Feshbach brothers—Joseph, Matthew, and Kurt—whose assets eventually reached $1 billion. Most of these short sellers, the Feshbachs included, faded away in the decadelong bull market of the 1990s. By 2007, there were less than ten, and Chanos has by far the greatest amount of assets under management.

His claim to fame, however, isn't survival. It's an uncanny knack for knowing when trouble is brewing. Chanos, forty-nine, was the first investor to voice concerns about Enron a year before it became the second-largest bankruptcy in U.S. history. That investment call was hardly Kynikos's biggest moneymaker, but it guaranteed Chanos a place in the financial annals as the nation's preeminent bear.

• • •

Chanos runs Kynikos from an office in midtown next to Michael's, the preferred eatery for the top names from all corners of New York's media world—magazines, newspapers, television, and publishing. Two long shelves of books line the walls of his conference room, displaying titles like *Iceberg Risk: An Adventure in Portfolio Theory*, by Kent Osband; *Of Permanent Value: The Story of Warren Buffett*, by Andrew Kilpatrick; and *Bubbles and How to Survive Them*, by John P. Calverley. A whiteboard, discolored from countless analyst meetings, dominates another wall.

Chanos is articulate and affable and not at all the dour sort one might expect of someone who is constantly doing battle with conventional wisdom. If he's a mostly solitary soldier, it's mainly because so few in the business have the right armor for short selling. "My philosophy on the psychiatric makeup of a short seller has done a 180-degree turn in the last twenty years," says Chanos. "When I was first starting to put out sell-side short research in the early 1980s, I believed that going short was simply the mirror image of going long. I assumed that all the attributes used on the long side could be reversed on the short side. I no longer believe that."

Chanos's change of view comes from hard-won experience and from studying behavioral finance and the ways investors and markets behave. It's also been influenced by observing the behavior of a whole cadre of people who've worked with him and by noting which attributes enabled them to make the transition from analyst to portfolio manager.

The successful short seller is not going to be the one leading the pack. He's the lone wolf, and many find that an uncomfortable role. "Studies have shown that human beings do not exhibit their best decision making under duress or in an environment of negative reinforcement," he says. Most people spend their lives seeking praise and approval, and generally the more success a person has achieved, the more praise and approval he or she is likely to have received. "If you've reached that level on Wall Street, you probably had good grades in school. You've been fed this pattern of success, and it's always been fostered by reaffirmation and praise," says Chanos. He describes Wall Street as a giant positive-reinforcement machine.

But most of what one hears is noise—facts that are already known or events that are already priced into the market. Chanos calls it the "Muzak of finance." "It's there, it will always be there, and occasionally there's a nice tune," he says. Except when you disagree with what everyone else is saying. "Then, Wall Street becomes an environment of negative reinforcement, and it's a rare person who can drown it out."

The noise comes from every direction. Chief executives threaten to sue you, and equity salespeople scoff. "You've got ten different research houses coming out recommending your stock, or analysts are raising the earnings estimates, or the CEO is on CNBC—just bullish blather all day long," says Chanos. "When you're a short seller, all you hear is a cacophony of 'You are wrong, you are wrong, you are wrong.'"

Even more intimidating is the added risk that comes from the very mechanics of selling a stock short. When investors buy stocks, they know that in the worst possible case, they can lose all their money. When a trader shorts a stock, traditionally by borrowing the shares and then selling them in the hopes they can be bought back later at a cheaper price, the loss is limitless because the stock can climb indefinitely. "You have to be able to say: 'The facts are the facts, and I am right,'" says Chanos.

Sometimes the list of those who think you're wrong includes your client. In the late 1990s, Chanos had to fire one. Kynikos was managing portfolios for other hedge fund managers who didn't feel they had the right temperament to bet on falling shares. One of these "wholesale clients" was a famous money manager, whom Chanos declines to name. The client manager gave Kynikos $50 million, which was 2 percent of the client's total assets of roughly $2.5 billion. Chanos was wagering on fifty companies at the time, so each position accounted for 4 basis points of the client's overall portfolio.

One of Chanos's short ideas was America Online, a position he eventually had to abandon after two years of watching the shares stubbornly refuse to collapse. He started to short the stock in 1996, when America Online was the largest Internet service provider in the United States. The company's revenue had grown to $1.1 billion in the fiscal year that ended June 30, 1996, up from $394.3 million in 1995. The company's costs associated with getting new customers and research and development had jumped just as dramatically. For 1995 and 1996, the company decided to expand the time it would take to account for these costs, thereby making the financial results look better. "We hated America Online because of its accounting, all the things that four years later caused the stock to blow up, although by then it was too late for us," says Chanos.

Kynikos had rigid risk limits—and still does. A position may be no larger than 5 percent of the portfolio, and when it gets to 4 percent, even if Chanos loves it, he trims it back so that a climbing stock like America Online won't run the firm out of business. But that didn't console Chanos's client. Four or five months after the client signed up with Kynikos, he started calling Chanos. "Are you sure you're right about America Online?" the client asked. "I just had lunch with an analyst from Merrill, and it's his favorite long."

Chanos assured him he was still confident about his position, but a couple of weeks later, the client called again: "America Online is up another 20 points." Chanos asked if the client would be more comfortable if he covered that position in the client's account. "No, I don't want to tell you how to run your portfolio," he said. But Chanos suspected that he'd not heard the end of it. He hadn't. Two weeks later, at 4:30 p.m. on a summer Friday, when Chanos was about to leave for his beach house in the Hamptons, he got yet another call. Before long, the manager was calling every day after the close.

"He was having an amazing year and we were making him money in the short portfolio," says Chanos. "America Online wasn't profitable, but we had Boston Chicken, Oxford Health, and Sunbeam. You will always have one position that's killing you. I could see it was driving him nuts."

The last straw for Chanos came when the worried client called on a Sunday night. "This is not working. If you want us to run the portfolio, let us do it," Chanos said.

"But I saw a news story about AOL in the *Times*," the client explained. "I just wanted to talk to you about it."

Chanos appealed to common sense. "You're obsessing about a position that's less than 5 basis points of your portfolio. You've had longs that are 8 percent of your portfolio. Why are you letting this get to you?" But logic didn't work. In the end, Chanos had to lay down the law: one more phone call, and he would fire the client.

Less than a week later, on a Friday afternoon, Chanos's phone rang. "I know what you said, but we have to talk about America Online," the client said.

"No. We have to talk about getting you your money back."

The former client and Chanos now look back and laugh about it. Still, the story illuminates how extremely disconcerting shorting can be for some. "Here was this world-class money manager, with a great track record, who had done nothing but hit home runs," says Chanos. "He knew he couldn't do the short side, yet even when he farmed it out it made him uncomfortable. If it's difficult for this guy, imagine how hard it is for others. I've seen him ride stocks down, and he would buy more, but on the flip side, the spectre of unlimited losses and the fact that all his buddies were long the stock made for an untenable psychological position. It taught me volumes about our business, and why I even have a business."

Chanos grew up in Milwaukee and graduated from Yale University in 1980 with a degree in economics, although his initial plan when he entered college was to become a doctor. His entry into short selling was a fluke. In 1982, at twenty-four years old, he was working for a firm called Gilford Securities in Chicago as an analyst. The first stock he wrote about was a company called Baldwin-United Corporation, a piano maker turned insurance and financial services company. "I wrote that report the day the market bottomed. I have great timing in all things short," laughs Chanos.

Written in the summer of 1982, Chanos's report pointed out that the company had a staggering debt load and "liberal accounting practices," a fault line Chanos would find repeatedly throughout his career of picking companies about to hit the skids. The stock kept climbing, going from $24, when Chanos first wrote the report, to about $50, before starting the inevitable tumble in early 1983, as everything that Chanos had laid out in his analyst reports came to pass. By September 1983, the stock was trading at $3.

Chanos hadn't planned on concentrating exclusively on short ideas, but his clients were intrigued. "Michael Steinhardt and George Soros were clients of the firm, and they called asking, 'What else does the kid think we should short?'" Chanos saw where things were heading—challenging as that direction would be. "I knew the problems inherent in being on the short side, but even when a stock was running up, it didn't bother me much. I knew I was right."

So he decided to make short-selling research his niche. "If I can do institutional research—well documented and well researched—on Fortune 500 companies where there is a flaw, people will pay me for this," he realized. Six months later, he moved to New York and took a job with Atlantic Capital, a unit of Deutsche Bank. Soon, Chanos had hedge funds and other large institutions like Fidelity Investments and Dreyfus Corporation wanting his research. "It was like minting money," Chanos says. That is, until autumn 1985.

That September the *Wall Street Journal* published a story that Chanos calls "the worst story in the paper's history." The article described a new breed of short sellers who used questionable tactics to drive down the price of stocks. "The short selling that raises some people's blood pressure is practiced by a relatively small, though also growing, group of speculators," wrote Dean Rotbart, then a reporter for the *Wall Street Journal*. "They specialize in sinking vulnerable stocks with barrages of bad-mouthing. They use facts when available, but some of them aren't above innuendo, fabrications, and deceit to batter down a stock."

The article included a graphic of concentric circles, depicting how the short sellers would create downward pressure on a stock. The outer circle was the analyst or investor building a short position, and then passing on the information to close friends, other investors, the media, and regulators. "Ripples can build into waves that swamp a stock: Falling price and lobbying by shorts prompt some large holders to bail out. Early shorts begin taking profits," the caption read.

Chanos, then twenty-seven, was one of the few bears who agreed to be quoted by name in the article. Most short sellers tend to keep a low profile to avoid retribution from corporate management.

His bosses in Germany wished he, too, had kept quiet.

Chanos got a call at home the morning the story ran, advising him to report immediately to the office. He hadn't yet read the paper. But the Germans had, his boss informed him.

"The Germans tried to fire us on the spot, but we had contracts," Chanos says. So the bank bought them out.

Soon after, Chanos got backing from Bill Brown and Glen Vinson, who wanted him to run a short portfolio for a wealthy family, and Kynikos was born. Brown had a two-year exclusive contract with Chanos, and he's still a client today. Short selling was a lucrative business for the next five years because it was largely virgin territory.

"There was not a lot of capital in the strategy," says Chanos. Their main investors at Kynikos were wealthy individuals because pension funds thought it was too risky. Kynikos's Ursus Partners fund returned 35 percent before fees in 1986, compared with 18.6 percent for the Standard & Poor's 500 Index. In 1987, it climbed 26.7 percent, while the benchmark index climbed 5.1 percent.

Despite institutions' reticence to go short, the strategy was perfect for tax-exempt investors like pension funds and endowments because profits from short selling are treated as ordinary income. The strategy also allowed these clients to lower risk on their equity portfolios and gave them an investment that wasn't correlated to the stock market. David Swensen, who runs Yale University's endowment, saw the advantages, and became Kynikos's first tax-exempt client. He remained one for five years. Ursus ended 1990 with its best record ever, returning 70.5 percent as the S&P 500 slipped 3.2 percent.

Over the next nine years, as the U.S. stock market climbed ever higher, Ursus fell a total of 75 percent. It posted only two positive years, in 1994, when the fund jumped 46.2 percent, and in 1997, when it climbed 5.4 percent. At the end of 1993, Chanos had about $200 million in assets. Many of his competitors, including the Feshbachs, had started adding long positions to their portfolios.

Chanos did two things to ensure his business didn't evaporate: He stopped using leverage in 1995, and he changed the fee structure. "I'm fighting this big bull market, and I can't do anything about it," says Chanos. "But I could be paid for outperforming the market." So if his fund was down less than the market was up, he got paid on that difference. Investors agreed to the new performance measurement. Chanos declines to disclose the fees investors pay.

The companies Chanos targets for shorting tend to fall into several broad themes. One is consumer fads; he has made money on companies associated with Cabbage Patch dolls, George Foreman grills, cigars, world wrestling, and Martha Stewart.

The second lucrative area is booms that go bust—debt-fueled asset manias in which the asset's price keeps rising even though the asset doesn't throw off enough cash to service the debt. That happened with real estate in the late 1980s and with telecom companies just after the turn of the century. These trends are great for short sellers because they tend to involve lots of large and liquid companies, allowing the short seller to ride the trend for a long time.

The third indicator Chanos looks for is accounting irregularities, like the kind he uncovered at Baldwin-United and later at Tyco, WorldCom, and Enron. These situations are often likely to arise at companies that expand through acquisitions. "Growth by acquisition is the last bastion of legalized accounting fraud in America," says Chanos. When a company buys another entity, it has quite a bit of leeway to revalue assets and book them immediately as profits.

Another telltale sign that there's money to be made is in technology obsolescence, when a new technology is undermining an existing business. Chanos has made bets against companies in analog businesses that are being elbowed out by the digital world. Distributors are especially vulnerable. They once had an oligopoly and are now getting crushed. Ripe for shorting have been companies like Eastman Kodak, whose margins on film shrank as consumers switched to digital cameras, and Blockbuster, whose profits have been reduced by the availability of movies on demand and consumers' option to buy DVDs inexpensively through large retailers like Wal-Mart. Hit hard as well are movie theater companies like Regal Entertainment Group and Carmike Cinemas, which are getting pinched as home theaters become more popular. "The slide has taken a while with Kodak and Blockbuster, but it's happening," says Chanos.

Chanos describes some targets as if they were no-brainers. "Look at Netflix. Consider the concept of having little old ladies in warehouses stuffing envelopes with DVDs," he says. "That might be a business for the next two or three years, but then it won't work." It faces the same pressures as Blockbuster, whose profits are dropping. "Why anyone would pay twenty-seven times earnings for that is beyond me."

In his crosshairs now are cable and satellite companies because Chanos projects that television shows will eventually be available over the Internet. "Everyone is grabbing his own content," he says. "The NFL Network is a great example. They are saying 'I own this content, so why should I give it to Comcast?'" Right now, cable companies pay the football network to carry the games, but in the next five years, predicts Chanos, every television will be plugged into the Internet, and the NFL will deliver the games directly to viewers. "All these cable companies buying each other are just shuffling the deck chairs on the Titanic."

Changes to the television experience will be revolutionary and soon, according to Chanos. "I grew up sitting on the sofa watching television. The idea of watching *The Simpsons* at 8 p.m. is over now. You ignore that at your own peril. In five years, it will be *your* programming, *your* network."

Value investors, the ones that own all the cable companies, prefer not to see it that way. "They're up in arms because these stocks are cheap, but you really have a business risk here," says Chanos. "Kodak was cheap all the way down too, trading at five times cash flow, from 70 to 24."

As is often the case, Chanos is early.

"So far we are wrong," says Chanos. Comcast is up about 30 percent since Chanos came out with this idea, and Cablevision stock has climbed as well. Satellite companies are all going up because they're going to be bought. The trouble is it's impossible to know exactly when a stock may begin its free fall, and because Chanos is the largest short seller around, it's essential for him to have a position in place before his hypothesis becomes apparent to the rest of the world. That's because an investor has to locate the stock to borrow it, which gets harder once everyone is convinced it's going to tumble.

"You'd be surprised, what with the borrowing restrictions, how hard it can be to get a trade on" once a stock starts to fall, says Chanos. In some instances, he's had to abandon his position, even though he eventually was proved right. "America Online was probably our most celebrated disaster." From the beginning of 1996 through the end of 1998, the stock rose 1,555 percent. "The trade probably cost 20 points of performance. That's the nightmare short. Those are tough to fight. Everything happened to come true, but by 1998, it had just worn me out. It seemed like no one would ever care." Indeed, it wasn't until the merger with Time Warner that investors took a more critical look. America Online bought Time Warner in 2000, and the stock eventually plunged by more than 70 percent between April 2001 and June 2002, as investors realized that America Online wasn't the money-printing machine that everyone had forecast.

Another difficult lesson for Chanos was his position in defense contractor McDonnell Douglas in 1991. "They had a bunch of planes, including the C-17 transport plane, on which they were facing cost overruns, and cash flow was outlandishly negative," says Chanos. It looked as if the company would have to restructure. There were rumors that the Air Force had decided to accelerate payments to McDonnell Douglas. The next 10K statement showed that the cash flow had completely turned around. Chanos didn't believe it would last. It did.

The final slap came in 1993, when the Pentagon's inspector general issued a report saying McDonnell Douglas had been improperly aided. "I now have a healthy skepticism that the government can come in and make things better," says Chanos.

Chanos's best-known call, though not his most profitable, is probably Enron. Chanos's antennae went up in late 2000 when an article in a regional edition of the *Wall Street Journal* written by Jonathan Weil, then an accounting reporter at the paper and based in Texas, discussed some bookkeeping irregularities at Enron. The company was reporting gains today that wouldn't be realized for years to come, if ever. Chanos started doing research, poring over the company's financial documents from the previous year. Doubts about Enron's future solidified as he realized that about 80 percent of its earnings came from energy trading. Worse, those wagers were returning only 7 percent, while the company was paying 10 percent to get access to capital.

Chanos holds an annual conference for a handful of bears every February in Miami at which everyone must present their two best ideas, including at least one short. At his 2001 "Hibernating Bears" conference, he named Enron and Williams Communications. By the next conference, Enron had fallen 99.9 percent and Williams was down 96 percent. "Enron wasn't even the most profitable trade that year," says Chanos, pointing out that he made more money betting on the tumble in telecom shares, including Lucent Technologies, than he did wagering on "energy merchant banks," as he calls them, like Enron and Dynegy.

"Enron got all the attention," says Chanos, but the Enron bet added only about 4 to 5 percentage points to performance. "In terms of its impact, the call on Enron will be considered a great call only because Enron captured the imagination of the country."

Enron, he says, was good for hedge funds in general, and short sellers in particular. "Hedge funds are pejorative and short sellers are twice as pejorative. Enron went a long way toward demonstrating: Short sellers are wearing white hats; it would be better if we had more people looking at companies the way they do. We should be celebrating these guys."

Chanos's approach to Enron also highlights a difference between Kynikos and other research-driven hedge fund companies. At most firms, the analysts come up with the ideas, do the research, and then pitch them to the top managers. At Kynikos, Chanos and his five partners generate the hunches. "Almost all of our ideas come from the senior level," says Chanos. "We come up with thoughts on things from reading articles or books and watching the markets. I'm the one with the experience. At most shops, the people who don't have experience and judgment are forced to come up with ideas and take true ownership of them. If they're responsible for coming up with ideas and processing them, what am I doing there?"

This atypical organizational approach probably helped Chanos uncover Enron's problems before others did. In Enron, he says, the problems were hidden in plain sight. He spoke to junior analysts at Wall Street firms, who were uncomfortable with the numbers, but they didn't know what was going on. Their bosses, who would have been in a better position to identify the problems, didn't have time to look at the details.

At Kynikos, after Chanos or another senior partner comes up with the idea, he'll then pass it on to an analyst. "They get the comparables, get all the bullish research together, get everything there is to know to become an instant expert in ten days, and then they come back up with their thoughts," says Chanos. "I think that's a more advantageous model. The risk-reward of the ownership of an idea stays at the top. I'm never screaming or kicking down the doors of the junior people. If they get facts wrong, or leave something out, I'll be mad, but I'm paid to have the opinions, and they're paid to do the research."

This approach accounts for there being so much less turnover at Kynikos than at other firms, Chanos says. "Our business is stable," says Chanos. "It's considered a great place to work, the bosses aren't screaming. We have very high expectations, but the junior people know they can speak their minds. If they are good at what they do, they can have lifetime jobs here, like being a tenured professor. The people who can do more take the next step up."

The partners have the skills to understand risk-reward models, portfolio structure, and how to size trades. "Those are rare skills. They come from being here a long time, and you have to have interpersonal skills and managerial skills," says Chanos. Rarer still among young people are the skills of shorting.

Withstanding the pressures inherent in taking stands so far outside the box is a tall order for those who thrive on the comfort of consensus, and Chanos is increasingly convinced that the ability to short is probably not acquired. "In most cases, I think you're hardwired for it or you're not," he says. "You're the type of person who's ruffled by the conflict, or you're not."

Chanos cites his experiences with his own pool of analysts in trying to identify who might have the requisite wiring for making the transition from analyst to portfolio manager. "I can tell within six to twelve months," he says. "When things start to go wrong with one of the ideas they're following, how do they handle it? And how do they handle it every single day, when Morgan Stanley, Merrill Lynch, or Goldman Sachs is recommending going long a stock we are short? Some are cool customers. It doesn't faze them." Others begin to waver. They're less certain at the analysts' meeting, less definitive in their research memos. "'Maybe I'm wrong,' they'll say. They start to question the position," says Chanos. And that reticence is rarely outgrown. "Even with a lot of coaching or hand-holding after two or three years, it doesn't change. They're either one way or the other."

Mentoring the analysts requires patience, something Chanos says he doesn't always have in huge measure. He points to Chuck Hobbs, head of research at Kynikos, who has a great ability to connect with the analysts. "You encourage them with positive reinforcement and tell them their facts are right," says Chanos. "When they're following something that works out well, it's important to say, 'You got it right for the right reasons.' They need to understand how important it is to stick to their convictions."

Even if someone isn't able to make the transition to being a portfolio manager who can sell short, it's not a sign of failure, says Chanos. "That doesn't mean that person can't be a stellar analyst."

One analyst who did make the jump is David Glaymon, who is now a Kynikos partner in its London office. Glaymon joined Chanos about five years ago from what was then J.P. Morgan Securities, where he was a telecommunications bond analyst. "He was thoughtful and hardworking, and I knew right away he was going to be a star," says Chanos. While he was at the bank, he had already shown signs of independent thinking. "At the height of the telecom lunacy, he went against the grain internally," warning, of the coming trouble in the sector. "That's a sign of courage if you can do that on the sell side."

Glaymon's courage is not in short supply. Chanos once decided to put him on airlines and steel companies for Kynikos, areas in which Glaymon had no expertise. "He was horror-stricken," says Chanos. "He said, 'I don't know a thing.' Within one year, whenever there was an airlines earnings announcement out, the sell side was calling here to see what David's take was. He had made himself an expert. He just did the work, went to the trade shows, went to the airplane manufacturing conferences, and that's all it took."

Chanos does not find many like Glaymon. "In a market downturn, I think long-short managers will be a disappointment because few managers have skills on the short side." Many managers made money in the downturn in 2001 and 2002, not because they did so well on the short side but because there were still a lot of stocks going up. "I think the jury is out. I don't think people did so well because they were shorting. They just avoided the stocks getting killed."

Chanos's choice of noteworthy up-and-coming managers hinges on the ability to short, a talent that for most contenders "remains elusive." Jason Ader, a former Bear Stearns analyst is one manager who has the skills.

Ader, thirty-nine, opened Hayground Cove Asset Management in 2003 after spending almost a decade at Bear Stearns, where he was a senior managing director covering the gaming, leisure, and lodging industries. As of June 2007, the firm managed a net $1.13 billion. Ader, who declined to be interviewed for *Hedge Hunters*, averaged returns of 15 percent with his Hayground Cove Institutional

Partners, between January 2004 and June 2007, compared with a 9 percent return for the S&P 500, according to documents sent to investors.

Despite his background in the leisure industry, Ader runs a diversified portfolio that includes computers, retailers, and tire companies. His portfolio was about 130 percent long and about 77 percent short, for a net exposure of about 53 percent, and most of his portfolio is in mid-cap and big-cap names, according to the documents.

"Ader loves the game and he loves digging for puzzles," says Chanos. "He's also a good short seller. He always gave us good short ideas, which is rare for a sell-side analyst. He's the kind of guy who will be able to run long-short institutional money for a long, long time."

AFTER THE CRISIS

A Nose for Losers

The credit crisis of 2008 made for a profitable year for Chanos, the biggest short seller in the world, with about $6 billion under management. As the Standard & Poor's 500 Index tumbled almost 40 percent, his fund climbed about 60 percent. Even his $150 million Opportunity Fund, which mixes in wagers on stocks he expects will increase in price, did well, returning about 15 percent, while other stock funds in the industry tumbled by about 25 percent.

In the first half of 2008, Chanos made money on the fall of financial stocks, as he successfully predicted that the likes of Bear Stearns, Lehman Brothers, Citigroup, and Merrill Lynch & Co. would be hammered by mortgage losses. As the bets paid off, he shifted focus in June and July to steel, industrial, and infrastructure companies. "The financials had fallen by 80 or 90 percent," since he put on the trade, he said of his reason for covering his positions at mid-year. "As I like to say, 'Let the last 10 percent go to someone else.'" Following that principle, he can shift capital to an idea with more potential for making money.

For 2009, Chanos is focusing on the deepening recession and what that means for companies who have benefited from government spending. Early in the year he was shorting defense companies and for-profit education companies, which get paid partly through government programs to retrain workers. He's also "dusting off files" of some banks that in March or April of 2009 rallied extensively. "It was a relief rally and some of these banks aren't necessarily good businesses," he said, without naming names.

In the Opportunity Fund, he likes to do what are known as pair trades, in which an investor chooses a winner and a loser in the same industry, shorting struggling car makers Ford and General Motors, for example, while buying shares in Honda and Toyota. He also bought preferred shares of some bank stocks, which were yielding 30 percent to 40 percent, and shorted the common stock.

For Chanos the biggest mystery related to 2008 is why Washington still thinks bankers have any credibility. "I don't get why the government continues to listen to the bankers, who got us into the mess," he said. "Bankers asked for a curtailing of short selling and loosening of accounting standards, and they got both."

He also has few kind words for hedge fund managers who suspended redemptions or limited withdrawals, a practice known as gating, in 2008. "The biggest black eye for the industry was gating. It did not have to happen," said Chanos, who faced about 20 percent redemptions despite his great performance. "It was a self-inflicted gunshot wound that really hurt relations with investors."

Chapter 17

Richard Perry
A Manager's Manager

THE OFFICES OF $14 billion hedge fund Perry Capital, nineteen floors above New York's Central Park, house about fifty pieces of Richard Perry's art collection, devoted to works of the twentieth century. The reception area combines the playful with the contemporary to create an ambiance that's hardly the norm at big-deal hedge fund firms. The place is studded with photos, paintings, and installations that would be quite at home at the Museum of Modern Art. On the wall behind a silver metal staircase is an installation of LED light tubes by artist Leo Villareal. Even the candy dishes are artfully arranged, filled with M&Ms that spell out *enjoy*. Perry's wife, Lisa, and photographer Martin Sobey designed the wallpaper for the kitchen area: a huge photograph of a grocery aisle at Kmart, a nod to Perry's board seat at Sears, which owns the discount retailer. The meeting room, with its view of the park's skating rink, is equally striking, with low-slung modern couches in beige and gray, accented with bright yellow pillows.

Perry and Lisa—a Fashion Institute of Technology graduate who launched a line of 1960s-inspired dresses in early 2007—are not only avid art collectors in their spare time; they also support causes popular among major hedge fund players: political candidates and charities. The couple have been generous backers of Hillary

Clinton for her 2008 presidential run—in their home they have a photographic diptych of Hillary taken by artist Chuck Close, as well as an autographed snapshot of them with the candidate.

On the philanthropic front, Perry sits on the board of Harlem Children's Zone, a charity whose goal is to provide services to children and families living in ninety-seven square blocks of central Harlem and to help end the cycle of poverty. The board's chair is hedge fund legend Stan Druckenmiller and industry notable Mark Kingdon, of Kingdon Capital Management, serves as director. Perry is also a trustee of Facing History and Ourselves, an organization that works with teachers to educate children about the evils of genocide, racism, prejudice, and anti-Semitism.

Since its launch in November 1988, Perry's flagship fund has returned 15.4 percent a year on average, compared with 11.6 percent for the benchmark stock index, and he's never had a losing year. He is a creative thinker, and over the years his investments have included real estate loans and private equity deals with partners like billionaire buyout executive Thomas H. Lee.

In choosing investments, Perry has turned to where the action is, in an event-driven approach that seeks out companies involved in mergers or acquisitions, emerging from bankruptcy, spinning off units, or going through some sort of restructuring. He has tailored that investment style over the years as more investors have entered the market. To stay ahead of the crowd, Perry has become more proactive, helping to create the events by working with management to make changes that will increase shareholder value. He will approach only executives he deems open to his counsel.

At fifty-two, Perry is tall and lean and athletic-looking—he's completed five triathlons. His manner is engaging, and he has the diplomat's skill of seeming to know everyone well, remembering tidbits from conversations he had with people six months earlier. With a directness honed from years of giving chief executives advice that's sometimes tough to hear, he has no trouble getting people to listen. He tells of calling up a well-known CEO, whom he asked me not to name, and saying: "You're the best manager in your industry, but you have the worst returns. Your shareholders don't trust you. Focus on your capital structure. You could add a lot of value and get your shareholders' support." The CEO eventually agreed and instituted a stock repurchase.

Perry's roots in the business are the stuff of hedge fund history. The hedge fund industry can, in part, be divided into family trees: Julian Robertson heads one of the largest. His Tiger Management produced scores of Tiger Cubs, who have themselves spawned another generation of managers. Another major branch stems from Robert Rubin's risk arbitrage desk at Goldman Sachs. As a member of the first generation of managers to work under Rubin, Perry helped hire the superstar team that went on to become some of the biggest successes in the industry: Edward Lampert, who now runs ESL; Thomas Steyer, head of Farallon; Daniel Och, who runs Och-Ziff; and Eric Mindich, who runs Eton Park. Rubin later left Goldman to serve as Treasury secretary under President Bill Clinton and is now chairman of the executive committee at Citigroup. Perry succeeded Rubin as an adjunct associate professor in the finance department at New York University's Leonard N. Stern School of Business.

To hear Perry tell it, it was his tennis game that got him the job at Goldman Sachs.

Even in high school, Perry had an avid interest in business. He had worked for a real estate investment trust as part of a student project and supplemented that by working a few days a week in the business office of his prep school, Milton Academy, in Milton, Massachusetts. Finance fascinated him. "It was practical and logical. There was a balance sheet and line items attached to a budget. You could change the line items and that would change the bottom line. I understood it immediately." After graduating, Perry headed to the Wharton School at the University of Pennsylvania. It was 1973.

With some help from his father, Perry landed a summer gig at Goldman Sachs, which was highly unusual for an undergraduate who had just finished his sophomore year. Perry's father, Arnold, who was in the office machinery business, knew some Goldman Sachs partners from tennis games in New York, where the family had lived since Richard was ten. "They thought I was a good tennis player," says Perry with a laugh.

That summer and the next, Perry spent much of his time on the trading desk for options, financial instruments that give investors the right but not the obligation to buy or sell a particular amount of a stock, bond, commodity, or currency within a specific time frame. These instruments were just coming into fashion on Wall Street, and the first options exchange in the United States, the Chicago Board Options Exchange, had just opened a year earlier in a smokers' lounge at the Chicago Board of Trade. Investors were getting a handle on how to value them thanks to the work of academics Fischer Black, Myron Scholes, and Robert Merton, who in 1973 published the Black-Scholes model for pricing stock options. Eleven years later, Black went to work for Goldman Sachs and Perry had a chance to interact with him.

Perry joined the options desk full-time after he graduated in 1977 and soon made friends with a fellow working on the arbitrage desk. His friend from arbitrage had a gift for the quantitative, and Perry was interested in investing, so the two young men organized a switch, and Perry began working with Rubin, who had taken over the arbitrage desk from L. Jay Tenenbaum, who had been running it since the 1960s.

Goldman's Arbitrage Desk. When Rubin joined the arbitrage desk in 1966, it was already a fabled place. Gus Levy, who later became chairman of Goldman Sachs, had built the original arbitrage group, whose aim was to make money off the differences in the prices of related securities, after World War II. That desk would buy shares of companies coming out of bankruptcy, going through mergers, or spinning off or selling business units. When Rubin joined, mergers and acquisitions were booming, and the desk would buy the shares of the company that was being acquired and sell short the shares of the company doing the buying. The trade was pretty much guaranteed to make money—as long as the merger was completed.

During Rubin's days on the arbitrage desk, which he describes in his autobiography *In an Uncertain World*, the deals were sometimes complicated, and an analyst had to get up to speed on many issues very quickly. Rubin describes the myriad questions that an arbitrageur needed to answer almost immediately: What might due diligence at the target company uncover? What antitrust issue might arise? Were shareholders likely to approve the merger? Would the target company miss earnings or get sued or go through some other event that would threaten the deal? Even though the decisions were based on incomplete information, they weren't made on instinct. Rubin carefully analyzed the situation to come up with a list of every conceivable event that could scuttle the deal and then calculated the probabilities of these events actually occurring.

Rubin looks at life as a series of probabilities, which gave him the ideal temperament to be an arbitrageur. He hired people with the same outlook. In arbitrage, you need to be right more than 90 percent of the time, and the best people are right 95 percent of the time. Being wrong increased the risk of losing a lot more money than you ever made on any deal.

During Perry's summers watching traders on the options desk, he had discovered that, like Rubin, he took a more intellectual or analytical approach to investing. "I never relied solely on instinct," says Perry, as did many traders he met. "There are a lot of people who do that and who are successful, but for me it was not a stand-alone tool for creating wealth." Yet options trading provided a good foundation for arbitrage because it too depends on understanding probabilities.

The years with Rubin proved to be a fantastic learning experience for Perry not only because of Rubin's talents but also because Goldman Sachs emphasized training in a big way. The firm liked to get their employees young, unadulterated by the influences of other organizations. When you joined Goldman Sachs, it was your first job, and higher-ups trained and molded you. The firm had little interest in hiring employees who had already proven themselves at other firms. Instead, they spent lots of time developing young talent.

On the arbitrage team, Rubin would add a new person every two years or so, and Perry was involved in hiring all of them. After Perry, the next entrant on the team was Frank Brosens, who joined in 1979. Thomas Steyer and Daniel Och came on board in 1982, Lampert in 1984, and Mindich in 1988. This A-Team had many qualities in common. "They were all extraordinary, they all worked very hard, they were high-powered, intelligent, and nice people too, with a strong desire to learn and to be cooperative and team oriented," says Perry. They understood something instinctively about investing, and they had the rare combination of being both intellectual and practical.

Team members didn't always agree on investment ideas, but they responded to the ideas in very similar ways. "Each of us would shake our heads at the same thing," says Perry. They all understood which issues were key. "When we heard an idea, we all had a sense of whether it was worth spending time on." If it was, the next step was to calculate the probability of various outcomes. "Investing isn't black or white. It's different shades of gray, and what was common to all of us was that we could see the different shades of gray and handicap them. There were very few second chances. The process had to be good." They called the process "expected value analysis," and it is still central to what Perry does today.

By 1988, Perry's experience at Goldman Sachs was no longer ideal. A key concern was his compensation. He didn't feel he was being paid appropriately. "I was being compensated well relative to my peers at Goldman Sachs, but relative to hedge funds, it was dramatically lower," says Perry. "There was no direct tie between my pay and how well our department did." His understanding was that even if he were made a partner, his paycheck would not rise dramatically. What's more, his bosses were pushing him to move to London for a job that would take him away from investing and uproot his family, which by then included two-year-old twins.

Encouraged by his wife and his mother's brother, Jimmy Cayne, chief executive of the Bear Stearns Companies, Perry decided to start his own investment firm. With two months left to go before bonus time, he told his bosses about his plans to leave, volunteering not to poach any Goldman Sachs employees. They paid him fairly, and he was on his way.

Perry set up shop with a part-time secretary, and his fourteen-year-old cousin filled in by answering the phones. It was a lonely climb. A friend from Boston, Seth Klarman, strongly suggested that Perry team up with Paul Leff, who was then working at Harvard Management Company, which oversees the university's endowment. Perry balked. While at Goldman Sachs, Perry had had a somewhat rocky acquaintance with Leff. Harvard had been a client of Goldman Sachs's during Perry's days on the arbitrage desk, and Leff was often looking to arbitrage merging companies. Unlike other desks at Goldman, the arbitrage department didn't have to heed customers' orders; in fact, it avoided most customer relationships, intending to invest in the stocks themselves. That meant that Leff put in a lot of orders on the desk but never got as much stock as he wanted. At a dinner with Perry, Leff complained about his treatment by Goldman Sachs. Perry unapologetically explained the situation. "The rest of dinner was very pleasant," says Perry, "but Paul was convinced that he should never do business with us again, which was logical."

Klarman found Perry's reservations understandable, but he was insistent, saying Leff's more macro approach to investing would be a good balance to Perry's bottom-up analysis. As Perry thought more about bringing Leff on as a partner, he realized that Klarman was right. "We thought the same way much of the time," he says. "He was always trying to do the same things that we were doing." Perry went to Boston, and they discussed the idea over lunch. Leff quit Harvard a month after Perry left Goldman Sachs, and they remain partners today, almost two decades later.

An early turning point for Perry Capital came in 1989, its second year of operation. About thirty or forty groups were trading merger arbitrage, and Perry's returns by midyear were smack in the middle. "That was depressing," says Perry. "Lots of guys who didn't do as much work were killing us. We weren't taking enough risk."

But with United Airlines, at least, caution paid off. The pilots' union and management had made a $300-a-share bid for UAL Corporation, the parent of the airline, and although the deal seemed expensive, everyone was convinced it would go through because Citibank, the buyer's lender, had never reneged on financing before. Many hedge funds loaded the boat with UAL shares. "We thought there was a 75 percent chance it would get done, but for us to invest, we needed it to be 95 percent," Perry says, given the stock was trading at $290 and the fund would make $10 if the deal went through but lose $200 if the deal broke up. Perry passed on it because he just couldn't see how the operating income would ever cover the interest on the loans. He was right. "The deal broke, and we went from the middle to the top of the tables." Within two hours of the release of the news that the deal had collapsed, the Dow Jones Industrial Average plunged 190 points, still one of the biggest daily declines in history. UAL stock plummeted from about $290 to $88 over the next twelve months.

Merger arbitrage, betting on the shares of merging companies, worked well for Perry until about 1992 when he and Leff realized that their strategy was too limiting. They set out to use their research to expand their investment horizons and make more money. Instead of focusing on the difference in prices between the stock of the two merging companies, they decided to focus on everything above and below that spread. Would the merged company, for example, be worth more or less than the price at which the deal was done? "Merger arbitrage was becoming too competitive," says Perry. "We were one of the first people to move out and to focus on the pro forma company."

Two years later, Perry entered what would become a ten-year transaction that changed the way he thought about investing and taught him that one of the hallmarks of a great money manager is patience. Even after more than a decade, Perry still enjoys telling the story of his takeover and transformation of FTD, the world's largest floral delivery service.

In 1994, FTD was a cooperative, and the company went looking for a buyer that would convert it into a for-profit business. Perry bought the company for about $130 million. He put in $20 million in equity, his partners Bain Capital and Bank of Boston together put up another $10 million, and they borrowed the rest. Nothing about the deal was easy. "We had a very acrimonious relationship with the bank, and the CEO of FTD quit before the bank financing was done," says Perry. "A lot of florists were hostile and angry because they felt their playground was being taken away. It was a very ugly conversion."

The nineteen-member FTD board approved Perry's bid by a single vote, but Perry couldn't complete the transaction unless he convinced more than 50 percent of the member florists to approve the deal. He visited flower shops and did interviews with the press about his plans to spend about $12 million annually on advertising and make other moves to get flower shops into the FTD network. The member florists were also given a chance to buy stock in the new company. "I hadn't been elected to anything since ninth grade," says Perry, who eventually won 61 percent of the vote. "I had a belief that I could understand the problems and convince the florists to do things the right way." He realized he needed to be patient and that the changes wouldn't happen overnight. They might take three or four years. "We created an enormous amount of value, and it took a lot of work and creativity."

During those years, FTD changed the ordering system from telephones to computers to connect the 24,000 florists in the network.

It protected the trademark domestically and internationally and also started an online unit, FTD.com, transforming the company from a flower vendor to a technology business. Revenues grew dramatically. In 2004, Perry sold FTD for $450 million to Green Equity Investors, about a 28 percent annualized return on his $20 million investment. The florists made good money, too. Those that bought nonpublic shares for around $2 when Perry first restructured the company got $24.85 a share from the new buyers. "It was a process that was financially rewarding in terms of making a lot of money and emotionally rewarding in terms of getting it right for all the people who trusted me," says Perry.

FTD was Perry's first experience serving in a position of corporate director, and he liked the view. Discussions inside the boardroom gave him insight into how companies are run and the confidence that he had solid advice to offer management. "I felt I could have a profound impact," says Perry, "whether it was about operations or financial structure, or how their sales force was operating." By 2007, he was sitting on four boards.

Before the Perry team invests in a company, they spend a tremendous amount of time talking to management, suppliers, and competitors, producing studies worthy of a consulting firm. Perry tries to understand why the company isn't making more money, what its main problems are, and whether they can be fixed. "I have close relations with the companies in which we invest. I know what issues they're confronting, and how they want to address those issues," says Perry. He tries to avoid hostile situations, believing they take too much time. Perry's criteria are that the chief executive recognizes there is a problem and has the desire to take action. Perry is willing to wait two to five years for the investment to pay off.

"The longer you're willing to hold, the less crowded the opportunities are," he says. When he first started Perry Capital, he and Leff looked for a definitive catalyst—a specific event that would send a stock rocketing or tumbling. Those opportunities are no longer so interesting for Perry because he can't get the 25 percent or 30 percent return he wants. "We've gravitated toward situations where operational fixes take time, where there is no clarity about what the catalyst is, but where there is a like-minded management team."

Perry focuses on buying assets at a discount but only when management is capable of creating profitability or eliminating liabilities to close that value gap. "You need both great management and a great asset," Perry says. "Having one or the other is a bad recipe." Without proper management, the asset's value will erode over time, making what was once a bargain price look much more expensive. "That's a value trap, not value investing."

Part of that job, as he sees it, is to provide CEOs—whom, he finds, often spend most of their time being cheerleaders rather than managers—with vital and sometimes painful information about their business, industry, or competitors. "CEOs get very diluted information. They're told what people believe they want to hear. We tell them the facts. We call a spade a spade. It's hard to get the facts because it's really difficult to know who's telling you the truth and who's camouflaging it."

Sometimes Perry must deliver his point of view succinctly and fast. In the 1990s, when privatizations were sweeping Europe, he would meet the heads of the companies about to be sold to the public after years of state ownership. He had less than five minutes to talk to them, and he asked them if they were interested in understanding why chief executives in the United States make so much money and what they needed to do to be equally successful. Some CEOs took the bait, and he advised them to align their own interests with those of shareholders. "Certain management definitely embraced our concept," he says.

Over the years, Perry has expanded the type of investments he'll take on and he now characterizes his style as opportunistic and contrarian. "Whereas typical investors are deterred by complex investments, we receive calls from CEOs and CFOs needing a quick resolution to financing problems," Perry's marketing brochure explains.

Perry's raison d'être is to generate creative business ideas. One of the days I interviewed Perry, he had just come back from a meeting with Harvey Weinstein, whom he backed when he and his brother Bob left Miramax Film Corporation in 2005, and Bill Ruprecht, the head of the auction house Sotheby's. The subject was a programming idea for Ovation, a cable network of which Perry Capital and Weinstein are backers. Perry had come up with the idea of an *Antiques Roadshow* meets *Project Runway* in which the television audience gets the behind-the-scenes dope on the artwork to be auctioned, watches the sale, and can even participate in the bidding over the phone. In exchange for providing access to a wider audience of art buyers, Ovation would receive a cut of Sotheby's auction take. Although he's not sure the show will ever become a reality, it's an example of the kind of brainstorming he does continually. One of his other ideas for Ovation was to have various ballet companies across the country do a bake-off of performances of the *The Nutcracker*, which will probably air in December 2007. "The goal is to constantly show executives ideas," says Perry. "I don't want to have any meeting, with anyone, ever, that is not a give and take. I want it to be as mutually beneficial as possible."

Perry promotes the give-and-take mantra within his own organization as well. Just as training was a huge part of the Goldman experience, so it is at Perry Capital. The hedge fund is perhaps unique in that it offers a two-year training program for analysts, after which it expects that virtually all of the trainees will leave.

Making promises he can't keep is not Perry's style, and a relatively small organization, where there are only about twenty portfolio managers—many of whom are partners in the firm— leaves little room for promotion. His solution is to manage the analysts' expectations up front by capping their stays at two years, after which they go off to business school or take jobs at investment banks or other hedge funds. Of the forty-five analysts Perry employed in 2007, only a handful are senior analysts who have stayed beyond the two-year program.

Perry trains by example. The investment staff doesn't have private offices, and the analysts listen in on phone calls and sit in on meetings to learn firsthand how the investment process works. The portfolio managers each have responsibility for their own pool of capital and manage the money following various guidelines that stipulate the amount of long versus short positions and the size of trades. When they have ideas they believe are worthy of a bigger investment, they make a pitch to Perry or Leff, who manage the core sixty to seventy positions—which Perry calls the master portfolio.

By and large, decisions result from consensus. "It's a very collective process. I almost never make a unilateral decision," says Perry. He meets with the portfolio managers to discuss the current positions, new ideas, and risk management. "We meet formally once a month, but we talk continually," he says. The bulk of his time is spent talking to his colleagues about the core positions. The portfolio managers generally do their own calls and meetings, although for the most challenging investments, they bring Perry in to talk to the chief executives.

Although Perry enjoys his conversations with corporate titans, he doesn't like to talk shop with other hedge fund managers, and he demurred when asked to name younger managers whom he respects. He claims it's tough to know who will make it over the long haul. "Most successful people are unbelievably challenging and complex. It's unclear whether or not they will be as consistently successful in the future as they've been in the past."

Aside from his own partners, the only managers he says he knows well are the Rubin-led team he worked with at Goldman Sachs. He remains especially close to Lampert, who asked Perry to sit on the board of Sears in 2005. "Eddie is the most successful guy of our generation," says Perry. "He has intelligence and commitment to work hard. He has a unique thought process coupled with an enormous drive. He is a phenomenal manager."

As for the rest, "I really try to avoid other managers as much as I can," says Perry. Their strong opinions invariably generate what he calls distracting "noise." "I don't want to hear it."

AFTER THE CRISIS

The Trouble with Truisms

In 2008, Perry experienced his first annual loss in his firm's twenty-year history. He ended the year down 27 percent and assets fell to $8 billion, down from $11.6 billion just three months earlier.

The market declines of 2008 were unlike any others he had witnessed, and the events that spurred them debunked a number of trusted investment maxims, Perry told his investors early in 2009. Notions long taken as gospel—*Buy on dips in the stock market; Buy and hold blue chip companies; In economic recessions, the rich will keep spending; Big banks will not fail*—all proved to be money-losing advice.

Perry has always been skeptical of at least some of these market bromides and was bearish going into 2008. Indeed, in 2007, he successfully bet that subprime mortgages would plummet. But he wasn't prepared for the scope of the market chaos. "We failed to execute on enough disaster-related hedges, and some of our hedges actually hurt us," he told investors.

Perry's fund ended the third quarter of 2008 down about 9 percent. He had already reduced his U.S. equity holdings to 19 percent of his long book—wagers on rising securities—down from 72 percent the previous year, and his net exposure to the stock market was very small. That turned out to be a good decision, given that the Standard & Poor's 500 Index tumbled 22 percent in the last quarter of the year. He was focusing his attention on credit, which at the end of September accounted for 26 percent of his longs. His cash balances stood at 31 percent of assets, at or near the highest levels the firm had ever held.

While holding a lot of cash was prudent given the market volatility, his credit bets tripped him up as the year came to a close. He had started buying too soon, thinking that high-quality bank loans and the debt of auto finance companies wouldn't fall farther. They did.

The fund was also hurt by illiquid holdings, which it was forced to write down and which he told investors may never recover to their former price levels.

As of January 2009, Perry had 29 percent of the fund's long investments in credit and was expecting that was to be his fund's "sweet spot" in the foreseeable future. Nearly 80 percent of the credit bets were in corporate bonds trading at 50 cents on the dollar, with the remainder in mortgages valued at even lower levels.

The firm was also sitting on a healthy cash position, which it planned to use to buy the securities of bankrupt companies and of distressed companies going through an event that would drive the price of the stocks or bonds higher. He was also looking to buy asset-backed securities like credit card loans, mortgages, and student loans, and to sell short credit that he thought would tumble.

Perry's decision to look toward the credit markets for money-making opportunities showed promise in 2009. Through September, Perry's flagship fund climbed 22 percent for the year.

Chapter 18

Daniel Loeb
Newfound Restraint

DANIEL LOEB OPENED Third Point in June 1995, and his fund returned 27 percent a year on average through July 2007—an eye-popping 16 percentage points higher than the Standard & Poor's 500 Index. Numbers like that certainly get Loeb noticed in the financial world, but what brings him notoriety are words like this: Irik Sevin is "one of the most dangerous and incompetent executives in America." Loeb shared this opinion of Sevin, then chief executive officer of Star Gas Partners, a heating oil distributor in Stamford, Connecticut, in a letter to him that went on to offer this advice: "Do what you do best: Retreat to your waterfront mansion in the Hamptons, where you can play tennis and hobnob with your fellow socialites."

Loeb's entertaining missives to chief executives and investment professionals alike have made him famous—or infamous, depending on your perspective—for the no-holds-barred approach he takes to getting his point across. He fired off an e-mail to Ken Griffin, head of hedge fund Citadel Investment Group in Chicago, warning him not to poach employees from other hedge fund firms. He called Citadel a "gulag," its employees "indentured servants," and closed by saying: "Good luck extracting exorbitant management fees and generating mediocre returns with your bloated organization and ego."

One needn't be prominent to trigger Loeb's ire. He made public an e-mail exchange he had with a prospective employee in Europe who hadn't responded well to Loeb's terse tone, finding it too brash and too American. The exchange ended with the erstwhile job candidate's one-liner "Hubris" and Loeb's retort "Laziness."

Given his epistolary antics, it's no wonder that more than a few industry insiders consider Loeb the bad boy of hedge funds. His reputation is larger than life in an industry that's become increasingly buttoned down. He hangs with rapper Fab 5 Freddy, and he paid $45 million for his penthouse on Central Park West in 2005—then the most expensive Manhattan residence ever purchased. Loeb has short, spiky hair that's starting to gray and a slight build. A native of Los Angeles, he's been a surfer since boyhood. Indeed, Third Point is named for a surfing spot at Malibu Surfrider Beach. He practices Ashtanga yoga, making time for trips every year and a half to visit a yoga school in Mysore, India.

In the entrance of his office in the landmark Lever Building on Manhattan's Park Avenue, where I spoke with him, visitors are greeted by a massive Andreas Gursky photograph of the interior of a prison and a ninety-inch-by-seventy-inch dollar sign painted by Andy Warhol, who once wrote: "Making money is art, and working is art, and good business is the best art."

Loeb, now forty-five, insists his strident days are behind him. Third Point, Loeb says, has evolved in its twelve-year history, and so has he. Misconceptions about his fund are widespread, he says, right down to the kind of investing he does. Loeb is often referred to as an activist whose mission is to bully companies into making changes that will boost their share prices.

"We're not an activist fund," he says. "We're a global event-driven fund with a long-short approach to investing," which refers to the strategy of investing in companies going through a corporate event, like coming out of bankruptcy or spinning off a unit. "I think I have a knack for identifying mispriced asset classes," Loeb says, whether it's distressed debt or small-cap stocks. "We have a really strong team of people who are specialists in a variety of industries, geographies, and asset classes, who have been imbued with our event-driven approach to investing. They are very good analysts and very good at understanding what differentiates a good investment from a bad one," he says in describing Third Point's edge. "And where we do take an activist stance, I like to think of it as being interactive with management."

To back up his statement, he points out that Third Point had ninety-six long positions in mid-2007. He had made public demands at only five of them, asking for the chief executive to step down or a company to be sold. "There are a lot of companies with whom we have ongoing productive dialogues. Sometimes they listen, sometimes they don't, but it's actually very rare that we have to take a more aggressive activist stance."

Third Point has applied its interactive, behind-the-scenes approach at companies like Martin Marietta Materials, the second-largest U.S. maker of road construction materials. At the beginning of 2007, Loeb owned a 6.1 percent stake. Because he had some business-improving suggestions for management, he filed a Schedule 13D with the U.S. Securities and Exchange Commission, required when an investor owns 5 percent or more of the company and isn't going to be a passive investor. Third Point's filing did not include any specifics about what the shareholder wanted to accomplish.

Loeb talked to management about ways to increase shareholder value, and the executives agreed, repurchasing more than 5 percent of outstanding shares by the end of the first quarter, helping to boost the stock price by about 30 percent. "We never went beyond our initial 13D filing," says Loeb. "We never wrote a letter. We never had anything further to say publicly about it. There was no need; we were on the same page," he says. In mid-2007, he had five 13D positions in which he had yet to make a public demand.

When conditions warrant it, Loeb insists he has no choice but to speak out. When he does, he seems to have toned down his rhetoric. In March and April of 2007, Loeb sent several letters to the board of PDL BioPharma, a biotechnology firm in Fremont, California, calling for the resignation of its chief executive officer, Mark McDade. In those epistles, he skewered McDade for moving his headquarters and building out 450,000 square feet of office space at a cost of nearly $100 million, contending he did so to shorten his own commute and provide a nearby slip for his yacht. He called the move illustrative of McDade's "empire-building philosophy, patho-logical selfishness, and poor business judgment" and referred to the new headquarters as the Taj Mahal.

The harsh words hardly support Loeb's claim to reform. Yet, in correspondence sent to directors in May 2007, a more tactful Loeb appeared. He mentioned that current and former employees of the biotech company had told Third Point they were concerned with the hiring and promotions of one Jeanmarie Guenot, PhD, the head of business development. "No acceptable explanation can account for her initial appointment or continued employment as head of business development," Loeb wrote. "In fact, the investigation uncovered at least one senior executive who left PDL BioPharma over what he considered unfairly favorable treatment of Dr. Guenot to the detriment of the company and its other employees." In the same letter, he stated that chief executive McDade "may have committed significant ethical breaches."

In response to my invitation to address Loeb's comments, a spokeswoman for PDL BioPharma said, "We aren't responding to any personal attacks."

Loeb's point regarding an inappropriate relationship was clear, but only between the lines. When I suggest that in earlier days, he probably would have done a lot less pussyfooting around and made his point in boldly flamboyant language, he laughs and tells me I'm making him blush. New persona aside, Loeb also mentions the firm's attorneys' influence on his language. "We are a bit less colorful, but we don't need to be as colorful," says Loeb, insisting that the kinder, gentler approach isn't about appeasing current and potential institutional investors, who made up about 80 percent of Third Point's clients in 2007. "I do what's right for the portfolio—whatever will maximize its returns," he says. "It's a natural maturity. We have a lot more teeth, I think, than we did before." McDade resigned in August 2007.

Influence, it seems, is directly related to size. In the last quarter of 2004, Third Point had $1.4 billion in assets. By August 2007, it managed $5.5 billion. With that heft, individual positions can reach more than $500 million, catapulting Third Point into the ranks of the top ten or twenty investors, even in large multinational companies. Large holders tend to be listened to, meaning Loeb has less reason to use what he calls the "shame lever." "Now we have audiences with people like the CEOs of Royal Philips, DaimlerChrysler, and Infineon Technologies," he says. "With those three companies, for example, we have very fruitful dialogues and interactions. We learn a lot about the businesses, and I think they gain a perspective from us that they find useful. To that extent, things have changed. We have the ears of these major companies."

Despite his growing influence with larger companies, Loeb primarily makes his money through traditional value investing in companies in which he might never speak to the chief executives. One of Third Point's most successful investments in 2006 was NYSE Euronext, which runs the New York Stock Exchange. "I think I shook John Thain's hand once at Davos, gave him a pat on the back and an attaboy, and just thanked him for all the good work he's done," says Loeb of his interaction with the head of the exchange. "I'd much rather stand on the sidelines and cheer management and the board for doing a great job, and that's usually what we're able to do."

He's willing to stand on the sidelines for years at a time. Loeb has owned Dade Behring, a medical diagnostic company, since 2002, when it was still in bankruptcy. In mid-2007, he held 4.8 percent of the outstanding shares, and nearly five years later, the stock was still going strong, jumping 90 percent in the first eight months of 2007. "Sometimes the best-performing things in your portfolio are things that you've owned for a long time," he says. "Dade Behring, for one, is an extraordinarily well-run company with a first-rate board of directors." Loeb bought the shares because Dade Behring was a leader among its competitors and the only pure-play diagnostics company. It traded at the lowest valuation, even while it was gaining market share and growing faster than its peers. "Nothing's changed in five years," he says, except that the stock has climbed an average of about 56 percent a year. The company is still significantly cheaper than its competitors, and it's trading at a price that's lower than where similar companies have been acquired, he says.

The characteristics of Dade Behring are typical of what Loeb looks for in the stocks he buys: companies with solid franchises that trade at an attractive valuation and generate a lot of free cash flow. "Even more important than all of that, we look for companies that are misunderstood by the market and mispriced," he adds. Typically, those sorts of situations occur around a big corporate restructuring like a spinoff or an emergence from bankruptcy.

That's because such companies generally have a more favorable operating model than they've had in the past, and managers have a greater incentive to make the businesses succeed, especially since they're generally given an equity stake in the new entity or options to buy stock. "I don't know if management teams do this consciously or unconsciously, but they tend to understate the performance of the company before the event; then afterward, the company surprises everyone on the Street except for us," says Loeb. "And it's a very long-term phenomenon that may play out over many years."

Loeb has been following stocks since he was a kid, a fascination that started when his maternal grandmother first showed him the stock pages in the newspaper. A social worker, she had invested her savings in the stock market—mostly in industrial companies—in the 1950s, and her nest egg grew to several million dollars by the time she died. "She was actually the first activist in the Loeb family," he says. "She used to show up at annual meetings at Westvaco, Union Pacific, and AT&T, and question why there weren't women on the board, or why there wasn't coffee and Danish available for the people who came to the annual meeting," he adds with a smile. When Loeb was thirteen, his father, a securities lawyer, helped him open his first brokerage account with money he'd saved from his allowance and from a skateboard company he ran with two partners.

Loeb started off his college education at the University of California at Berkeley, transferring to New York's Columbia University two years later. He traded stocks throughout college, amassing $120,000 by his senior year, when he lost it all on one stock, Puritan Bennett, a maker of medical respirators.

After graduating in 1983 with a degree in economics, he started working, first as a private equity analyst at Warburg Pincus and later for Island Records, once the biggest independent record label in the world and home to reggae artists Bob Marley and Burning Spear. There he headed corporate development and set up debt financing for the label.

Loeb landed his first real money-management job in 1988, joining a hedge fund run by Barry and Alan Lafer in New York. After three years he moved on and, not finding a gig at another hedge fund, ended up as an analyst at brokerage firm Jefferies & Company. Drexel Lambert had gone bankrupt the year before and there was money to be made in the distressed debt that came out of the junk-bond boom of the 1980s. "The bankruptcy of Drexel itself was my first big analytical coup because I had gone through the disclosure statement and figured out that there were these obscure securities called 'Drexel CBI-As,' or certificates of beneficial interest, which were entitled to proceeds from the liquidation of the firm," he says.

In essence, CBI-As were trade claims—accounts receivable—and loans that would get paid under bankruptcy laws. Loeb saw that the certificates were worth a lot more money than the price at which the European banks that held them had valued them on their books, so he convinced the banks to sell them and found buyers among hedge funds like Farallon Capital Management and investment banks like Goldman Sachs. "In one fell swoop, I became analyst, bank loan trader, and started covering accounts," Loeb says. He was right about the value. His customers acquired the claims for a cost of about $0.03 on the dollar and earned $0.30 or $0.40.

This transaction ultimately led to the relationships Loeb developed with the people who later became the biggest names in hedge funds: Eric Mindich, who runs Eton Park Capital Management; David Einhorn, who heads Greenlight Capital; Jeff Altman, at Owl Creek Asset Management; Tom Steyer, at Farallon Capital Management; Jeff Aronson, at Angelo, Gordon & Company; John Bader, at Halcyon Asset Management; and David Tepper, at Appaloosa Management.

Loeb continued as a researcher and salesman for the next two and a half years, until looking for a bigger paycheck, he jumped to Citibank to become a high-yield-bond salesman. The pay was better, but he missed the world of distressed investing and he wanted to get back into that business. "I was criticized at my previous jobs for spending a disproportionate amount of time investing and thinking too much like an investor rather than like a salesman, although I was a very good salesman," he adds. "Because of the research I had done and the relationships I had formed, I felt prepared to start my own fund, which was always my passion."

So he did. From the weight room of David Tepper's office in Chatham, New Jersey, in June 1995, he launched Third Point, later moving to digs in Manhattan.

• • •

The initial mandate of the fund at Third Point was to invest in special situations in distressed debt and equity, and that's still how the firm invests today, although it has expanded its horizons outside the United States as well. Loeb seeks out shares to buy, or ones to sell short, which will produce a 30 to 50 percent annualized return.

Third Point runs a fairly concentrated portfolio, with the top ten holdings accounting for close to 50 percent of its long positions. Loeb uses a modest amount of leverage, with the portfolio's gross exposure at 100 to 200 percent of assets and net exposure between 30 percent and 70 percent. He has four partners and together they run industry groups specializing in biotechnology, energy, telecommunications, media and technology, consumer companies, financial services, and metals and mining. Teams also focus on geographic areas, covering Asia, India, and Europe. Another team is dedicated to short selling. The partners have discretion to buy or sell short up to a certain position size, and if they think a bet is worthy of a bigger stake, they bring the idea to Loeb. If he agrees, the position can grow as large as 10 percent of assets.

Many of Loeb's larger holdings in 2007 were in biotechnology. "I've always been intrigued by the biotech industry because it's one of the ultimate event-driven games out there," he says. The company founders in this area are very smart, but they don't always have a lot of experience in running a business. "There's an opportunity for us to add value to those types of companies," he says. Loeb expanded the firm's expertise in the industry by hiring a medical doctor, Brigette Roberts, as an analyst a few years ago. She has since become a partner in the firm. "She's one of the most astute investors I've known in the business," he says.

The pharmaceutical sector became the first in which Loeb made a foray into using what he calls the legal lever—that is, staging proxy fights to get board seats when the company management won't listen to reason, rather than shaming it into submission. In 2005, he and two other directors nominated by him joined the board of Ligand Pharmaceuticals, which makes cancer and pain drugs.

Loeb is pleased with Third Point's track record in proxy contests. "We've never initiated a process whereby we either didn't win seats or were granted seats when we wanted them. And most important, once we get on the boards, even if we don't control them, we've had a high level of success in persuading the directors, even though we're in the minority, that the course of action suggested is a good one and should be pursued."

Sometimes the action is decisive. In August 2006, David Robinson resigned as CEO of Ligand Pharmaceuticals, eight months after Loeb joined the board. In November 2006, chief executive Thomas McLain resigned from Nabi Biopharmaceuticals, four months after Loeb won seats for two directors.

Victories aside, joining the board is the option of last resort for Loeb. "We don't want to serve on boards. First of all, they're time consuming. You have to get on a plane, the meetings are unbelievably tedious, and it just takes a long time to get things worked out. It also limits your flexibility financially" because, as insiders, directors are restricted regarding when they can sell or buy shares. As of July 2007, Loeb was on the boards of Pogo Producing and BioFuel Energy, a company that had just gone public.

At the start of 2007, Loeb also sat on the board of Massey Energy, the United States' fourth-largest coal producer. It represents his most disappointing activist investment to date. "We stayed one song too long at that party," he says. He and his team underestimated the cyclicality of coal prices as well as some of the company's production issues. "We were a little surprised by how dramatically its cash flow deteriorated" in 2006, he added, when the stock dropped 39 percent.

Initially, Massey seemed to be on track to improve. Following demands by Third Point and another hedge fund, Jana Partners, in November 2005, the directors of Massey agreed to buy back $500 million of stock. Yet the company was dragging its feet, and by early 2006, Loeb, discouraged by the slow progress, decided to run for a board seat along with his colleague Todd Swanson. They won, but Donald Blankenship, the chief executive, had yet to approve more than $50 million in share repurchases as of 2007. The stock was up about 50 percent in 2007 from its lows. "We made a good chunk of the money back, but if I could do it over again, I wouldn't have invested in Massey," he says. He resigned from the board in June 2007.

When the democratic process for initiating change doesn't work or gets stymied by poor corporate governance, Loeb resorts to the poison-pen tactics. "Companies that have erected unnatural barriers such as "poison pills" and staggered boards and make it impossible to call special meetings leave us with no alternative but to pursue the social-pressure angle, and that's a phenomenon of their own creation," he says. "We would just as soon put it to a vote."

Loeb wrote his first 13D letter in September 2000, when he was managing $136 million. Corporate raider Carl Icahn had been writing angry letters to corporate management since the 1980s, but in early 2000, a hedge fund manager named Robert Chapman, who runs Chapman Capital in Los Angeles, caught Loeb's eye after he shot off a letter to J. Michael Wilson, chief executive of American Communities Properties Trust, a real estate trust in which Third Point also owned shares. Loeb found Chapman's sarcastic style a potent weapon, and a few months later, Loeb sent his own biting correspondence to William Stiritz, chairman of Agribrands International, an animal feed company. Ralcorp Holdings, maker of store-brand breakfast cereals, also chaired by Stiritz, had just agreed to buy Agribrands for $39 a share, a price Loeb thought was too low. The deal didn't go through and less than three months later, Cargill made a $54.50 bid for Agribrands, making Third Point $20 million.

Although Loeb gets noticed for his long positions, at least 50 percent of the fund's assets are wagered on companies whose prices he expects to tumble. Loeb's investors say he's a talented short seller, borrowing shares and then selling them in the hopes that the stocks will tumble and can be bought back later at a cheaper price. Even in the years of the Internet bubble, Loeb managed to profit on the short side, specifically in companies that later faced investor lawsuits over inflated profits or stock prices, including Actrade Financial Technologies and Chromatics Color Sciences International. Another company, Computer Learning Centers, was penalized for illegally paying commissions to school admissions officers.

Many of Loeb's short ideas came from a stock promoter named John Liviakis. "We used to go through his client list because it was a particularly fruitful universe of attractive short candidates," he says. He still finds such questionable companies to short, although he declined to talk about any currently in his portfolio.

Although Loeb, unlike many managers, likes shorting shares, he finds the strategy a lot harder than buying stocks. "I think making money on the long side is a more fruitful activity, but from a portfolio-management standpoint, the shorts give you the staying power to live through difficult market conditions. In a perfect world, you should be able to make money on both your longs and your shorts in the long run."

Third Point's endurance also stems from having become more institutional, with what Loeb calls a "best of breed" operations group and a strong team of investment professionals. "We've had to be more institutional in order to grow the business and to appeal to the investor base that we have," he says, "and frankly, the environment that we're in today is one in which having more capital is actually a competitive advantage because it facilitates exposure to different geographies." One of Loeb's big goals is to move away from a United States–centric approach to investing. In June 2007, Loeb said he would list a fund on the London Stock Exchange, one of only a handful of funds to make such a move.

The key to success, Loeb says, is to maintain that spirit of entrepreneurship and creativity in investment management. "We don't have firmwide meetings about how we should approach investments. These things are decided by two or three people at any given time."

As an example of the kind of talent Loeb looks for, he points to Rehan Jaffer, thirty, a partner at River Run Partners in New York. Jaffer, who declined to be interviewed for *Hedge Hunters*, was formerly an analyst at Third Point and left in late 2004 to join River Run, which was started by Ian Wallace, a friend of Loeb's who had been renting space from Third Point.

Loeb tried to keep Jaffer at Third Point by making him a portfolio manager, but Jaffer wanted more independence. "He is superhungry," says Loeb. "He's got a good nose. He's very intelligent. So he's got a great combination of having a high IQ, really strong financial analytics, a great nose for value, and great trader sense."

To find those qualities in new hires, Loeb looks for academic excellence, creativity, good financial analysis, and common sense. He hires most analysts straight out of business school or from a Wall Street training program. Many don't have any investment experience per se, but Loeb prefers it that way because he trains them in the Third Point way himself.

Although Loeb might seek out candidates with special degrees, like his partner Roberts, he's not one to seek out candidates with unusual backgrounds. To land a spot at Third Point, "you almost have to start preparing when you're thirteen or fourteen years old," he says. "You have to be the best student, go to the best school, and go on to the best banking programs and distinguish yourself there. That has become the typical career path."

And one he didn't follow. "I wouldn't have gotten an interview at Third Point. I'm the first to admit it," he says. "I wasn't the best student in college, and I don't have an MBA."

He does, apparently, have a few other skills—and, of course, a way with words.

AFTER THE CRISIS

Charting a Way Back

Loeb's flagship Third Point Offshore Fund tumbled 32.6 percent in 2008, the worst annual loss in the firm's history. Assets shrunk to $2.3 billion as of January 1, 2009, from roughly $5.5 billion in August 2007, a consequence of losses and client withdrawals. Even with last year's decline, Loeb has averaged a 20 percent annual return since starting Third Point in 1995, compared with 6 percent for the Standard & Poor's 500 Index.

Although Loeb fully expected that the credit crisis would hit the housing market and financial institutions hard in 2008, knowing what lay ahead wasn't enough to keep him from losing money. "One of our most fundamental mistakes was underestimating the speed with which the economy could deteriorate," Loeb told his investors at the start of 2009. That miscalculation led him to stay in some bullish positions too long.

In the first half of 2008, he made money buying energy stocks, and he increased his holdings in companies including Plains Exploration & Production Co. in June, as oil prices shot up toward $150 a barrel. In early July, crude began to tumble as the global economy slowed, dropping to $100 a barrel by mid-September. Loeb quickly cut his exposure to these stocks, but his earlier profits disappeared.

Loeb also learned how dangerous investments in hard-to-sell positions can become when markets turn volatile. Throughout his career, he's made lots of money buying less-liquid holdings, including investments in private companies such as Radia Communications, a semi-conductor start-up. In 2008, with the economy in a tailspin, such positions cost him big. A large debt stake in ailing carmaker Chrysler lost almost all its value, as did an investment in a fund that owned retailer Target, which he was locked into for two years. "Needless to say, we won't make this type of investment again," he told investors.

In 2009, Loeb has been getting back to his roots, concentrating on so-called event-driven and special-situation investments, which include stocks—both those he expects to rise and those he is wagering will fall. He's also focusing on distressed debt and high-yield bonds. Coming out of the previous recession, Loeb shifted much of his portfolio into distressed investments, reaping returns of 51.5 percent in 2003 and 30.2 percent in 2004 as markets rebounded.

During the first half of 2009, he bought the senior bonds of a bankrupt company at 84 cents on the dollar and expects to trade them at 100 cents on the dollar by year-end. His purchase of the shares of Sun Microsystems after a deal with IBM fell through was an event-driven investment he made "on the thesis that someone would scoop up this gem of a company." He made a quick profit just weeks later, when Oracle Corp. stepped up to buy the computer maker.

"After suffering through a year like 2008, the best thing to do is to stand up, take your lumps, and clear the portfolio of dead wood," says Loeb. "With that exercise sufficiently behind us, I am liberated to focus solely on making this a profitable year for our investors." By the end of September, Loeb had done just that, with his flagship fund up 29 percent for the year.

Index

About the Author

Katherine Burton has covered hedge funds for Bloomberg News for more than a decade. Before joining Bloomberg in 1993, she lived in Paris, where she wrote for the *International Herald Tribune*, *U.S. News & World Report*, and Bloomberg. Burton received a Bachelor of Arts in French from Drew University and a Master of Business Administration from New York University. She is a winner of the 2001 Society of American Business Editors and Writers Award for breaking news and the 2005 New Jersey Chapter of the Society of Professional Journalists Award for Excellence in Journalism for business writing. She lives in New York City.

About Bloomberg

Bloomberg L.P., founded in 1981, is a global information services, news, and media company. Headquartered in New York, the company has sales and news operations worldwide.

Serving customers on six continents, Bloomberg, through its wholly-owned subsidiary Bloomberg Finance L.P., holds a unique position within the financial services industry by providing an unparalleled range of features in a single package known as the Bloomberg Professional® service. By addressing the demand for investment performance and efficiency through an exceptional combination of information, analytic, electronic trading, and Straight Through Processing tools, Bloomberg has built a worldwide customer base of corporations, issuers, financial intermediaries, and institutional investors.

Bloomberg News®, founded in 1990, provides stories and columns on business, general news, politics, and sports to leading newspapers and magazines throughout the world. Bloomberg Television®, a 24-hour business and financial news network, is produced and distributed globally in seven languages. Bloomberg Radio℠ is an international radio network anchored by flagship station Bloomberg® 1130 (WBBR-AM) in New York.

In addition to the Bloomberg Press® line of books, Bloomberg publishes *Bloomberg Markets*® magazine. To learn more about Bloomberg, call a sales representative at:

London:	+44-20-7330-7500
New York:	+1-212-318-2000
Tokyo:	+81-3-3201-8900